WITHDRAWN

LOOKING
FOR ROBBIE

LOOKING FOR ROBBIE

A Biography of Robbie Coltrane

NEIL NORMAN

ORION

For Susannah

First published in 1999 by Orion Books Ltd
Orion House, 5 Upper St Martin's Lane,
London WC2H 9EA

Typeset in Great Britain by Selwood Systems, Midsomer Norton
Printed and bound by Butler & Tanner Ltd, Frome and London.

ACKNOWLEDGEMENTS

Given the unusual circumstances, under which this book was written, I freely confess to using a variety of published sources. Suffice to say, I owe a debt of gratitude to every journalist and critic who has written about Coltrane, interviewed him, or voiced an opinion whether I have quoted them or not. These include the usual suspects, William Leith, Andrew Billen, Gordon Burn, Tom Hibbert, Jan Moir, Robert Crampton, Colin Wills, Christine Eccles, Garth Pearce, Angela Levin, Louise Gannon, Ginny Dougary and Michael Owen. In addition, I have referred to a variety of books. I am indebted to John Crace whose book *Cracker: The Truth Behind the Fiction* was a source of inspiration and information; and *Coltrane in a Cadillac*, the book accompanying the television series, which provided excellent background material for the chapter Coltrane in America. Finally, the support network of friends, editors, colleagues who cajoled, encouraged, scoffed, admonished, harassed, soothed, black-mailed, wept and generally took whatever action they deemed necessary to get me to finish this book is wondrous. I thank in particular my tireless editor Yvette 'don't Hide Behind Your answerphone' Goulden, Julian Alexander (the coolest literary agent on earth), Pandora White for organising pictures, Camilla for organising money at inappropriate moments and my colleagues on the *Evening Standard* Arts Desk for putting up with whinging throughout (Alison, Zoe, Pete, Mary Ann). Finally, Adieu Kirsten and Hello Lucinda.

Pictures supplied by: The Kobal Collection, Rex Features London, Pictorial Press Ltd., Big Pictures, Mail Photo Library and Granada Television.

CONTENTS

Acknowledgements v
1 Robbie and Me: Who Would You Most Like to Have a
  One to One With? 1
2 Fragments of a Childhood 10
3 From Posh School to Art School 16
4 Fat Fab Rab: The Big Times of a Fat Actor 23
5 In Pictures: Coltrane's Early Movies 32
6 Fun With Nuns and Other Religious Persons 47
7 More Politics: Some Heroes 53
8 Robbie and Romance: The Girl Who Got Away Eventually 59
9 If the Cap Fitz 64
10 Coltrane Prepares 72
11 Coltrane, Cars, Cadillacs 88
12 The Later Movies 100
13 American Movies 121
14 Television and Radio Highlights 129
15 Cracker: Blow by Blow 134
16 What Have You Got? 214
  Appendix: List of Coltrane's Credits 220
  Index 223

Chapter 1

ROBBIE AND ME:
WHO WOULD YOU MOST LIKE
TO HAVE A ONE TO ONE WITH?

I swore I'd never write another biography. It always seems to produce disappointment. You start off with the best intentions, having selected someone you really like in the vain hope that this will sustain you through the peaks and troughs, wrong turnings, culs-de-sac, and downright refusals that face you on the journey through A Life. But it seems to pan out the same. You end up resenting, despising, even hating the subject you began by liking, admiring and wanting to write about.

It begins with a telephone call. My agent, a fellow of almost infinite patience, if not jest, enquires gently how the magnum opus is progressing. By this he means the ongoing novel that has drifted in and out of my extra-curricular working pattern, occasionally staying around for half a chapter before going back to sleep in the bottom of the word processor.

After the usual pleasantries he idly enquires if I might consider doing something else: something for money, something that is already being bandied around by a publisher. A biography. I mean to say no, but it comes out as 'who?' The answer is Robbie Coltrane.

It is at that moment that the fatal, fateful hesitation occurs. He knows he's got me. All he has to do is reel me in, play the line a little bit, and land me. It's simple.

Why did I say yes?

The question is easy; the answer difficult. Split into several shards of response, many of which are connected to the ego, the self-esteem, the layer upon layer of motivation that stratify every answer. But above all, the abiding motive is that I like Robbie Coltrane. I like his work, I like the man, I like his location in the (in)human landscape of celebrity.

OK, I thought. Given that there is a body of work that appears to be operating on an upward, cumulative curve, given that he is quite extensively and regularly interviewed, given that he appears to have a large reservoir of friends, allies, colleagues.

I said yes.

FLASHBACK
Rewind the tape back to May 1991. I am conducting an interview at Rogano's seafood restaurant in Glasgow with Robbie Coltrane. We are having lunch to discuss his role in *Perfectly Normal*, a Canadian film of attractive quirkiness in which he plays an opera-loving restaurateur with a shady past. Aside from the fact that I am a wee bit late, having missed the flight I'd intended to catch, all is progressing well. I have prepared assiduously, even down to the framing of the possible trap questions.

Here is my introduction:

Popular Myths One: Fat men are funny because it's a defence mechanism learned at an early age.

'Absolute nonsense,' roars Coltrane (he really does roar). 'I wasn't a fat man at an early age. I was always a big strong guy. If I had to defend myself against anyone I just hit them.'

As always when I am interviewing a subject, I am half engaged in 'casual' conversation and half alert to the nuances of character, sudden shifts of mood, clothing and body language. This isn't arrogance, it's a question of survival. Sometimes, if you don't read the signs, you can come an awful cropper. In Coltrane's case, a man not given to suffering fools or journalists (yes, Robbie, there *is* a difference) gladly, it is wise to have your wits about you. Which is not quite the same thing as being witty; when you're in Coltrane's presence, he is the only one who is allowed to be witty. Otherwise, it can become a little competitive.

To continue:

The other diners, frozen in various attitudes of apprehension by the outburst, relax and return to the business of eating. Coltrane may be a formidable presence, but as he's a regular they have become used to him.

He is currently in Reformed Character mode. He is drinking nothing stronger than 'freshly squeezed orange juice' and is (literally) watching his diet. Sure, he still smokes like a trooper but he's cut down on swearing.

Note the scene-setting devices at work here. I am clearly attempting to paint a picture of the context in which we are talking; also, to convey, with as little fuss as possible, Coltrane's current state of mind – or at least an idea of what his state of mind might be. Of course, writing in retrospect, I am at an advantage. I already know what his state of mind is, or was, during the interview. It's a curiously underhand business, this interviewing lark.

'I've lost a stone and a half in a month and three days with Weightwatchers,' says the not-so-big man. 'I do it on the phone. They run it rather like Alcoholics Anonymous. You get a counsellor and can call him any time day or night if you're being tempted by a packet of chocolate biscuits.'

Observe at what point I place this quote. Right near the top of the article, just following his outburst and a description. Here is the first example in the interview (and there are many more) where Coltrane reveals his funny side. What's more, in the space of one quote we get a hint of his alcoholic intake as well as his appetite for more solid nourishment. Plus a joke. Coltrane doesn't waste words, which, for someone who talks as much as he does, is little short of remarkable. It is this facility, of course, which should make him a dream interview – as long as he's in the right mood.

Back to Rogano's.

Squeezed behind a table in Rogano's seafood restaurant in Glasgow, Coltrane peruses the menu. 'Dieting's easy,' he says. 'Basically you take all the things you like and stop eating them.'

Robbie Coltrane may not be the man he was these days, but his star is unquestionably in the ascendant. With a film opening this week,

Perfectly Normal, another one in the cutting-room (*The Pope Must Die*) and one just about to begin filming (*Alive and Kicking*), he is very much in demand. Not to mention receiving the Peter Sellers prize for Comedy at last year's *Evening Standard* Film Awards, numerous offers from America – where he is regarded in the same heavyweight league as the three Big Johns, Goodman, Candy and Belushi – and a book and a television sitcom he is in the process of writing. In addition, he's an ace mechanic, regularly servicing friends' cars as well as his own fleet of vintage American autos.

All this and Persil commercials too. If there is one thing that is putting on weight, it is the Coltrane bank balance.

So there it is: a condensed synopsis of his latest work, a brief catalogue of his talents and recognition (with a sneaky self-promoting insert for the *Evening Standard*), topped off with a mildly sardonic comment on his current status. By this stage, the reader should know where he, Coltrane and myself stand. I have established a certain relationship with Coltrane – on the page – have allowed him the luxury of cracking a few funnies and also revealed that I reserve the right to comment on him, his words and the situation. Not bad, even if I do say so myself.

The least attractive of all the options open to Coltrane is the American connection about which he has a scarcely concealed contempt. His last American film, a comedy thriller made with Richard Dreyfuss, *Let It Ride*, was never released in British cinemas.

'What do I want to go to Hollywood for? I can eat here every day of my life. That's all I've ever wanted. If I worked in America they stitch you up for five years. If you become a big movie star you stop getting interesting parts.'

This will be the last digression for a while, I promise. But I would ask you to pay particular attention to this last remark. Given Coltrane's extraordinary facility with American accents, given his fondness for American cars, given his addiction to American movies and movie stars from Marlon Brando to Spencer Tracy, is it not curious that he should reject the notion of at least attempting to crack the American market? It isn't as if he'd be forced to live there, after all. Is there some veiled reticence here? Fabulous as Rogano's is, *any* restaurant would get a mite tiresome if one actually ate there every day. Interesting parts are all very well – they're on the wish list of every actor I've ever met – but Coltrane could as easily find interesting parts in America as in Great Britain. Of course, this interview was conducted before *Cracker*, before Coltrane became the star that he was subsequently to be. Now let's return to the one and only conversation between Robbie Coltrane and Yours Truly.

His impressive girth appears to have been no hindrance to his work. Quite the contrary. He has, reputedly, 300 accents at his command, and a quick scan of the 28 films he has made – quite apart from his work in the theatre and television – reveals an almost indecent diversification. A Pope, a cardinal, a rock and roll singer, a cop, sundry crooks, a couple of transvestites and Ken Livingstone; it's not the mileage that impresses so much as the terrain.

Certainly his role in *Perfectly Normal*, as a shady Italian/American restaurateur with a disastrous history and an obsession with opera, falls into the category of 'interesting parts'. A sweet and edgy comedy, it depicts what happens when a stranger in the shape of Coltrane's Alonso Turner comes crashing into the life of an innocent young man and completely overturns it.

'Alonso is a bit like Bilko. He has the instincts of a complete shyster but the soul of a decent chap. You know the kind of guy I mean. Most end up as film producers.'

He pauses for breath. Like most big men, Coltrane has a tendency to wheeze slightly, though doubtless that has as much to do with cigarettes as his weight. Being tall, he appears more big than rotund, though he admits to feeling the weight as he gets older (he's 41). 'It's no good for the old jam tart. Also, I've done all the fat men parts. Falstaff, Samuel Johnson.'

His Johnson appeared in the critically acclaimed one-man show *Your Obedient Servant* (I love that: where was the rest of his body? Rehearsing *Hamlet* at the National?), for which he researched assiduously.

In the last review of her career, Pauline Kael said of Coltrane in *Perfectly Normal* that 'he comes on like a low-rent Orson Welles'. He beams at the recollection. 'I thought, "That's it. I can retire." ' Fat chance.

Although he maintains a flat in south London, he moved back to Scotland two years ago after a long period of London residency. Now he lives in newly discovered domestic monogamy with his 'girlie' Rhona (20 years his junior) in an idyllic cottage just outside Glasgow. He was becoming increasingly depressed, he says, about the unhappiness in London, the growing climate of envy and greed that was making life intolerable for many people. But was the world changing around him, or did his growing celebrity mean that people reacted to him differently?

'I asked my mum about that, and she would know. She said I haven't changed.' He even gets around to saying (though I was hoping he wouldn't) that he went back to discover his roots. Uh oh.

'Glaswegians have a policy of humiliating those who they think are getting above themselves.' Otherwise, it was a case of where else could he go? 'The alternative is to go and live in France where nobody recognizes you. But then you don't recognize anybody either.'

Sitting in the restaurant, engaging in earnest conversations with the waiter ('Where do you get fresh basil in Glasgow?') and mischief with a television producer on a nearby table, Coltrane is neither as relentlessly funny nor as elusive as previous reports have suggested. Between the funny accents and the vocal legerdemain, he will talk, articulately, about anything – work, humour, politics, dieting, his personal life (up to a point) – only becoming dangerously animated when he gets on to the subject of the health service. Coltrane has never been shy of stating his political leanings nor his contempt for the Tory Government.

Quite recently, it reached the stage where it appeared he might follow in the footsteps of Glenda Jackson and stand for Parliament.

Popular Myths Two: Actors make lousy politicians.

'Lousy actors make lousy politicians,' he counters. 'I find it deeply insulting that actors should be considered brainless flibbertigibbets. Why should lawyers make better politicians? There are a lot of shyster lawyers about.' In the event, his incipient political career has been put on the back burner. He prefers, he says, to express his views through his work.

'I've been accused of being a Marxist. Actually, I'm a utilitarian. I believe the greatest number of people should have the best possible life. I don't think there has ever been an agenda for anything in this country. Nobody will address transport properly, especially in London; nobody will address education or health ...'

As he starts to relate a couple of hardcore anecdotes relating to the health cuts and the failing education system, his huge, oil-stained hands clench into fists on the tablecloth. His face alters from the squashy, familiar man-of-good-humour into something altogether more lethal. There is no denying his commitment.

Which brings us to the washing-up commercials. How does a man with such strongly held political principles reconcile these with a series of commercials for washing-up liquid? Coltrane gives what, on anyone else's face might be called a wry grin, but on his looks more like a seismic rift.

'Ah. I thought we'd get around to that. What people who accuse me of selling out for Persil don't realize is that I turn down half a million quids' worth of advertising a year. And it also happens to be good stuff – I tried it out. Anyway, I'm not doing a personal endorsement of this product. It's an acting job. And it's not the usual sexist crap you see in commercials. It shows a guy doing the washing up while the woman sits on her arse.' Neat, huh? Coltrane shores up his credibility the instant it has been breached; occasionally, he turns the siege guns on himself. He is suffering from a painful torn ligament suffered while leaping lightly over a wall during *Nuns on the Run*. After spitting blood about the state of the NHS – 'the envy of the world' – he ruefully admits he is going to pay to have it sorted out.

Popular Myths Three: All great clowns conceal fathomless depths of tragedy and depression.

'There is truth there somewhere, if you take the Zen view that every coin has two sides.' He hesitates, a rare thing to witness. 'Johnson said, "If you are melancholic, be not idle. And if you are idle, be not melancholic." When I'm feeling sad and blue, I take the suspension off my Cadillac.'

(Had I but known it at the time, Coltrane was misquoting Johnson but, more interestingly, surreptitiously revealing something very significant about himself in this quote from Johnson. Realizing this, he immediately put a jocular spin on it, effectively occluding the depth of the meaning and distracting the listener from venturing too far along that path. Now, I see, there is something there. Although he rarely makes reference to it, he has occasionally called himself a manic depressive. Certainly, there is the suggestion that the reason he works so hard is to fill up the time that might otherwise be taken over by the black dog of depression. It would also suggest the reason why he has what might be described as an addictive personality. This constant need to fill in space and time is a characteristic of the 'aware' depressive personality. Lecture over; last tranche coming up.)

Over cappuccino, the conversation turns back to Great Men and Coltrane muses on the likes of Sean Connery ('I like him. There's no shite about him. Why he plays golf with Jimmy Tarbuck I'll never understand, but . . .') and the late Sir David Lean.

He remarks that during a recent documentary on Lean, everyone who knew him said what a great man he was without actually admitting that they liked him. 'I think I'd rather be a less than great man and that people wept at my funeral.'

Popular Myths Four: Size doesn't matter.
   'Only nice girls say that.'

So there you have it. The result of my one and only previous professional encounter with the subject of this book. I include it here for several reasons: it is a timely reminder of the kind of combative, amiable, changeable, wary and funny nature of Coltrane. It is a reminder of the fact that I once warmed to him and found him a winning personality. It is a reminder of the body of work that, even then, he had amassed, and the variety of it. Above all, it is a reminder of why I agreed to write this book.

Believe me, many and oft is the time when I shall be grateful for these words; they will console me when everything around me is falling apart, when friends, colleagues and lovers refuse to talk to me;

when I wake up in the middle of the night with the panic sweats, wishing that I'd never embarked on this book, times when I'd rather be doing something – anything – other than slogging through a biography.

It will by now be evident that 'biography' in this case is a misnomer. Rather than abandon a book that I have in good faith begun, I have redirected my attention, come up with an alternative method of dealing with the subject. I shall attempt to discover the nature of Coltrane through his work rather than his life. This approach, I am sure, will cause me many difficulties and allow me to draw conclusions which may be completely fatuous. But I also hope that it will provide some insight into the man whose talent and personality are inextricably linked. A man who, through the actor's concealment of accents, characterization, jokes, performance, inadvertently reveals more about himself than he believes.

That's the pitch. That is how I will proceed.

Hello Robbie.

Chapter 2

FRAGMENTS OF A CHILDHOOD

Note the heading: fragments, shards, bits and pieces of Coltrane's early life, when he was still little Robbie MacMillan, are what's on offer here. This, as I pointed out, is not a conventional biography. In fact, it is hardly a biography in the true sense at all. My mission, now that I have chosen to accept it, is to attempt a portrait of the man from the outside in, to study his work and determine his real character from the roles he chooses and the manner in which he plays them. This may prove an impossible task, or one beyond my capabilities, but I am not going to let that stop me from having a go.

Meanwhile, I will dredge up and put together such facts and data as are available to sketch in the background whenever I can. Bear with me on this. Coltrane, like many artists, can be flamboyant with the facts of his life when he isn't being outright parsimonious. Any failings of accuracy must, of course, be laid at my door. I simply crave your indulgence for those passages which do not deal with my own observation; in the end, it is the only thing I can trust.

'Being born was my first big mistake' is one of Coltrane's favourite openers. And it is guaranteed to put you off before you begin. But it also hints at the darker side to Coltrane's personality. There is little doubt that he is a complex human being, a shadowy, multifaceted personality with a voracious mind and abrasive, strongly held opinions.

'My old man and my mother are fairly typical Scottish Calvinists.

They don't have a lot of fun, but they do have a very strong sense of what's right and wrong.'

Coltrane's earliest memory is of lying beneath a piano listening while his mother played. As a teacher, it behove her to be reasonably proficient in several disciplines rather than just the single trajectory of teaching that seems to be the norm nowadays. Clearly, the MacMillan household was an enlightened one, where books, literature, music and films were part of the normal diet rather than an occasional treat.

The arts were taken care of. But it was by no means an exclusively artistic household. His father, Ian, was a doctor, and this fact introduced another element, another world, into Coltrane's early life.

'I look back on my own life and I don't think I ever spoke to my own father until I was about six. He went off to morning surgery and when he came back I was in bed. I only ever saw my old man in the holidays and on occasional weekends.'

As a GP and a police surgeon, Coltrane's father was on call 24 hours a day and was often summoned in the middle of the night to go to a murder scene and determine the cause of death. Coltrane remembers this well and has often referred to the feelings he had when he awoke in the dead of night to hear his father leaving the house with his medical bag.

Coltrane's father wanted to take his son to view dead bodies at the age of eleven. 'Dad thought people had forgotten how to deal with death, partly because we never see any dead people any more. He was going to show me some gas victims, but my mother wouldn't let me go.'

In addition to literature, the bookshelves held medical books of clinical authority, and Coltrane often ventured to the top shelf to shudder deliciously through the pages of *Medical Jurisprudence and Toxicology*. 'That was the one you were never supposed to open,' he recalled. 'It had colour photographs of people who'd blown themselves up or thrown themselves off buildings.'

At first, it was the gruesome pictures that had a forbidden allure. As time went on, it was the descriptions themselves that caught the young boy's imagination. Herein lay horrors beyond imagining, flayed bodies and pathological descriptions of such casual cruelty that only those of a very limited imagination could fail to have been affected by them. And Coltrane possessed a vivid imagination from an early age.

'We had books by people like Glaister and Churchill in the house. John Glaister more or less invented pathology,' he recalled. 'And Chur-chill did the same with ballistics. It left me with a fascination about why someone could commit murder, cold-blooded murder. How can someone get like that? I can imagine, like most people, murdering someone in defence of my family. Or losing my temper and hitting someone. But to think, "I'll kill someone today. I'd better buy a knife and get some gloves" requires the sort of mind that is fascinating.'

The gruesome stuff was not his to explore alone. Born on 30 March 1950 in Rutherglen, Glasgow, Coltrane was the middle child of three. The elder of his two sisters, Annie Rae, was born two years ahead of him and is largely responsible for encouraging her brother's artistic aspirations.

In a very rare interview in *The Sunday Times* 'Relative Values' series, Annie Rae recalls something of their childhood years: 'From the age of three he always had such presence. He was the boss and I'd trail around after him, getting the blame. Robbie would get out of trouble by being funny. He'd make my parents laugh so much the situation was defused. He always knew he had an audience.'

Both Coltrane and his elder sister shared a taste for movies and painting and it was inevitable that one would nourish the other. But Annie Rae also recalls another obsession of her brother's which is quite enlightening: 'As a child his heroes were all actors, but he was equally obsessed with long-distance lorry drivers. It was all about escape, one way or another. Both of us reacted strongly against our background.'

When a *Time Out* interviewer referred to him as a fat slob, Annie Rae leapt to her brother's defence. And there is plenty of evidence to suggest that Coltrane is a workaholic, that he somehow uses work to fill up time which might otherwise hang heavy on his hands.

'My upbringing gave me an exaggerated work ethic – I can't even enjoy a holiday – and I really am very shy. I'm always afraid that I can't be spontaneously funny, that I will dry up. It's true that I only feel safe expressing myself with people I know well. Perhaps I hope the comedy work will eventually bring me out of myself. I may seem confident and have this big body, but the insecurities I feel go back to childhood.'

Insecurity is an overused word, especially when it comes to describing the actor's motivation. But in Coltrane's case, again, there is plenty of evidence to suggest that it is true. His extraordinary workload, his professional restlessness which sees him bouncing around between England, America, Canada and Europe in a variety of wilfully random roles in film and television, the expanding catalogue of accents and voices and his obsessive indulgences – alcohol, food, women – all indicate a deep-rooted desire to escape from himself; either to become somebody else or to distract himself from his own thoughts by plunging himself into work.

The atmosphere in which he was brought up at home – though far from unhappy – clearly contributed to this. Professional, artistically inclined parents, middle-class values and aspirations and being the only boy between two sisters – all contribute to Coltrane's ultimate stance of armchair rebellion. This was undoubtedly exacerbated by his time spent at Glenalmond public school in Perthshire, where, by his own admission, he spent the unhappiest days of his childhood. The authoritarian regime at Glenalmond did not prevent him from continuing in this rebellious mode, however.

Clearly, the fact that his parents felt compelled to send him to Glenalmond was indicative of their fears about how Coltrane might develop without some serious discipline. But if they thought that the regime of public school would curb his anarchistic tendencies, they were sorely misguided. On the whole, with most exuberant children, the more you try to hem them in, the deeper the need for rebellion roots itself. It is a feature of Coltrane's personality that informs much of his work and his adult character. For most of his life and career, Coltrane has fostered the notion of unresolved rebellion. It is evident in the roles he chooses, the manner in which he conducts himself, his behaviour towards the press and his general demeanour. Part of this rebellion is clearly 'borrowed' from his American icons, the heroes that he keeps in his personal dossier; and part of it is rooted in his formative years.

He revealed an inclination for performance from an early age. Aside from keeping the family amused and using humour to wriggle out of trouble, he made his first appearance on stage at school at the age of twelve, reciting speeches from Henry V clad in a costume of chainmail that had been knitted for him by his mother, Jean.

The young Coltrane also developed an interest in films and the cinema. His father, Ian, used to take him to the cinema regularly and one of Coltrane's earliest film memories is of seeing *Dr No* at the impressionable age of thirteen. And, like any young man who experienced 007 at a similar age, he imagined himself, if not in the role, then certainly in a Bond movie. I myself recall vividly being taken by an aged aunt to see *From Russia With Love* at the tender age of eleven. She was under the impression it was a musical about Anastasia. Boy, was she ever surprised. But from that moment on, I have always been a Bond fan, for good or ill. Coltrane's experience is not so very different.

'I have always wanted to be in a Bond film [he told Garth Pearce]. The first one I saw was *Dr No* with my dad when I was about thirteen. I remember Ursula Andress walking out of the sea in that incredible bikini and the whole place went mad. As a kid, I just wanted to be James Bond. All that sex and having a licence to kill people. This is something all young boys aspire to. We used to leap up and down in the streets, pretending to be him. I would imagine having an Aston Martin DB5 and going to a casino and knowing exactly what to do. As an adolescent you always wonder what you should be doing. But James Bond even knew what wine to order, how to drive fast and how to chat up girls. Of course, the chatting up girls was particularly important.'

Schooldays and young teenage years went by in a flurry of fights, movies, putative girlfriends, the usual stuff. Clearly, Coltrane was heading towards the artistic side but he still had little idea of what he might want to do. He was a passable artist and considered going to art school. He was hooked enough on movies to seek out those above and beyond the usual Hollywood fare, occasionally delving into the repertory cinemas to catch old and unusual features.

Until the age of sixteen, however, the world of acting and the possibility of a career in the business called show had never occurred to him. It was a movie that changed all that. Or rather, an actor. It was the day he went to see Marlon Brando in *The Wild One*, the biker picture that had been banned for fourteen years in Britain. 'There was a scene where he's wearing his New York Rebels leather jacket and a blonde asks him what he's rebelling against. He tells her, in effect, "Whatever there is to rebel against!" I thought "Yes, YES!" And I walked out of the cinema ten feet tall. From that moment, I knew I would never take any flak from anyone. And I haven't. I decided I would not become a doctor or a solicitor and I wouldn't do anything that was expected of me. I'd always thought that acting was for jessies. But I didn't let that put me off.'

After all, what was good enough for Marlon Brando was good enough for Robbie MacMillan. The acting bug, having bitten, lay dormant for some years afterwards, however, while Coltrane tried his hand at painting and went to Glasgow Art School.

Chapter 3

FROM POSH SCHOOL
TO ART SCHOOL

Coltrane's primary education at a local state day school was pretty much par for the course for the son of a respectable middle-class couple from Glasgow. But a combination of Coltrane's irrepressibility, the fact that his father spent a lot of time away from home and the fact that he had two sisters – all persuaded his parents that he should go to public school where he might undo the soft influences to which he was subject at home. This turned out to be a huge miscalculation.

'They tried to turn me into a gent, which proved a total waste of money.'

Obsessiveness came easily to Coltrane. Later tales of extraordinary self-indulgence, not to say self-abuse, with legendary episodes of him drinking an entire crate of strong lager, without apparently getting drunk can be sourced in his early years. Compare this with the way he discovered the films of Luis Bunuel while at art school; he simply gathered all 26 works together and watched them one after the other. And later, when researching his one-man show on Dr Johnson, he read 22 books on or by his subject. When Coltrane says he's 'a bottle of whisky a day man or nothing', he isn't joking. And this refers to everything he would consider worth doing. If it's worth doing, it's worth doing to excess.

Coltrane was thirteen when his parents sent him to 'The Eton of Scotland', Glenalmond, in Perthshire. To the ebullient tearaway with the fast mouth and the facility to amuse it came as something of a shock to land in an environment of strict discipline and rigid rules. According to accounts, Coltrane was chubby, not sporting and not very happy during his early years at the school. It was also during this period that, according to some of his schoolfriends, he became interested in being funny.

The humour and wit that he had deployed at home to make his parents and sisters laugh and to divert potential trouble were clearly honed in an environment where bullying and a tough authoritarian regime were the norm. But it was also noted that Coltrane, while not academically distinguished, already had the makings of an enquiring mind. He was interested in things and he was not satisfied until he had discovered how the things in which he was interested actually worked. In another life, Coltrane might have made a decent physicist, cataloguing, analysing and speculating on everything from the workings of a coffee percolator to nuclear fission.

Euan Kerr, his first friend at Glenalmond, says of the thirteen-year-old Coltrane (then MacMillan): 'He was phenomenally keen on lorries – he used to pretend to be a lorry. He knew all the makes, where they went, everything about them. He had a very enquiring, curious mind.'

The young Coltrane, or 'Fat Rab' – 'He probably christened himself that,' says Kerr – was bright, witty, a bit of an oddball and plump. 'He was . . . chubby,' says Kerr, who is still a friend of Coltrane. 'He was the classic chubby young boy. He was the fat boy who started telling jokes to protect himself.'

'He could be both melancholy and happy,' says Alex Grieve, another contemporary at Glenalmond. 'He wasn't conformist, although he wasn't the most rebellious boy, by any means. When he was in charge of the school dormitory, he used to rule it with a fairly good rod of iron.'

According to William Leith, Coltrane's least favourite journalist, Coltrane's schooldays 'sound as if they were intense, mildly prankish, and a trial to him, offset by a few glorious moments on stage, in revues, making people laugh. Once, he stole gowns from various prefects and hung them on the clock tower. In his last year, he got "reasonably fit", and won a place in the First XV, as tight-head prop.'

While he may have been considered 'a bit weird' by some of his schoolmates, he was far from an outsider. He was part of a schoolboy gang called The Curry Boys and they engaged in the customary disgusting rituals for initiates.

'We had a special ceremony,' recalls Coltrane, 'using a dead crow's head which we kept buried. It had maggots coming out of its eyeballs and we'd make people kiss it.'

When things got a little out of hand and Coltrane was threatened with expulsion, he recalls, 'The head was warned there'd be a riot if they did. They called me Fat Rab. At fifteen, I was 6ft 1in. I was in the First XV, head of the debating society, I won an art prize and played rugby for Scotland Schoolboys on tour in Canada.'

For all the good times at Glenalmond, there were plenty of bad ones. During his five years there, he was frequently subjected to bullyings and beatings. And it wasn't just teachers who beat the recalcitrant Coltrane. The prefects drew blood, too, with their vicious canings.

Coltrane has described his time at the now £11,000-a-year college as 'like being in Borstal. It was a prison – only there were no screws, so the prefects beat you up. I remember it as a place of unmitigated cruelty, it was just legalized violence. Luckily I was quite a tough kid.'

Coltrane has since called for all public schools to be abolished and has vowed never to send his son, Spencer, away to school ('Not unless I hate him').

Another of his schoolfriends revealed: 'Prefects were allowed to beat the younger boys and one particular prefect took a real dislike to Robbie and really laid into him.'

Once, in a desperate bid to escape the bully-boy prefects, Robbie was forced to hide in the school chapel. His old history teacher, David Perry, said: 'I remember going into chapel one evening to play the organ when Robbie emerged from the shadows and I asked him what on earth he was doing – I knew he couldn't be praying. He said it was the only place he could get away from the prefects. He was right, they were forever getting at him for something.'

Coltrane, however, proved to be too tough to be broken down by successive beatings. One former master who admitted beating him on a regular basis said: 'I only realized when I stopped beating Robbie that it did him no good at all. It had no effect.'

David Perry added: 'Robbie was slightly different from the other boys. He was lively and full of fun – very engaging. He was very popular because he was a bit of a lad and rebelled against the rules.'

Surprisingly, in the end Coltrane was persuaded to become a prefect himself. Another teacher explained: 'At first he refused because he thought it would ruin his anti-Establishment image. But it worked. He made a good prefect. He could exert authority and get the youngsters to jump to his command. But he was not a bully, he knew too well what it was like to be bullied.'

To say that Coltrane was unhappy at Glenalmond public school is the understatement of his life. He absolutely hated it from stem to stern and lost very little time making his opinions felt at the school. He hasn't stopped digging away at it ever since. What pissed him off even more was the separation from his sisters, especially Annie Rae, who had gone off to art school in Edinburgh to study graphic art and was leading the kind of life that Coltrane really envied.

'I went to public school and was terribly unhappy. It was a rigid, disciplinarian, extremely right-wing environment. On days off I used to visit Annie in Edinburgh, where she was an art student. She used to introduce me to all her arty friends in the most unpatronizing way and I suddenly thought, "Jeez, I'm art too. *That's* what's wrong with me!" It was entirely down to Annie that I realized I had some kind of creative potential. When I left school, I went to art college, too.'

Life at Glenalmond was made almost bearable by this contact with Annie Rae – who used to send pictures of Orson Welles to Coltrane at school as she knew he was utterly obsessed with Welles as an actor and director.

The five years at Glenalmond forged Coltrane's character into what he has now become. In spite of his hatred of the regime and his desperate unhappiness throughout his time there, he managed to discover and explore aspects of himself which were to prove fruitful. In terms of future prospects and incipient careers, Coltrane had two prime choices, acting and painting. While he enjoyed performing and making people laugh, it was art and painting that first got under Coltrane's skin. He had a certain facility for drawing and painting and determined to become an artist.

When Coltrane enrolled at the Glasgow School of Art, he did so at the prompting of his elder sister, who seemed to be having such a good time at art school in Edinburgh. Coltrane viewed the prospect of actually making art and having a wild time in a completely unfettered environment as something close to heaven. But he was serious about his ambition, took his art seriously. He wanted to be a painter. It was not to be and Coltrane had to make a very difficult decision.

'I was painting portraits, which I was never very good at, but I had it in my head, somehow, that you had to be good at portraits to be a great artist.'

To be just a good artist wasn't enough for Coltrane, even at this early stage. 'I had this epiphany. I looked at my work one morning and thought, "This is not what I had in mind at all. This is nothing like what is going on in my head." It was no good. And I didn't want to be anything other than a brilliant artist, of course. I mean, what young man sets out to be mediocre at something? I wanted to be a fucking great artist. I didn't want to be an artist who was content to be not very good. That's fair enough, isn't it? It depressed me for a long time, although the outside world didn't know. They thought I was fine, that I'd get a lovely wee draughtsman's job, design some nice posters. They didn't realize there was a more important way of making a living.'

Following his stint at art school, Coltrane attended Moray House College of Education in Edinburgh. In Scotland universities did not traditionally train teachers, so all graduates – of universities, art colleges, whatever – who wished to become teachers had to spend a year following their degree in a college of education. Sean Hignett was a lecturer in arts at Moray House in the 1970s and recalls: 'Robbie MacMillan was one of my students in the Seventies, spending a year in the college following graduation from the art college. I used to mix a great deal with the art graduates who were the most unconventional bunch of students in what was at the time a very sedate country and very sedate college – one that had tried to kick me out for writing an "obscene" novel. Robbie used to turn up in a battered leather motorcycle jacket, looking like a rocker. He was quite talented, actually, but he lost a lot of his drawings in a fire and I think that discouraged him.'

Whatever the reason, Coltrane abandoned his aspirations to be an artist and decided to pursue his alternative ambition to be an actor. Without formal training, Coltrane simply began hanging out in the vicinity of actors on the Scottish scene, shuttling between Glasgow and Edinburgh, entertaining the Edinburgh Festival crowd at Bannerman's bar with his incessant anecdotes, accents and general comments, running through a succession of MacJobs before meeting up with playwright John Byrne, who cast him in the *The Slab Boys*, his trilogy about three foul-mouthed Glasgow boys. It was the aspiring actor's first major break; he changed his name to Coltrane and started getting small roles on stage and in films.

Then, in 1976, a personal tragedy occurred that devastated Coltrane and has left a deep psychological wound on him ever since. His sister Jane – at twentyone, five years younger than Coltrane – committed suicide while studying at York University.

A gifted English student, Jane appeared to have everything to live for. But she suffered from deep depression that led her to make her first suicide attempt when she was only eighteen.

A friend of hers at university, Robert Mason, revealed that she wanted to become a social worker but was worried that her middle-class background was too different from that of the people she would be working with. He also said that Jane had confided to him that she'd had a mental breakdown during her first year at university and tried to kill herself with a drugs overdose. She survived that first attempt, but two years later was still on anti-depressants and finally swallowed a handful of Ludiomil tablets after a late-night drinking session at her student digs.

Like Coltrane, Jane engaged fully with life's pleasures, possibly as an antidote to the depression that dogged her towards the end of her life. 'She was a bit of a tomboy,' recalled York neighbour Mary Dent. 'There were numerous rowdy parties and late-night comings and goings at the house.' Another friend, Catherine Loughley, said Jane would often do wild things when she'd had a drink – like making a cake in the middle of the night, going for a midnight cycle ride, or taking a moonlit swim in the river.

Jane's suicide, coming just seven years after the death of Coltrane's father from lung cancer at the age of 56, placed an intolerable burden on Coltrane. He was very close to Jane and subsequently took on the task of travelling from the family home in St Andrew's, Scotland, to York to collect his sister's clothes and possessions. It was an ordeal that left him grief-stricken, and on the return train journey to Scotland in May 1976, as he sat with Jane's things beside him, Coltrane snapped. A close friend of the family recalled the incident.

'Robbie was so deranged with grief that he went berserk and vandalized the train carriage. He was about as broken up by Jane's death as it is possible to be. They were very close, and for a while I think he seriously considered following suit and killing himself, too. It took him a good three years to even start to come to terms with Jane's death – his mother, Jean, just pulled the shutters down and withdrew into her own grief, and Robbie had to deal with it by himself. Where he comes from the attitude is: "Pull yourself together, and if you are feeling down, go in the bushes and come out when you are feeling better. But don't bother us with your troubles." That is basically what he had to do, and to this day Robbie won't discuss Jane's death.'

There is little doubt that her death had a profound and lasting effect on him. It was a trauma that shattered his world, deeply affected his attitudes to family life and has informed his emotional life ever since. His surviving sister, Annie Rae, was the only person with whom he could share his grief at the time, and the catastrophic event bonded them together even more closely. If ever Coltrane is attacked or misrepresented in the press, Annie Rae is the first to leap to his defence, in spite of the fact that she places an even higher value on privacy than he does.

Coltrane has never spoken about it in public and rarely speaks about it even to his closest friends. There is something Stygian here, a dark lake of anxiety, guilt and fear. No one loses a sibling under such circumstances without carrying the scar for the rest of his life. It is a legacy of loss that must be borne, even if, over the years, it is buried deep. Clearly, Coltrane's occasional admission that he is a manic depressive is an expression of the same fear that his sister was not strong enough to contain.

Coltrane's reaction was understandably violent. But wrecking a train carriage was not the action of a destructive child or a rock musician. Nor was it a catharsis. It was simply the mute expression of a grief and rage too terrible to bear, too shattering to comprehend.

Chapter 4

FAT FAB RAB:
THE BIG TIMES OF A FAT ACTOR

Everyone makes fun of the fat boy. He is the class scapegoat, the one who has to parade his blubber in the showers, the one who has to puff into last position in the compulsory cross-country running, the one who everyone knows – no matter how bad it gets for you personally – is always going to be worse off than you are, because he is fat.

Is Robbie Coltrane fat? Or is he just big? And anyway, what the hell does it matter?

Actually, it matters a lot. How much space a person displaces in the air can determine the way in which he or she is perceived. Can we imagine a thin Fitz – even with the knowledge that Robert Lindsay was supposed to play him? What would happen if Coltrane suddenly stepped from a '47 Cadillac in a new, slimmed-down, streamlined form? It would be like Nigel Lawson – having got used to him one way, to see him in another, radically altered guise leads one to believe that he has either been terribly ill or has had some kind of radical cosmetic surgery.

There are times when Coltrane is fat, and times when he is not. There are also times when he seems fat and those when he seems not. As a buffoon, in a comedy role like *Nuns on the Run* or as the transvestite in *The Fruit Machine*, Coltrane acts fat. He is fat, therefore he is funny. The only conceivable way of making him funnier is to make him wear women's clothes.

But put him in a suit and a serious role and he doesn't appear fat any more. Big, certainly, but fat? No. Can it be that Coltrane is that good an actor? Is it possible that a man can create the illusion of weight and corpulence and redistribute it at will? While it is not unusual for actors to appear larger than life, and while it is true that the camera does in fact lie at every given opportunity with a little help from the lighting cameraman, the property department, wardrobe, carpenter, trench digger and so on, Coltrane sustains these illusions as if by magic.

There are occasions when he seems bigger in real life than he does on film. It is as if the screen is not big enough for him; he needs more space. Even Robert de Niro had to put on weight physically to play the ageing Jake LaMotta in *Raging Bull*; and then had to lose it all again. Coltrane, on the other hand, has only to think himself thin in order to play someone who is not fat. His weight fluctuates totally independently of his *modus operandi*. It's a non-Method thing.

Largeness is part of Coltrane's presentation to the world. He is an expansive human being in many ways, generous of appetite, encyclopaedic of knowledge, a voracious reader and hunter/gatherer of facts and fancies, both trivial and significant, a man given to the grand gesture and the loquacious anecdote. In other words, not a shrinking violet.

Which is not exactly the way he sees himself. Coltrane is on record as claiming that he is, by nature, quite shy and retiring, a man somewhat fearful of social situations and constantly aware that he will be expected to be funny. He has said that he worries about drying up, about being unable to contribute. Which may explain why he often dominates a gathering, delivering a torrential patter of stories, observations and comments in a bewildering variety of different accents, simply to damn up the silence that (he feels) perpetually threatens to engulf him. Clearly, this is not such a worry in his home environment, where it must come as a relief not to have to bow to the pressure of being Robbie Coltrane every five minutes of the day. But that doesn't stop him from attempting to remodel himself in a new image – lose weight, stop smoking, and clean up his act.

There is something about fat actors that delivers a variety of messages without them trying; they can be funny and sinister simultaneously; they can be slobbish and gross or surprisingly delicate to the point of fastidiousness; and they can be either warm and heroically cuddly or truly madly menacing. Think of Sidney Greenstreet in *The Maltese Falcon*, John Goodman in *Barton Fink*, Willoughby Goddard in television's *William Tell*; think of John Candy, John Belushi, Fatty Arbuckle, Oliver Hardy, W. C. Fields. The Fat Man is alternately the figure of fun or the figure of fear. Sometimes, he can be both at once.

The thing about fat men is that they often delude you into thinking they'll be friendly; Shakespeare put his finger on it in *Julius Caesar.* 'Let me have men about me that are fat; sleek-headed men and such as sleep o' nights. Yon Cassius hath a lean and hungry look. He thinks too much: such men are dangerous.'

As all outsized actors know, this is one of the great natural advantages of their appearance. Coltrane had the additional advantage in *Cracker* of having been known primarily for his comic roles; the shock to the system of having a fat comedian suddenly playing a dark and dangerous dramatic role was of course rather delicious casting. And it is a situation with which film-maker and casting directors have flirted time and again in the past.

Coltrane has always been big, even if he wasn't actually fat. It is only in the last two decades that it has become problematic. 'Even when I was thin I was big,' he has said. 'As a sixteen-year-old – and I was an athlete then – I couldn't get shirts that fitted round my collar.'

This would be a matter of no consequence but for two things: the reasons offered by his friends and colleagues as to why he put on weight and the increasing concern about the state of his health as a result.

Clearly, it is a matter of concern to him. Otherwise he would not continue to go on diets from time to time; usually in the same context as giving up alcohol and, whenever possible, smoking.

'It's giving up smoking,' he told Andrew Billen, when asked abut gaining weight after a period of wife-inspired dieting. 'But in terms of life-threatening behaviour, smoking 80 cigarettes a day is tip-top. You can lose the weight but they are not going to give you a new set of lungs. My dad died of lung cancer.'

There are other problems associated with the weight, as Coltrane remarked to Gordon Burn, when the writer asked him if his (then) current weight bothered him.

'Considerably. I'm really going to have to lose some. Because I'm putting on about a stone a year. You can laugh. It's serious. It's a strain on the old heart and there's the possibility of diabetes and thrombosis. All the possibilities. There's a quote in, I believe, *Henry V part 2*, where he talks about Falstaff and he says, "Everybody knows that the grave opens wider for a fat man." Which is so very true. That's why my physical for every movie I'm going into is so thorough. "Jeezus. We're investing eight million quid and this fat bastard might keel over halfway through." '

The trouble is, Coltrane has a very hearty appetite, as most of those who have interviewed him over lunch – myself included – can testify. He loves food – the preparation, the savouring of it and the final ingestion. There is even a Robbie Coltrane recipe for French Toast lurking on the Internet, the details of which kind of sum up his attitude to food.

New York Diner French Toast

I got this recipe from a short-order cook in a New York diner many years ago. It's very simple and delicious and although everyone thinks they can make French toast it ain't necessarily so! The secret is the thickness of the bread, the ratio of milk to egg (which should be 50/50) and the vanilla. There are lots of ways to serve this. My favourite is with a sprinkling of lemon or lime juice, then dusted up with icing sugar. You could spread maple syrup on the toast and serve with crisp bacon, or top it with two fried or poached eggs and a sprinkling of grated cheese.

2 large eggs
4 fl oz/110 ml milk
1 tsp vanilla extract
A pinch of salt
1 small white loaf (must be good quality), cut into slices 0.5 inch/1cm thick
1 oz/25 g butter

1 tbsp oil

METHOD

Beat the eggs, milk, vanilla and salt together until smooth, then pour the mixture into a wide shallow dish. Dip each slice of bread briefly into the mixture, until wet but not soaked through. Melt the butter and oil in a frying pan and fry the dipped bread over a fairly high heat until golden brown, turning to cook the other side.

Serves 2 to 3.

Contrary to what his schoolfriends claim, Coltrane himself says that he wasn't fat as a child and tends to lay the blame on his excessive drinking.

'I wasn't a fat kid and I didn't start putting on weight until I was 27 and took up drinking, I do try to keep my weight down – but it's difficult when you're filming. You get there early in the morning and there's a big breakfast, then there's elevenses and lunch and tea and dinner. You can't not put on weight! It's not fair, I had a flatmate once who'd have a fried breakfast, three pints at lunchtime and a big dinner – and he was always slim. I don't eat any breakfast, I rarely eat lunch, but I'm fat. What can I do?'

What he did, and continues to do, is go on diets. In October 1986 he flew to Mexico, where he attended a special health clinic near Guadalajara in order to get his diet under strict control.

He again blames drinking for his massive weight gains in an interview he gave Steve Absalom in the *Daily Mail* in April 1990, 'All this is not from stuffing my face. I don't eat that much. Booze is my undoing. I can drink a gallon of beer and not feel the least bit drunk. The one thing about being fat is that it's rather like the *Portrait* [sic] *of Dorian Gray*. I have this terror that there's a lined, boring old man under this chubby exterior.'

More recently he has been motivated by his love for his son Spencer and his 'wife', Rhona Gemmell.

'It's the baby,' he confessed when Spencer was ten months old. 'I started thinking about when he's five years old and wants to run around the garden. I don't want to be sitting indoors like some wheezy beggar saying, "You just run away with your wee friends, son, I'll waddle over later." Spencer deserves more than that, and if anyone is going to be kicking the ball around with him, then it's going to be me.'

Towards the end of 1993 he had apparently lost seven stone and was determined to keep it going until he had dropped ten stone. Not that he was in danger of becoming obsessed with his body image.

'If you open trendy men's magazines, then they're full of half-naked men selling aftershave with absolutely perfect-looking bodies. Well, I take enormous consolation in the fact that most of them are gay. No real man would spend that much time looking after his body because women aren't that impressed. Whether you've got 16-inch biceps or 21-inch biceps really doesn't interest a woman. What women want is someone big enough to defend the home. Someone like me. It makes me laugh watching all those slimming drink adverts on the telly. Someone will twirl round saying, "I've lost a stone-and-a-half." I shout back at them, "Hey, what do you know? I lost a stone-and-a-half off my dick!" The diet has been a nightmare, though – especially being around people like the guys who are in *Cracker* with me. They're very sociable types and are always saying, "Let's go for a drink." But, of course, I can't because alcohol is absolutely forbidden on my diet. It's not that I want to get drunk – getting up at 6.00 a.m. to start filming has meant I couldn't do that even if I wanted. But sometimes I think, "Christ, what I'd do to be able to go out for a curry with them." It does take a lot of discipline. But hell, it's only a year of your life and I just had to make my flaming mind up. You have to have a vision of yourself when you've finished. It's an act of imagination as much as anything else and I've got a picture of a tall, slim me in my mind's eye. There's a thousand nice things that happen to you when the weight starts coming off. I got in a plane today and I had absolutely no problem getting the lap strap on. I can go up and down stairs and get in and out of cars without any trouble. I'm wearing a suit now that I haven't been able to get on for the last five-and-a-half years. I can always do something if I make up my mind. After the weight, my next goal is to quit smoking.'

The comparisons with other large stars in no way disconcerts Coltrane. On the contrary, he appears to lap them up, even playing Oliver Hardy at one stage. But he doesn't care for the association and accusation of self-destruction that occasionally accompanies them.

Just before setting off for the States to make a movie, he revealed in early 1988 why it was that the Americans – who tend to like their stars whippet-thin and squeaky clean – were encouraging him.

'They think they've got another John Belushi. I'm not a John Belushi. My God ... poor, sad, man. I won't self-destruct. But I'm a Celt and we do have our dark sides.'

Indeed, Coltrane's dark side turns to face us every now and then – especially in the company of the press – and one wonders whether or not he sees the warning in Belushi's life and untimely death. Belushi was a gifted comic whose obsessive nature drove him to the drugs which finally killed him. Coltrane is a gifted comic whose obsessive nature drives him periodically to alcohol, cigarettes and food. It would be difficult to establish which of the two lifestyles is more likely to shorten your life.

'I'm afraid to say I was something of a hellraiser,' Coltrane has admitted on more than one occasion. 'And if you're out having a Good Time, all you're fit for the next day is tidying the flat.'

'The problem is,' he continued, 'that I don't enjoy exercise. I have a boat, and I enjoy sailing, but that is mainly arms and torso. I go fishing, and have to walk miles to get there, but then it's just standing around. I don't wheeze like some fat people, but I feel the heat and I know now I'm 40 that I have to be careful about heart attacks [Coltrane said in 1990] I'm never going to be a wee skinny guy, but I'd like to look in the mirror and see myself as I was ten years ago when I was fit and thin and could take out a bus queue.'

Like all people whose size is constantly a subject for comment, either to his face or behind his back, Coltrane has an equivocal attitude to his girth. There are times when he simply laughs it off, referring to his past successes with women 'How come I'm not a virgin?' was a particular refrain – times when he sheepishly admits to being a serial dieter, even times – hidden from public view – when he becomes seriously depressed.

And yet his tremendous physical energy belies the fact of his size. When a *Time Out* writer referred to him as a 'slob', his older sister,

Annie Rae, was incensed. 'A slob is someone with a beer belly watching television all day,' she told *The Sunday Times*. 'Robbie does five times more than anyone else and he was like that way before he was famous.'

In an article for *The Times* magazine in 1993, Ginny Dougary found his size vehemently distracting from his seductive powers and his apparent ease with women. She cited in particular the dubious context of Coltrane in America in the road series, *Coltrane in a Cadillac*:

'My pulse fails to quicken. I am not in a position to be unkind about fat people, but there is something unfortunate about the sight of a man of Coltrane's girth holding forth in America. For this is a continent which boasts some of the most obese people in the world. And Coltrane is right up there among them. As he zips down the highway in his open-top Cadillac, his face is so roomy that it billows in the wind like an astronaut's at take-off. It is hard to concentrate on what he is saying – which is not exactly funny, anyway – because he looks so uncomfortable in his over-tight suits (described by William Leith, Coltrane's least favourite male journalist, as the split-condom look), folding himself in and out of his elegant, svelte car with difficulty.'

Dougary then goes on to say that Coltrane in the flesh is actually rather sexy, reminding her less of a 'slormy couch potato' and more of a languorous Roman emperor or blown-up cherub. It is, she says, his zest for life that carries his bulk above and beyond the accusations of slobbery with malevolence and into a region somewhat more rarefied – a man with a Rabelaisian relish for life, '100 per cent vivid'.

Coltrane's enjoyment of life's pleasures is offset by his ferocious work ethic. He plunges into his projects and work with the fanaticism of a zealot rather than the hesitancy of a dilettante. The cliché of the person who works hard and plays hard is particularly, spectacularly true of Coltrane.

The weight can work both ways, too. It gives him metaphorical weight on the screen, which he is able to dominate simply by his sheer size; also, it grants a psychological weight that many less substantial actors would have to convey in a different manner. When Coltrane made his entrance as the Russian gangster, Valentin, in the James Bond film, *GoldenEye*, he delivered a bigger performance than the role probably merited. But he was so keen to maintain a profile in James Bond that he persuaded the screenwriters not to kill off his character, in order to allow the possibility of Valentin appearing in other James Bond films. This appears to have worked, as Coltrane has just been signed up as the chief villain in the forthcoming Bond film, *The World is Not Enough*.

Chapter 5

IN PICTURES:
COLTRANE'S EARLY MOVIES

After buggering about in Glasgow and hanging around the fringes of
the movie business in Edinburgh, especially during the Festival, where
he worked as an official chauffeur, driving directors, stars and other
celebrated visitors from the airport to their hotels and around the city,
Coltrane finally sidled into film himself.

His first appearance on the big screen was an uncredited walk-on
role in Bertrand Tavernier's *Deathwatch* (1980), the screen version
of D. G. Compton's science fiction novel *The Continuous Katherine
Mortenhoe*. Shot in Glasgow, it starred Romy Schneider (in one of her
last roles) as a woman suffering from a fatal disease who is secretly
filmed as she dies by a documentary cameraman (Harvey Keitel) with
a camera implanted in his brain. Set in the future when all diseases
and life-threatening illnesses have supposedly been eradicated, it is
deemed greatly in the public interest to record this unique event, no
matter what the cost in dignity to the suffering woman. It is a dark
and brilliant futurist work, almost as good as Godard's *Alphaville*, and
benefited greatly from being shot in Glasgow by a French director.

Film guide archivist Leonard Maltin describes it as 'a biting commentary on media abuse and manipulation, with solid performances,
direction.'

In the same year, Coltrane got a walk-on role in *Flash Gordon*. Billed
as 'Man at airfield', it was a cough and a spit. In the opening sequences
of the film, when Flash is sitting in his car at an aerodrome, Ming the
Merciless (Max Von Sydow) is playing games with the Earth's weather,
sending showers of hot hailstones like miniature flaming meteorites

down on to the face of the planet. As they bounce off the roof of his car, Flash looks up into the windows of the aerodrome's control room and sees the controller walk towards the window. It is none other than Coltrane, blue shirt open at the neck, who peers out at the unusual weather conditions.

Shortly afterwards, as Dale and Flash board the aircraft, Coltrane walks up behind them and closes the aeroplane door, locking it shut. And that's it. Coltrane's big-screen first *credited role* in movies? It was hardly an auspicious event, though, looking back, it should have been.

Having hung around with musicians, film-makers, playwrights and assorted punks in New York at the tail end of the 1970s, Coltrane naturally found himself being courted by some of the fringe dwellers who wanted to use his considerable presence. Among the most creative of the New York underground film-makers, Amos Poe was also probably the most highly regarded. Poe was born in Tel Aviv in 1949 and his family emigrated to the US eight years later. He made his first series of photographs in 1968 on the subject of the Russian invasion of Czechoslovakia. In the early Seventies he made Super-8 films and worked for a time in film distribution. Shortly afterwards, he teamed with Czech musician Ivan Kral (of Patti Smith's band) to document the exciting Punk Rock scene in downtown Manhattan. Their film, *The Blank Generation*, is one of the handful of seminal works on the subject. Poe's central dramatic theme of the newcomer struggling with an alien environment is intriguingly explored in the loose trilogy of *Unmade Beds*, *The Foreigner* and *Subway Rider* – films which are immensely popular on the festival circuit.

His short films had established him on the late-night circuit, and he and Coltrane formed an attachment based on love of film that was to blossom into a professional relationship leading to the actor's first leading movie role.

Poe, like Coltrane, was a big fan of *noir* thrillers and his knowledge of the roots of *noir*, from German Expressionist cinema through early Hollywood, was encyclopaedic. He envisioned a punk *film noir*, set in New York, that paid tribute to his favourite directors while capturing something of the dark subterranean river of urban paranoia and violence that runs through the city. Gathering together a number of luminaries of the New York music scene, Poe fashioned a tale about a psychotic saxophone busker who goes on a murder spree and hides out in the New York subway. He hired a saxophonist and actor John Lurie as the killer and Coltrane as his nemesis, a hardbitten detective who went by the allusive name of Fritz Langley. This was a none-too-subtle reference to the great German director Fritz Lang, whose early Expressionist films included the monumental silent science fiction film, *Metropolis*. Lang had moved to Hollywood in the 1930s and into the classic *noir* genre, directing films like *The Big Heat*. To Poe, he was a god among film-makers.

The random, virtually plotless movie was saved by the brooding atmosphere of menace that was a result of Lurie's haunting score. Coltrane does very well as Langley, but the odour of underground movie clings to it in the wilfully grainy cinematography, the cavalier approach to narrative and the random street characters and trashy punks who people the movie. Consequently, it works better as a quasi-fictional document of the New York scene at the time (it was released in 1981) rather than as a coherent movie.

But it gave Coltrane the impetus he needed to kick-start a career as an actor. Back in Britain, he began to pick up small parts in films purely on the basis of his looks and presence. He was a heavy in Mai Zetterling's *Scrubbers* (1982) – the female version of *Scum* set in a girls' reform school – which also contains notable performances from Miriam Margolyes and a very young Kathy Burke. Although it suffered from comparisons with the superior *Scum*, Zetterling's film ventured into territory rarely explored outside of American exploitation movies.

Coltrane appeared briefly in *Slipstream* in 1989. Starring opposite Mark Hamill was Bill Paxton as a roguish black marketeer who opens the film by hijacking Byron, the killer android whom cop Hamill has just captured. With Byron by his side, Paxton returns to his settlement, called Hell's Kitchen, before turning in the android himself to the authorities for the large reward on offer for his apprehension. As Paxton enters the somewhat curious set-up, which resembles a cross between a circus and a post-Armageddon tent city like those featured in *Mad Max* movies, Coltrane and several other inhabitants are seen cavorting in a hot tub. Coltrane, somewhat eccentrically, is wearing a vest. The conclusion is that to save water everyone bathes together and does their laundry at the same time, while still wearing their clothes.

It has to be said that Coltrane looks mighty uncomfortable in this sequence, an observation given credence when he begins to speak. He opts, for no good reason, for a somewhat unlikely urban American accent, though it is difficult to place. It sounds bogus, a rare thing for Coltrane.

Clearly, he is one of Paxton's 'gang' of outlaws. This is confirmed when he is next seen leading a handful of the other guys through the woods like post-Apocalypse Sherwood Forest outlaws. They come across Hamill and his partner (Kitty Aldridge) and challenge them. It is at this point that we realize just how bad the dialogue is. Even the resourceful Coltrane cannot bring a great deal of conviction to lines like: 'This is forbidden territory. What are you doing? Answer, or die.'

'You hear that, boys? We're all under arrest. Well, I could just die of embarrassment.'

Indeed. Coltrane leans on 'die' with more than necessary force, leaving one in no doubt that he could just die of embarrassment from having to spout such turgid stuff. Luckily, a brief gunfight later, most of his band are dead and being buried by Hamill and Aldridge who, being the heroes, are quicker on the draw and more accurate than any old bunch of outlaws.

In 1982 he also appeared in *Ghost Dance* – the English equivalent of a New York underground movie – written and directed by Ken McMullen. A kind of existential meditation on the nature of death and the afterlife as viewed through a Marxist lens, *Ghost Dance* boasted a wildly fashionable Anglo-French cast which included Pascale Ogier, Dominique Pinon (to whom we had just been introduced as the shaven-headed punk in Jean-Jacques Beineix's *Diva*) and Leonie Mellinger, who concludes the film by making love on top of Karl Marx's grave in Highgate cemetery. What attracted Coltrane to it is anyone's guess, though perhaps it was the political hue of McMullen's script. Or maybe he was lured by the promise of making that rare thing, a British art-house movie. Either way, it sucked.

Moving from the ludicrous to the ridiculous has never proved much of a problem for Coltrane, whose choice of projects sometimes makes one question his judgement. At this stage of his career, he may be

forgiven for the seemingly haphazard nature of his roles; screen experience was his most pressing need, and he didn't mind making a fool of
himself in order to achieve it. So it was out of a no-budget art movie
and into a big-budget sword and sorcery film.

Krull (1983) was directed by Peter (*Bullitt*) Yates, not that you'd
know it. A truly dreadful contribution to the genre, it suffered from
anonymous and anodyne leads (Ken Marshall and Lysette Anthony),
a silly, uninventive script and some mindbendingly inappropriate
casting. Coltrane plays a character called Rhun, and all one can say is
that he is in good company in a bad film; Freddie Jones, Liam Neeson,
Alun Armstrong and Francesca Annis are also involved in this farrago,
though you rarely see it on their CVs. Bernard Bresslaw plays a
Cyclops, which sort of says it all.

In the same year (1983) Coltrane found himself once again in
prestigious company in Richard Eyre's amiably eccentric comedy,
Loose Connections. Lindsay Duncan plays an English feminist who
with her cohorts build their own car so they can all drive to a big
convention in Germany. Unfortunately, her friends are unable to go,
and so she substitutes an apparently gay fellow who turns out to be
an incredibly chauvinistic pig in disguise. It's significance for Coltrane
is that it gave him a chance to show off his knowledge and enthusiasm
for cars as well as his prowess as a mechanic.

Former *Time Out* film critic Chris Petit then cast Coltrane in his
obscure and enigmatic thriller, *Chinese Boxes*. Set in West Berlin
(before the Wall came down), the film features Will Patton as an
innocent American who finds himself in the middle of an international intrigue. What precisely that intrigue is never becomes clear,
although Coltrane's character Harwood, among many others in the
supporting cast, is clearly a charlatan or, at the very least, a chameleon,
given to playing games and disseminating disinformation about
himself and the plot. Once again, Coltrane must have been lured by
the dense script, which may have read like an intelligent twist on the
genre but which becomes completely incomprehensible on the screen.

Chinese Boxes in which Coltrane gets fourth billing, was Chris Petit's
third movie, following *Radio On* and *An Unsuitable Job For A Woman*.
Produced by Stephen Woolley and Nik Powell, it marked a low point
for Petit, an intelligent man with a taste for genre obscurity and

political paranoia, both of which are excessively indulged in this low-budget thriller. Producer Stephen Woolley recalls the film with some reluctance.

'Chris came to us with a great idea. He wanted to do a low-budget thriller for around £200,000 and set it in Berlin. It was a mystery that was supposed to have an intricate mechanism to unlock it, hence the title *Chinese Boxes*. I went over to Berlin about three weekends and it was clear that things were going wrong. The only thing that cheered me up was going out drinking with Robbie.'

Unfortunately, Petit, an erudite and immensely likeable man, was not terribly good at dealing with actors and pretty well allowed them to get on with it without giving them any guidance. Consequently, says Woolley, 'the actors were all going over the top. There was no coherence.'

Even Petit today admits that it was not among Coltrane's favourite movies or experiences. 'I don't think he'll thank you for reminding him of it. It rarely appears on his CV nowadays.'

In spite of this, Coltrane comes out of it with some dignity as an actor. Having opted to play the role of Harwood, the mysterious Customs and Excise officer, in what Woolley fondly recalls as his 'Orson Welles mode', Coltrane is at least consistent in his performance and consistently watchable in the film, which is more than can be said for his fellow actors.

We catch a glimpse of him during the opening scenes as a group of men stand around in a Berlin street at night smoking and drinking from a tequila bottle. One of them, Frank Wolf, appears to have just emerged from prison and his friends are celebrating his release. Further down the street, unbeknown to them, a man sits in a car smoking and studying them. This is Harwood, and Coltrane presents him at once as a contemplative mystery, short hair slicked back, light suit and quizzical gaze. He looks like a private eye or a police detective.

Shortly after the friends take their leave of each other, Wolf is seen driving through a tunnel being pursued by another car. The car draws alongside and the man in the passenger seat (Chris Petit, the director, doing a Hitchcock) stares coldly at Wolf before pulling a gun and shooting into his tyre. In the following scene when one of Wolf's friends, an American called Marsh (Will Patton), is taking leave of his girlfriend, we gather that Wolf is dead.

A variety of men, including Marsh, are then seen gathering in a bar or club. They are Americans and Germans. Snippets of conversation are heard, from which we deduce that they are somehow involved in drug smuggling, possibly from Amsterdam. There is reference to 'mules', the people used to carry the drugs from country to country, and a slightly mad girl enters, wanting to use the bathroom. When Marsh finds the bar owner, Zwemmer, and his drunken friend roughing her up, he tells them to leave her alone. Zwemmer complains she's been selling drugs in his bar. 'Frank's new junk route. One of his mules.'

She goes home with Marsh, who wakes the following morning to find the girl dead on his bathroom floor, having apparently taken an overdose of heroin.

Marsh does a runner, rings Zwemmer to meet him in a hotel and help him out. But Marsh's old girlfriend Sarah arrives instead, telling Marsh that by the time Zwemmer arrived at his apartment the girl was gone. She must have been alive and regained consciousness. As Sarah persuades Marsh he should be on the plane out of Berlin, the door is kicked in and two men with guns pin them both down.

The next scene is Coltrane, sitting behind a metal desk. He is smart, slick and wearing a light grey suit. He gives a profound sniff and addresses Marsh, who is seated before him, in a low, gravelly, staccato American voice. He sounds very much like Orson Welles.

'Mr Marsh. Sorry about the quick pick-up. Told you were alone. Had to speak to you kind of urgently.'

Marsh asks after Sarah, and Harwood (Coltrane) tells him she has been released.

'Now let's talk about your tough luck, Mr Marsh.'

Harwood throws a photograph on to the table between them. It is the dead girl lying on the bathroom floor exactly as Marsh had found her. Harwood goes on:

'Number one. Donna Rae Johnson. Fifteen years, seventeen months. Female, white, approximately a hundred and thirty pounds. No history of drug addiction. Died of a heroin overdose this morning, approximately five eighteen.'

Coltrane rattles off the facts like a policeman, which is what we assume he is. 'She was skin-popping. Had a bad shot. In your apartment. Mister Marsh. Terrific, huh? In your apartment.'

Harwood puts the photograph back in the envelope.

'Two. You know what a vaginal smear is? What it can show? Shall I quote you the autopsy report on that? Shows signs of forced entry. Also known as rape. Three. The heroin all over your apartment. Four. You're a kinda, kinda dealer sometime, eh? Two years ago nothing big – a little grass, a little hash. No record of dropping skag on fifteen-year-old girls, but hey, might be the time to start. And five. Miss Donna Rae Johnson's daddy is in the American diplomatic office. Could be a kinda sensitive situation for you there. This adds up. What we used to call bad weirdness. They could put you away for it so long, pal, you'd end up in another dimension.'

It's a long speech. Especially for an introduction to a character, and Coltrane does nothing but sit and make it, occasionally fiddling with the photo. But it is sublimely effective. Coltrane approaches it like a piece of music, breaking up the speech with an odd wheezing breath – just like Welles – which makes him emphasize odd words, alien inflections. Its clipped telegraphese also gives the impression that he is some kind of official – but what we are not sure. Plus his use of understatement: 'Could be a kinda sensitive situation for you there' is flipped out like a coin, nothing heavy. It is, in short, not only a brilliant impersonation of Welles but a brilliant bit of screen monologuery in itself.

Coltrane's unwavering stare, the way he holds his head tilted slightly upward in a position of superiority and the smart, casually lethal way he flips the dialogue is the mark of an actor secure in what he is doing. Petit, whose inexperience or lack of interest in working with actors is more pronounced in this movie than almost any of his other work, struck lucky with Coltrane. He is the only one on screen who doesn't let him down by going over the top, indulging himself in thespian tricks or otherwise making an embarrassment of himself. It is this quality in him that attracted Stephen Woolley and persuaded him to champion him in *Mona Lisa* when all around him scoffed that Coltrane was nothing but a comedy actor. A funny man.

There is something else. What we see in early screen performances by Coltrane – and this one in particular – is the development of a performer before he has made the transition into actor. In spite of his protestations ('I am an Ac-tor'), Coltrane spent much of his early professional life being an impersonator, not a true actor at all. The accumulation of accents, voices, anecdotal material, the ready put-downs and verbal sparring techniques – these are all the accoutrements of someone who cannot, either through lack of training or fear of self-analysis and exposure (i.e. vulnerability), reveal elements of himself in order to create and sustain a character in the way most actors are trained to do. The reason why Harwood is such a successful character and so consistent has nothing to do with Coltrane's understanding of the man and everything to do with his refined technique of imper-sonation – in this case, of Orson Welles. It is almost undetectable, but a trained eye (an actor's) can spot the difference immediately. Coltrane's performance is seamless, consistent, but it bears no relation to reality; or rather its 'reality' is at one remove – it is a second-hand reality, formerly used by Orson Welles. This realization does not, however, make it any less enjoyable. Rather, it heightens my admir-ation of Coltrane and the way he has progressed. His evolution from performer to actor is therefore far more dramatic and intriguing than one would have guessed. But it is by no means a clear arc, an unglitched trajectory.

The one good thing to come out of the *Chinese Boxes* experience, says Woolley, who managed to sell the world-wide rights to Vestron Video for more or less what the film cost, was the series of encounters with Coltrane. The two got on famously. The diminutive, pony-tailed producer and the massive, ebullient actor made a strange pair, but their nocturnal jaunts in Berlin clearly forged a bond that has lasted to this day.

And it was Woolley who first spotted Coltrane's potential as a straight actor. 'I realized watching him work that he was much more than a comedian, which is how he had been perceived until then. Subsequently, when we were casting *Mona Lisa* I insisted that he was the one to play Bob Hoskins's friend. It took a lot of persuading to get him into the audition because everyone thought of him as a fat funny man. However, I managed to persuade them to see him. The funny thing is, Robbie was so nervous that he'd gone to the pub before the audition and subsequently fucked it up. So I had to go through the whole process again. I just knew he could do it.'

As it turned out, Woolley's instincts were sound. Coltrane was cast and he delivered one of the first major straight performances of his career. 'I also put him in *Absolute Beginners*,' recalls Woolley. 'Blink and you'll miss him. But he's there. I think I gave him a bottle of whisky for that.'

During the early Eighties, Coltrane seemed to be testing the waters, slipping into small roles and performing without any undue commitment. It was a period of adjustment, when he was attempting to find a conduit for his talent, without being quite aware of what that talent was. Coltrane always was an actor, and thought of himself as such, before he ever considered himself a comedian. The comedy and humour were by-products of his personality and his observational powers rather than his ambition or aspiration. Even today – especially today – Coltrane will always correct someone who refers to him as a comic with the stentorian, cod-Sinden-like intonation: 'I am an Hack-Taw!'

It was in the mid 1980s, after a series of cameo roles and walk-ons and odd leading roles that Coltrane finally began to make his mark on the big screen. 1985 and 1986 were key years for him, in which several films emerged featuring Coltrane in increasingly interesting roles.

In *Defence of the Realm*, David Drury's terrifically engaging British political thriller, Coltrane played Leo McAskey, one of the many journalists depicted on the screen. He was in excellent company. Apart from Gabriel Byrne's troubled investigative reporter Nick Mullen, there was Denholm Elliott's priceless depiction of Vernon Bayliss, a drunken old hack who still has a nose for a good story. Elliott won a Best Supporting Actor award at the BAFTA ceremony that year and it is easy to see why. It would take Coltrane a little longer to start winning awards, but it was a good start to be seen in such exalted and professional company. The plot, meanwhile, about a government cover-up which is exposed (or attempted) by the British press was a subject that must have been dear to Coltrane's heart.

As Mullen investigates the connection between a government minister and a KGB agent, he uncovers a conspiracy to conceal the truth about the death of a young man near a secret air force base. Threatened and misinformed at every turn, Mullen finally acquires vital information from his colleague Vernon Bayliss, who is then found dead from a mysterious heart attack. With the help of the minister's secretary (Greta Scacchi), Mullen exposes the cover-up of an accident which almost precipitated a nuclear disaster. Before he can see the results of his investigations, he dies when a bomb explodes in his flat.

The part of Leo McAskey is not much of a stretch for Coltrane, but he fits in well with the rest as the garrulous, shaggy dog story teller of the newsroom who likes the sound of his own voice a little too much. Some way into the film, he arrives in the newspaper office and sits down opposite Byrne, who is in the process of receiving an anonymous telephone call, leaking him vital information about the story he is working on. In a manner which is revealed later as typical of McAskey, he ignores anything important and appears more concerned with the expenses he has accumulated in Grimsby, from where he has just returned.

'Eighty-four quid for dinner for two. You think they'll buy that upstairs?' he asks Mullen.

Later, in the pub where the assembled reporters are watching a television news report about a ministerial resignation that Mullen's news story has precipitated, McAskey is telling a very long-winded joke. He thinks he is holding court, but in reality very few of the hacks are listening to him. Eventually, when the minister appears on screen, one of them simply says: 'Shut up, Leo.' It momentarily silences him while the news item runs, and then he's up and running again, taking up the joke from where he left off.

His last scene in the film is at the traditional 'banging out' of a retiring employee. Because of the noise – the printers hammering the print trays with lead blocks – Coltrane has to write a note and hand it to Byrne, although he's standing right next to him.

Coltrane speaks in what sounds like his natural Scottish burr, and doesn't do any spectacular 'performing' here. But the film is so well cast, and the ensemble playing so seamless that Coltrane looks as comfortable as a garrulous journalist as he has in almost any other role.

That same year Coltrane was one of numerous good actors on

board *Revolution*, Hugh Hudson's overblown, over-budget epic about the American War of Independence, which went down with all hands. Coltrane was cast as one of the 'New York Burghers'; in other words, little more than a spear-carrying townsperson. Nonetheless, he was cast in an American role, and the interminable time spent hanging around the set gave him ample opportunity to practise other shades of American dialect.

Another oddball bit of casting: Coltrane appeared as 'Man in the bathroom' in *National Lampoon's European Vacation*, a dumb sequel to *National Lampoon's Vacation*, with Chevy Chase and Beverly D'Angelo reprising their roles at the head of the Griswold family, whose successive vacations are destined to be turned into decreasingly funny films.

It was now, following his television appearances in classic work like *Tutti Frutti*, that Peter Richardson finally persuaded him on board to film a series of *The Comic Strip* movies and specials. Coltrane can be seen in several *Comic Strip* television specials, notably as both the Hollywood producer and as one of the militant miners in *The Strike*. When Richardson, who is an all-round, all-purpose megalomaniac with a creative soul and a diabolical ego, began work on movies, shifting his aspirations up a notch, he invited Coltrane to contribute to *The Supergrass* (1985), as Troy, a chainsaw-wielding detective.

Coltrane appears around half-way through the movie, stepping from a bus at night in the rain in a remote Cornish sea resort. It is an intriguing introduction, mirroring the first appearance of Charles Bronson's character Harmonica in *Once Upon a Time in the West*. In Sergio Leone's film, a train draws up and stops at a station where three gunmen are waiting for their victim. Nobody descends, and the train draws out. As the last caboose leaves the station, Bronson is revealed standing on the other side of the track, holding a large travelling bag. Richardson follows precisely the same pattern. We are waiting for someone to arrive, and it has been suggested that he will be a hired assassin. A bus arrives, and we confidently expect to see a killer disembark. But nobody does. As the bus pulls away, Coltrane is revealed standing on the other side. He, too, is holding a case of some description, though in this instance it is a cello case, which carries connotations of gangsters and Tommy guns. The white mac he is wearing and the sinister music that accompanies his every appearance all add to the impression that Troy is a dangerous man who has come looking for trouble.

Given Richardson's propensity for looting images wholesale from other movies and then playing them up to the point of cliché, it is remarkable that Coltrane manages to maintain both the comic and the sinister aspects of the character. When the landlady opens the door to his late-night knock and he tersely demands 'bed and breakfast' in a South London bad guy accent, he is shot in half-shadow, heightening the menace of his huge frame. As if in mockery of the artifice, the first thing that Coltrane does when entering his room and locking the door is to turn out the light, maintaining his shadowy perspective. The last thing he does is place the cello case beneath the bed.

The following day we see Coltrane walking across the sandy beach in his black suit, a spectre at the holiday feast. He sits and drinks whisky from a bottle – a sure sign of a ne'er-do-well -while looking menacingly at a boy building a sandcastle. The kid walks away and Coltrane gets up, picks up the spade and builds a bit more of the sandcastle. The kid returns, says, 'Can I have my spade back?' and stamps on the turret Coltrane has just made. Coltrane picks up the kid, holds him dangling in front of his face and says, 'Do that again and I shall take you out to sea and drown you.' Having delivered these immortal lines he simply chucks the kid backwards into a pool of water and walks off.

It's a great scene and one of the funniest in the movie. Coltrane doesn't miss a beat, keeping a level of menace and sheer physical threat even when exposing the 'child within'. Returning to his digs, he complains to the landlady in the same terse manner as before: 'Sheets are damp. There's no hot water.'

By this time Coltrane and Richardson have convinced us that the mysterious Troy is one bad dude. The only question is: who has he come to kill? The drug dealers? The cops? Or, most likely, Adrian Edmondson's self-styled Supergrass?

As Edmondson emerges from the shower the following morning, all becomes clear. Coltrane is sitting in Edmondson's bedroom, talking to Richardson. He is introduced as Detective Sergeant Troy. A couple of fat jokes later ('Too fat to be a drug dealer', 'I don't think you're fat;

I think you're just well-built'), Coltrane has Edmondson on his knees in front of him and is painting a red swastika on his naked chest for no apparent reason other than to scare the living daylights out of his victim and to maintain his status – albeit in an official capacity – as a borderline psycho.

After searching for the £30 that Edmondson has confessed to dropping in the sea, attached to an empty bottle of washing-up liquid, they are all extremely surprised to haul up a sack containing thousands of pounds. Back in the hotel, Troy, who is clearly the 'bad cop' part of the 'good cop/bad cop' routine, interrogates Edmondson with some violence, bemoaning Richardson, his partner's softly-softly approach: 'Bloody wet liberals.' Finally, he goes up to his room and opens the cello case. This is the moment we have been waiting for, the reason for casting Coltrane in the first place. As he strides purposely forth across the beach and on to the concrete promontory clutching his cello case, the sound of Frankie Goes to Hollywood's 'Two Tribes' rises on the soundtrack.

This scene, where Coltrane walks along a sea wall which is being battered by waves, carrying the cello case, must rank as one of the most memorable and reckless scenes Coltrane has ever performed. The sea wall was wet and very slippery, the water rough and very cold. Had Coltrane slipped and fallen in, it is unlikely anyone could have got him out.

It looks a solid heroic moment, and Richardson makes the most of it, shooting Coltrane from above, the side and in silhouette. It ends with Coltrane reaching the end of the sea wall and simply sitting down, waiting as the sun goes down.

In the morning, as he wakes up, he sees a yacht approaching; the vessel he's been waiting for. He bends down, unlocks the case to reveal a shiny chainsaw. Unhurriedly, he clips it together like an assassin's rifle, finally standing up with the thing like a well-dressed Leatherface. He promptly jumps into the water and begins to chainsaw the yacht to pieces, in spite of the protestations of those aboard and, indeed, of Richardson from the shore. It is, of course, the wrong boat. When it is finally destroyed, Coltrane wades back to shore and shrugs his shoulders: 'Yeah, well. It's done now, innit?'

There is something magnificent about this scene, ludicrous as it is, and in Coltrane's contribution to it. It is both a classic punk/rock and roll gesture and an evocation of unfettered power. Coltrane has been in many better films, has delivered more articulate scripts, but he has rarely had a moment to equal this for sheer no-holds-barred bravura.

Chapter 6

FUN WITH NUNS AND
OTHER RELIGIOUS PERSONS

Old habits die hard. Religion-baiting is one of Coltrane's favourite pastimes, not because he lacks spirituality but because he views it in the same light as he does all organized, regulated institutions: with deep suspicion. The Catholic Church in particular provides an ample target for a Coltrane pasting, if only because of the hypocrisy embedded in a Christian organization worth millions upon millions of pounds whose business is conducted with cloak and dagger secrecy and the majority of whose followers are far from affluent. Indeed, many of them, especially those in Third World countries, still live some way beneath the poverty line.

Thus Coltrane is unlikely to turn down any opportunity to have a crack at the ancient hypocrisies of such an edifice, given his own militantly held socialist views that once got him nicknamed Red Robbie. Religion was one of the many targets fired upon by Peter Richardson's *Comic Strip* team in the course of their mini-features and television series. Coltrane's first shot at sending up religion occurred with the farcical comedy caper, *Nuns on the Run*, written and directed by Jonathan Lynn.

Coltrane and Eric Idle star as inept and bungling bank robbers who – more by accident then design – make off with £1m and hide out in a convent in order to escape from a hit man whom Coltrane has double-crossed. Naturally, they are forced to dress in nuns' habits to mingle unobtrusively with the sisters, most of whom, it need hardly be said, appear to be young, nubile and rather attractive – especially when discovered soaping themselves in the showers.

47

Released in the UK on 4 May, *Nuns on the Run* was a success both in the UK and at the American box office, where it gathered in £3m (the cost of the movie) in its first two weeks. The combination of Lynn (co-writer of television's *Yes Minister*), former Python Idle and Coltrane was fortuitous; the wonder was that it took so long before a collaboration between the comic factions of different eras occurred. Each knew the other's work, from different perspectives.

'When I was at university I used to watch *Python*,' recollected Coltrane during the publicity round for the film, prompting one sharp-eared journalist to remind her readers that her subject attended art school and not university.

Coltrane admitted that he could not distinguish one Python from another – with the exception of John Cleese – but knew enough about Idle to recall that he had 'that cheeky music-hall thing in him'. Consequently, he accepted the part when it was offered.

Having been involved with *The Comic Strip*, who – for better or worse – were the sons of *Python* in terms of television comedy, Coltrane was experienced in working with a small group of actors and writers who, by virtue of working together over and over again, had developed their own comic shorthand. Coltrane also discovered that, although the humour might have been different in approach and execution, the targets of *The Comic Strip* were fundamentally the same as those of *Python*.

The *Python* targets were general, rather than specific in their satire. 'All political systems are the same,' said Idle, 'like churches. They are formed by people who should be locked up. Comedy can sometimes suggest things about the human condition, but not very often or very easily. Robbie attacks me for being an old has-been and I attack him for being an alternative, and therefore not very funny, comedian.'

Coltrane, on the other hand, says he liked *Python* because it was cruel to the people who deserved it. The essential difference between the two was that *The Comic Strip's* humour was far more political: 'It all grew out of punk. Our humour was different from the Oxbridge lot, not so literate. You don't get my generation doing parodies of Proust; our sketches were about things like catching buses. We were really only alternative in the things we didn't do, like make sexist or racist jokes.'

Coltrane's social concern and his vociferous defence of his attitude won him plenty of Brownie points with Idle: 'He is prepared to stick his head up and be shot at. I keep my head down and keep moving fast.'

Oddly enough, during an interview conducted with Cassandra Jardine, it was Coltrane – the non-university attender – who gave the impression of having thought more about the business of comedy, i.e. what makes people laugh and why.

'Humour has to be very obvious,' said Coltrane. 'You have to see the banana skin to laugh at someone falling over.'

There is something disingenuous about this remark. Coltrane may have played obvious comedy moments in his career, but there are levels of subtlety within his performances that go far beyond this simplistic definition.

Certainly, he knows that to stick him in drag – as in *The Fruit Machine* – or inside a nun's habit is an easy way to get a laugh or maybe two; but there is a lot more to it if you are going to sustain the comedy and keep people laughing. And one of the aspects of the comedy is to create a sense of reality, however far-fetched it may seem. This, it seems, was achieved in full measure in *Nuns*.

'Ninety per cent of the film was shot on location. Eric and I were lounging around in our habits most of the time. People kept coming up to us and saying, "Good morning, sisters." We used to bow back solemnly.'

Under different circumstances, and in a different country, Coltrane had a similarly discombobulating effect on bystanders when he was dressed as the Pope in *The Comic Strip* movie, *The Pope Must Die*. Shot in Yugoslavia, the production often caused gasps of amazement among the locals as they watched a gaggle of cardinals and the Pontiff himself all standing around, with leather jackets slung over their robes, smoking cigarettes and trading jokes in between takes.

Being a serious film buff, Coltrane knows more than your average actor about the business of film-making. Quite apart from the fact that it appeals to the technician that lies within him, it also saves time during the shooting process.

'That helps enormously. If you see people doing film work who are not used to it, they very often have to do it ten times for the machinery.

But once you're in command of that, all you have to worry about is your performance. You don't have to worry about throwing shadow and people being out of focus, out of frame. I always remember my own continuity, things like that. Technique shouldn't get in the way. In all the best films it disappears. You have to liberate the ghost in the machine – that's what it's really down to. I think that's why I like making movies, because the great Scottish talent has always been breathing life into machinery. And for me it's the perfect thing because it's a machine that's desperately trying to capture something that is essentially spiritual in a way.'

Herein lies a clue to Coltrane's enduring interest in machinery and engines; it is a combination of intrigue over the practical function and admiration at the aesthetic form. When the two combine in perfect harmony, Coltrane is there to appreciate it. Cameras add another dimension in that they are designed to capture images in an extraordinary trade-off of aesthetics.

'The great thing abut film people,' said Coltrane, 'is that they're very quick to share their expertise with you. If you ask most people who have a job that involves a certain vocabulary of knowledge, they won't tell you. Like sailors never tell you what a bowsprit is for, or a halyard. They go, "Yes, well . . ." But I've worked with some of the best cameramen. I've said, "How does that gate work?" And they've said, "I'll show you," and taken the bloody thing out. And it's wonderful, because it's got these two little claws and – do you know how it works? – what it actually does is, it takes 24 still photographs a second . . . It's beautiful, beautiful. And, you know, 35 grand's worth, just for the wee driving bit. These guys are all kind of coy about it, all very macho about their stuff, but when you get them going they're dead interesting. They're like painters – it's exactly the same as painting. It's balanced light. When you're matching one shot to another they still measure it in candle power, they measure it in kelvins.'

The Pope Must Die was clearly going to upset a few people along the way, even if all they witnessed was the title, but Coltrane was in no way concerned about the probable problems the film might encounter in some areas.

'Not at all. In fact we sent it off to the Catholic Thought Police, not because Peter Richardson had any intention of altering it to please them. But it was actually quite a curious thing, because there's an office in London and an actual person whose job it is to read scripts, and he will tell you completely unjudgementally how much shit is going to hit the fan. They don't say, "Don't you dare make this film." They just tell you, "The fundamentalists will burn the cinemas in Idaho." But there's nothing offensive about the film. It's a fantasy, it's a comedy. It doesn't say the Catholic Church is corrupt, it says like all organizations it is capable of being corrupt.'

While he may not go to the lengths of Brando or De Niro to inhabit a character, he takes his research seriously. Even for *The Pope Must Die*, perhaps not the most serious depiction of the Vatican and all within it in the history of cinema, Coltrane nonetheless spent three weeks in Italy watching priests, 'because you don't want to fuck up on day one by having the cross in the wrong place'. In fact, even for something as outrageous as this, Coltrane does his homework with the assiduousness of a Method actor approaching Hamlet.

'I spent time in Italy just watching how the priests behave. How they greet each other. Body language and so on. It's something De Niro gets absolutely right.' Not only that, but he read all the books he could lay his hands on about the Vatican financial scandals, just to get into that Calvi mood.

Having played a cardinal in Derek Jarman's *Caravaggio*, Coltrane has some earlier experience of religious roles. His role as Pope Dave the First may be one of farcical invention, but the accuracy of his depiction of the day-to-day life of Father Dave, the small-time priest who is elected Pope through a clerical error, is a tribute to his powers of observation and a measure of his commitment to even the silliest film.

Even the title seemed guaranteed to provoke outrage. While shooting in Yugoslavia, the film went under the fabricated working title 'Sleeping with the Fishes' to avoid offending devout Catholic locals.

'Anyone who sees it as an attack on Catholicism is being paranoid and perhaps feeling a bit guilty about something,' said Coltrane. 'I was brought up in a heavy Protestant area of Glasgow, my parents were committed Christians and I went to an Episcopalian School. The result is that I'm agnostic. I won't accept that this film is offensive because I believe that most people go to church as a convenience – to relieve their consciences. My Roman Catholic friends are conditioned by the morality of the Church and I don't agree with conditioning.'

And Coltrane was perceptive and funny about the difference between Catholics and Protestants: 'You can't imagine a bunch of Orangemen forming the Mafia, because they wouldn't have the style for those ritualistic murders. It wouldn't occur to a Scotsman to kill a man and put a fish in his mouth – "That's a perfectly good herring, Alistair." '

Chapter 7

MORE POLITICS: SOME HEROES

Coltrane is a fan and a fairly reckless one at that. It was his love of jazz that urged him to change his name from MacMillan to Coltrane, in honour of John Coltrane; it was Marlon Brando's performance in *The Wild One* which persuaded him that acting could be a career path for him; and it was his love of Spencer Tracy that prompted the name of his first child, Spencer.

There is something almost childlike in the way Coltrane reveres certain people and personalities. He conveys genuine awe, genuine affection for several people time and again in interviews and articles. There is something humble about this attitude, or it may lurk deeper. It is possible that Coltrane desperately wants to be seen as an original (thinker, artist, actor) but is afraid that he isn't. Hence the need to copy a thousand others through accents and performances, to revere those to whom he aspires but cannot quite stop comparing himself with. Take this comment on Brando:

'I loved Brando because he was vulnerable and sensitive, and his feelings were terribly strong, but if you crossed him he'd beat the shit out of you. The Warrior Poet. That was the role model for me ... Somebody said to me the other day, "I think Brando is all very homoerotic," and I said, "Well, it's homoerotic if you want to fuck Marlon Brando." I didn't want to fuck Marlon Brando, I wanted to BE him.'

By adopting the rebel rocker image at art school, complete with battered motorcycle jacket and greasy rock and roll quiff, Coltrane got as close as he ever would to inhabiting Marlon Brando's image –

though it has to be said that he could play Brando now as a younger slimmer man, so enormous has Brando become.

This 'fan-ness', this appreciation of others, is a particular Coltrane trait. It gives him the opportunity to slip into an anecdote or an accent of the favoured one, as he frequently does, repeating many of his personal favourites. Often, these are connected with injustice in some way; something that makes his blood boil.

Take his oft-quoted anecdote of Muhammad Ali. 'There's some lovely stories about him. Like he went into a Manhattan restaurant in '62, when they were still segregated, and the waiter says, "I'm sorry, sir, we don't serve Negroes." And Ali says, "I'm glad to hear it, I don't eat them." Ha! This is from a guy who could beat the shit out of a Transit. A great combination, that; a big, strong man with a great mind.'

Herein lies a clue to Coltrane's hero worship; what turns him on is not just physical presence and power but also deft wit and courageous intelligence. In the film world, Coltrane is particularly fond of Orson Welles for these reasons and more besides. Coltrane and Welles share much in terms of size and worldview, the main difference being that Welles made his mark at a much earlier age.

Even so, it gave him a real thrill to be described by Pauline Kael in her last ever review in *The New Yorker* as 'a low-rent Orson Welles' for his performance in *Perfectly Normal*.

'Isn't it marvellous,' he told Tom Hibbert. 'I've been resting on that, dining out on that. It is great because she is one of the few film critics that I would ever take seriously. I've got all her books.'

And to me, over lunch at Rogano's in Glasgow following the release of *Perfectly Normal*, he beams at the recollection of Kael's description of him. 'I thought, "That's it. I can retire." '

Clearly, Coltrane would rather be considered a low-rent Orson Welles than a RolyPoly Comic or Red Robbie, both of which he has been labelled in the past.

'It pisses me off. I mean they don't say Tory Tarby, do they?'

Maybe not. But Coltrane ran into trouble even with his admirers when he took the Persil shilling for a part in a long-running television advertising campaign for washing-up liquid. In much the same way that Bob Hoskins got a hard time from the tabloid media for his BT commercials while the public got sick of the sight of him and the sound of him ('It's good to talk'), Coltrane ran the risk of undoing much of his good work. The Persil commercial was at least well-scripted, featuring Coltrane as a leather-jacketed biker in a cottage with his dear sweet old mother (or granny).

There are things that Coltrane will not do, roles he will not play. When it was suggested that he was pencilled to play the part of former Paisley South MP Gordon McMaster, Coltrane made it abundantly clear that he would not be attaching himself to the film.

'Just because I'm a Jock and I'm fat doesn't make me the natural choice,' he said. 'I wouldn't want to do it because it's a desperately sad business and nobody has found out what really happened yet, so what's the point? I'm always a bit suspicious of making dramas out of people's real lives when their friends and family are still around showing their pain.'

The body of Gordon McMaster was found by his elderly father four days after he committed suicide by suffocating himself with carbon monoxide fumes from his car in his garage at his home in Scotland in July 1997. He had been the victim of many accusations over his health and sexuality in the time leading up to his death.

Considered one of the brightest young stars of the Labour party, McMaster stood for Paisley South in 1990 following the death of Norman Buchan MP, having been the youngest leader of Renfrew District Council two years earlier when he was appointed.

In a report following his death, Benedict Brogan and Simon Houston of the *Daily Mail* reminded their readers of McMaster's character: 'A 30-year-old former horticultural lecturer renowned for his sharp mind, jovial manner and resemblance to Robbie Coltrane, McMaster had two years earlier become the latest leader of his council. He was marked out by party chiefs as a potential star of the future.'

By December the same year, there were rumours that Coltrane had signed up for the role in a forthcoming ITV television film tracing the events leading to McMaster's suicide. In spite of the fact that the film was to be made by the hugely respected Joan Bakewell, presenter of the BBC's religious programme, *The Heart of the Matter*, there was a huge furore concerning the film from both the government and members of McMaster's family.

One of the strongest attacks came from Scottish Minister for Education, Brian Wilson, who called the proposed programme '... cheap, intrusive sensationalism, and no attempt to dress it up in pseudo-intellectual claptrap will alter that reality.'

Not wishing to engage with anything so sensationalist or politically embarrassing, Coltrane turned down the opportunity to play McMaster.

His politics and his strong identification with Scotland have not prevented him from taking on some unlikely roles, however. There is a superb irony in the fact that Coltrane, Scottish through and through, should have played the Scots-baiting Londoner, Dr Samuel Johnson, with such depth and relish. If anyone can have been said to have fostered and encouraged the notion of the north/south divide, it is Johnson, whose metropolitan parochialism is best conveyed by his own words: 'If a man is tired of London, he is tired of life' and 'The noblest prospect that a Scotchman ever sees, is the high road that leads him to London.'

'Basically he was a snob about anything north of Watford,' said Coltrane about a man with whom he has little in common. 'He thought that people in Scotland were savages who lived in poverty. People often say he was a Scots-hater, but Johnson just had an amusing contempt for them.'

Written by John Byrne, *Boswell and Johnson's Tour of the Western Isles* was a television play loosely based on the two men's accounts of their trip to Scotland in 1773. It gave Coltrane and one of his best friends, John Sessions, the opportunity to play the parts they had been improvising for the entertainment of their friends in various West End pubs for years. (October 1993 transmission).

Coltrane had done more than a little preparation for the role. In 1987 he appeared in a one-man show about Dr Johnson, entitled *Your Obedient Servant*. It opened at the Lyric Hammersmith on 9 April. Up to that point, Coltrane's career had consisted almost entirely of comedy roles, with the odd villain thrown in for ballast. Playing Dr Johnson – lexicographer, literary biographer, wit and melancholic – represented a total departure.

'I'm doing it because – well, actually, simply because I like the play. I like the idea of playing somebody I admire that much.

He was a tremendously original thinker. And a man with tremendous inner resources and strength. In pain half his life, blind in one eye, almost blind in the other, deaf in one ear, almost deaf in the other … a terrible depressive. Imagine going to bed for three weeks because you couldn't bear to wake up.

Probably the funniest man in England at the time. And the way they lived. Boswell and a couple of other boys would come to pick him up at 3.00 a.m., they'd go to Covent Garden, have a few drinks with the market boys, rent a boat, go to Billingsgate, have a few drinks with the fish market boys – oh, he was game for a laugh all right.

A radical Tory, in a lot of ways. Very funny about the Colonies, hated imperialism, also hated the Americans for wanting independence and keeping slaves. He was given a man as a slave once – that went down a storm.

It is incredibly presumptuous, don't you think, to try to get inside a great man like Johnson? But by the time this show's over I'll probably know more about him than anyone who isn't an academic. You see, that's the kind of thing you get to do if you're an actor. I'll never get bored with it, and when I'm sixty, I'll play sixty-year-old men.'

Given the fact that as we have seen Coltrane read 22 books by or about Johnson by way of preparing for the role, one can see his boast justified.

'I know, I know, it sounds so pretentious, doesn't it? But the thing about Johnson was to be asked to play him was an enormous honour because I've always been a big fan of his – and I mean that in the real sense of the word. A fan!' And this in spite of Johnson's apparent and well-documented dislike for Scotsmen and all things Scottish. Coltrane even has a riposte to this.

'A man who didn't like the Scots wouldn't have spent two thirds of his life being followed around by Boswell, a man who was about as Scottish as you'll ever get – a classic Calvinistic old bugger. When Johnson went to the Hebrides, he fell in love with the place. He was terribly moved by people's simplicity and hospitality. They let him sleep with a dog, which was a great honour, and he discovered whisky when he was up there. Yes, I'm a big fan of Johnson.'

Not everyone, however, was such a fan of the programme. As an example of how the critics were divided the *Daily Mail* takes some beating. On 27 October 1993 Elizabeth Cowley included it in her previews of the day's programmes: 'In *Boswell and Johnson's Tour of the Western Isles*, Robbie Coltrane strides the Hebrides in 1773 looking more like a cartoon of a bloated Queen Victoria than the famed (and fat) philosopher Dr Samuel Johnson. John Byrne's delightful odyssey – co-starring John Sessions as Johnson's biographer James Boswell – closes the *Screenplay* series.'

The following day, the *Daily Mail*'s television critic Peter Paterson was moved to write: 'The less said about *Boswell and Johnson's Tour of the Western Isles* the better. It starred Robbie Coltrane, fresh from his acting triumph in *Cracker*, as Johnson and John Sessions as Boswell, and was a disaster. How producer Nicholas Barton could take a classic like Boswell's *Journal of the Tour of the Hebrides* and turn it into this nonsensical farrago – still less how it could have been accepted by the BBC – is a complete mystery. It treated Johnson as a buffoon, Boswell as an idiot and the hospitable Highlanders as boors. Only the cameraman, Denis Crossan, emerged with any credit from this lamentable production.'

Chapter 8

ROBBIE AND ROMANCE:
THE GIRL WHO GOT AWAY, EVENTUALLY

John Sessions has, on more than one occasion, suggested that Coltrane's dietary problems, his excessive eating and drinking, his bingeing episodes that made him put on a stone a year in weight during the Eighties, were due to the fact that the great love of his life refused to marry him.

Coltrane had steadfastly denied this suggestion, labelling it cheap psychology whenever reminded of it by journalists, but the fact remains that his original paramour was a guiding factor in his formative years. His first love, Robin Paine, like his wife, Rhona Gemmell, was an artist. When Robin finally left him in 1987, Coltrane confessed he got into a bit of a state.

'I have been in love with this beautiful girl for fifteen years. I've been going out with another girl for the past year. I can't sort out what is going to happen. They don't know about each other. I'd like to marry them both. But what can I do? Tell the truth and lose them both? I met the second girl when I broke up with the lady I have been with for fifteen years. During that year I acquired the other girl now I am sodding about with the first. I don't live with either of them. I saw the girl I have been with for fifteen years a couple of weeks ago and spent a weekend in Glasgow with the other one. It is havoc.

I met the first one at art school in Scotland sixteen years ago. She is a twin and twins are born married. She has her twin brother and she doesn't really need me. I spent all last night with this guy Alistair, a mutual friend, and he was telling me that I was wrong and that she was crazy about me. He said he had spent all the previous evening with her and all she had talked abut was me. I asked him, "If that is so, why won't the silly bitch marry me?" I want to marry her but she is an independent spirit. I would like to get married and have children. I have come to that point in my life. I get fed up with empty hotel rooms and coming back to an empty house when I have been away for a while.

There's a terrible smugness about married people. They think people who aren't just don't go through any emotional traumas. They see you with two girls in a year and they think what does he know about real feelings, he's never been married. That is absolute nonsense. It can be shattering.

I never used to believe in marriage. I could never understand why people did it. I have changed my mind about it because I want children. I wouldn't like my kids to go to school and be called illegitimate and that is the only reason I want to get married. I know a girl whose wee boy came home from school and told her that one of the other kids had said, "I've got a daddy and you haven't." I don't want that to happen to children of mine. It is supposed to be the woman who wants the security but my woman won't marry me. I have asked her often enough. Though we have known each other for fifteen years our relationship has been very on and off. I suppose we have been together for about five of those years. I have been out with lots of other women.

Although we have known each other for fifteen years, which is longer than a lot of people are married, we haven't shared our lives as man and wife. We lived together on and off but neither of us ever abandoned our own places. We didn't marry because we both wanted our independence. It is as simple as that. It is quite possible to be in love with somebody for a very long time and not want to marry them.

I used to think that marriage was largely a financial institution, but I have changed. I am 36 – I am not a boy anymore. She is 33 [this was in March 1987]. If we are going to have a baby she is going to have to do it soon. My liking for independence is running out. There are just so many nightclubs and you can get tired of things like that after a while. She doesn't want to give up her independence. She is an artist – one of the finest portrait painters. If she won't have kids it might happen with someone else. I have been out on the town because I am broken up about this woman. I should have been sensible and gone home at ten o'clock last night – but I didn't. I stayed up all night talking about her.

I am a manic depressive. I go down as far as I go up. When I get depressed, I work on my old cars, or go fishing. I do all the solo things.'

There is little doubt that Robin Paine was the love of Coltrane's life. But she adamantly refused to marry him despite his many proposals. They met at Glasgow School of Art and were together on and off for fifteen years. Robbie, the romantic, the man who would be a father, pursued her relentlessly, as he began to feel the need for a family of some kind. Robin, who is four years younger than Coltrane, wanted the status quo to remain the same. She suspected that marriage to Coltrane would be a disaster; she was an independent, artistic spirit who could just about put up with Coltrane's many dalliances within their relationship, but feared the entrapment of marriage and children with Coltrane. As long as she was not married to Coltrane, Paine could at least control her own destiny.

A friend who knew them both said: 'It's not that Robin wasn't in love with him. It was just one of those situations where, if they had married, something was going to have to give. They had a very stormy relationship, and marriage was going to be more destructive than positive. Robin is a ferociously independent woman with her own career. Her main objection to marrying Robbie was her fear of always being in his shadow.'

Coltrane was furious when it was suggested by the same friend in an interview in the *Sunday Mirror* (18 September 1994) that Rhona Gemmell was a kind of substitute for Robin Paine. Clearly, however, the two women have much in common.

'I don't doubt that Robbie loves Rhona, but in my opinion we're talking substitute here,' said the friend. 'Robin was the real love of his life and from day one he went down on bended knee and got nowhere.'

Being madly in love with Paine (whose twin brother, Tom, is also an artist) did not stop Coltrane from pursuing other women during their relationship. She knew about the other women and put up with them in the realization that this was just the way he was. But it also warned her away from marriage.

'There were lots of women,' said a friend. 'He had casual

relationships, heavy relationships, one-night stands, one-week stands.

I have known Robbie a long time, and in my opinion he was completely without morals in those days. It is just the way he was and Robin Paine knew that. She put up with it, but that's not to say she didn't mind. She did mind, what woman wouldn't? But she is not the kind of person to be possessive in that way.

Robin was the one he loved. It was Robin from art school days right the way through to Rhona. It's no coincidence that Rhona is amazingly like Robin Paine. They are both great fun and, most importantly for Robbie, both are redheads. He finds redheads a real turn-on.'

Coltrane and Paine lived together on and off in London and in Scotland, leaving many opportunities for Coltrane to play the field.

'Robbie has a giant appetite for everything, including women. He is something of a debauched sensualist. I can't remember the names of half the women he slept with and I bet he can't either.'

When the relationship finally ended some time in the late Eighties, Coltrane went on late-night drinking binges to ease his broken heart. 'In the end Robbie just ran up the white flag of surrender and gave up chasing Robin Paine.'

Luckily, he had just met Rhona Gemmell, and before long they became an item. Coltrane's pal John Sessions says: 'Rhona saved his life. Without her Robbie would be dead. She taught him what it means to need other people.' Other friends agree. 'Rhona has been a terrific anchor.'

It was Christmas Eve, 1988, when Gemmell walked into his life. Coltrane was in a pub when she came in and sat on a stool next to him. It was, he recalled, the only stool not occupied by a drunk. It was, he confessed, lust at first sight. 'Love came later.'

Gemmell was eighteen, a student and living with her mother in a village outside Glasgow. When she accepted Coltrane's invitation to accompany him to a Hogmanay party, he picked her up in a red Cadillac convertible. It was a very smooth move.

'She's terribly funny,' said Coltrane, when asked about Gemmell. 'She's quite shy, but if she's with people she really knows, she can be outrageous. A sense of humour in women, of course, is completely *de rigueur*.'

Their son, Spencer, was born in February 1993, and it was a momentous event in Coltrane's life. Aware that he had a proper responsibility, a family to take care of, he began to take more care of himself, losing weight, attempting to give up smoking and cutting down on alcohol. He's been continuing the process with varying degrees of success ever since. And Gemmell, who is a vegetarian, has introduced him to some dietary ideas previously undreamt of in Coltrane's philosophy.

Robin Paine now lives in America, and teaches at the art school attached to the Boston Museum of Fine Art, but her life-sized portrait of Coltrane still has pride of place in the £350,000 converted barn he shares with Rhona.

'I know that Robin doesn't regret splitting up with him,' said a friend. 'Robbie is a very difficult person to be close to. It's not a matter of nastiness, it's just that he has a huge appetite for life and that means people have often been overwhelmed by him – he likes everyone to do what he wants.'

Chapter 9

IF THE CAP FITZ

Odd as it seems now, *Cracker* was born out of the desire to find a television hero for the New Age. Until *Cracker*, detective thrillers and police drama series tended to concentrate on police procedure or the well-trodden path of mystery whodunit structures. In other words, they were *Z-Cars, Softly, Softly, The Sweeney, No Hiding Place* and *Inspector Morse.* Strangely enough, even with the advent of progressive American police series like the ground-breaking *Hill Street Blues,* British crime drama series were stuck with both feet in the past.

Towards the end of 1991, Granada's Head of Drama, Sally Head, issued an edict requesting a dozen new ideas to be given to the commissioners before the end of the day. Gub Neal, who became the producer of the first *Cracker* series, had been working on possible storylines involving a forensic psychologist detective. He had in mind a kind of latter-day version of Sherlock Holmes, though the idea had been put on the back burner when it was discovered that much of the work and process of current forensic investigation was done via the computer screen – not an enticing or appropriate dramatic prospect. However, Head's memo inspired Neal to resurrect the idea, and he hurriedly scribbled the following proposal:

'A series of two-hour dramas about a totally New-Age detective.

Working class, but an academic; a self-made man who teaches in a university in the north of England. He's in his mid-forties, popular and well-liked by his students. He is, however, deeply resented by the police. His success at cracking cases they have found impossible is second to none.

How does he do it?

He's the first of a new breed. A criminal psychologist, making a science, and sometimes an art, out of studying criminal behaviour. Unlike the 'intuition' of the detective's hunch, he uses anthropology, animal psychology, but mainly his own mind as a drawing board for penetrating crime. Brash, daring and sexy, he's a latter-day alchemist with a 5K megabyte brain which he uses as a torch to peer into the murky depths of the human psyche.

The town marshall with a pocket full of Jung. He uncovers the mysteries behind the criminal mind. What makes a person put razor blades in baby food, or climb 30 flights of stairs to rape an old woman? The question for this man starts not with who but why.'

Although this bears only a superficial resemblance to the profile of Fitz that eventually emerged on to the screens, it captured Sally Head's imagination sufficiently for her to give Gub Neal the go-ahead to commission a pilot script.

There was little doubt in Neal's mind whom he wanted for the job: Jimmy McGovern. McGovern had learnt his television screenwriting craft on *Brookside*, just won the Samuel Beckett award for his one-off drama, *Needle*, and was currently working on a drama series for the BBC called *Priest*.

'Even though I was going through a really bad time with *Priest*,' said McGovern, 'with my script lying on Michael Wearing's desk, I was reluctant to abandon it. So when Gub first approached me with *Cracker* I refused it, but he's a persistent man, and he came back to me again, and after a lot of thought I said yes because I recognized its potential. I'd seen *Silence of the Lambs* and had been taken by the idea of getting into the heart and soul of a killer through a man who knew about the dark side of life.'

McGovern had his leading character in mind as he drafted the first script. He had a vision of a 'thin, wiry man with a sense of danger – a John Cassavetes type'. With this description in mind, Gub Neal approached the actor Robert Lindsay, who had just been seen to great effect in the political drama series GBH as a neurotic politician modelled on Derek Hatton.

Lindsay, however, had other ideas. He was currently in a successful stage production of *Beckett*, was scheduled to star in another production as Cyrano de Bergerac and was unwilling to sign up for a television series playing a character that he read as being too similar to his role in GBH. He turned the offer down flat.

Sally Head and Gub Neal were faced with a problem. They needed a major star in the role of Fitz, but they did not as yet have a script. It would be impossible to get anyone of any calibre to commit purely on the basis of a treatment or an idea. McGovern had to finish a script. He spent all of August polishing off the first draft. It was the basis of the first two-parter, *The Mad Woman in the Attic*.

Head and Neal took the unusual step of taking the first-draft script as their lever towards a star's commitment. Under normal circumstances, it would have taken another two drafts at least before they were happy to show it around, but both felt so inspired by McGovern's work that they took the gamble. 'Jimmy's script felt as if it had wings,' said Sally Head. 'He had written with such intensity that we hardly needed to change a word.' Both Head and Neal were agreed that the actor who would best fit the role of Fitz was Robbie Coltrane. He may have seemed like a far cry from Robert Lindsay – physically, at the very least – but they had recently witnessed his first major straight acting role as a former junky in *Alive and Kicking* and felt that he had all the necessary qualities to bring Fitz to life.

What they were looking for was an actor who was a major presence, who commanded respect and who wasn't afraid of being feared and, if necessary, disliked. Coltrane's own formidable persona fulfilled many of the criteria laid down by McGovern's script and, in particular, his character description of Fitz:

'His problem is he's easily bored. He drinks heavily. He chain smokes. He gambles compulsively. All because he's bored. He chases women, but as soon as he's caught one, he's bored again. Why don't they just shut up and lie back and think of England? Why must they insist on conversation? So he attacks them. He attacks them because they're middle-class and don't know what life is. He attacks them because they're working-class and so parochial...

He's a criminal psychologist lecturing in a northern university. He's probably the best in his field and he's got a string of publications to his name, but fellow professionals think he's a maverick. That doesn't bother Fitz – they're just a bunch of boring old farts.

Fitz understands crime, you see. There's nothing immoral about it whatsoever. Crime is just big-league gambling. At stake is your liberty; the prize could be millions of pounds, or a wife six feet under – nothing to do with morality at all, just a simple calculation of risk and reward. That's the trouble, you see: no one is prepared to say things like that (bar Fitz). The whole world is living a lie, and Fitz will tell you that he sees it as his duty to challenge the world, to expose lies and hypocrisy, to get to the core of what people really feel. But the truth's a bit different; Fitz takes on the world because he's bored.

Maybe it's all down to his Catholic upbringing. My God, how he hates the church. Those Jesuits taught him how to think, yeah, and argue, but they really screwed him up in other ways. The Virgin Mary, for instance – the only woman he's ever really trusted. And then all that examination of conscience and analysing motive. He's the world's leading expert on conscience and motive. Did you know, for instance, that nobody has ever, in the whole history of the world, done anything for a pure, decent motive? Quote Fitz an example and he'll destroy you. Soldiers laying down their lives for others? Only because they were too fucking terrified of being called a coward, too cowardly to be a coward. And conscience? *Schadenfreude* – well, there you are. The bloody Krauts have got a word for it – for the way you laugh your balls off when you hear that someone has fallen down a lift-shaft. But the English, the pious, anal-retentive English ... hypocrites, all of them...

Fitz never stops. He just cannot stop. Occasionally a massive depression might strike – particularly after he's just lost a small fortune on a horse that should have won by half the track. When that happens, he'll drink and drink and listen to J. J. Cale, but eventually someone will say something (his wife, for instance) and he'll be off again, defending, challenging...

He doesn't drive. When people ask why, he says it's because he's never been sober enough, but the truth is he's never trusted himself behind the wheel of a car – it's just too tempting to put your foot down and close your eyes and gamble that you won't hit anything before you've counted to twenty. So his main form of transport is taxi. But when he's skint (as he very often is) it's the bus. Now that's a problem for him because he just can't stand still, so he's always walking to the next stop and then the next and, sure enough, that bus always comes racing along while he's between stops. And it's no smoking upstairs and down these days, but he lights up anyway and, of course, someone protests and there's a row but these health fascists are all the same, the country's full of them ... So that's a little taste of Fitz – dynamic, charismatic, hurtling along the road to self-destruction ...'

The curious thing about this hastily contrived yet full-blooded character description is that it draws on some of the character traits not only of McGovern but also of Coltrane. The principal reason to get Coltrane involved was that Neal and Head realized that he could make such a monster actually likeable without losing any of his innate edge. 'Even though Robbie has never compromised on the roles that he's taken, or maybe even because of it, he's always been held in great affection by his audience. With Robbie playing Fitz, people would be predisposed to liking him.' Which meant, of course, that Coltrane could get away almost with murder.

McGovern, however, needed some persuading about Coltrane. And it eventually came from a source much closer to home.

'When Robbie was mentioned, I didn't know that much about him,' he said. 'I didn't know if a fat, middle-aged man would have much appeal. But I have two intelligent daughters, more aware of modern culture than I am, and they told me how brilliant he was, so I felt safe writing for him.'

Naturally, shifting from the image of Robert Lindsay to Robbie Coltrane necessitated some changes in the script.

'Robbie hasn't got the figure for all-action cops and robbers stuff, so I made Fitz wittier – and so did Robbie. His arrival also made the part more violent. Robbie has such a legacy of affection that I knew I could make his character much darker.'

Coltrane liked the script but was wary of giving his final

commitment. A one-off television drama or a film is one thing, a long-running play or a television series quite another. Coltrane is not a man who likes to be tied down. Like Fitz, he gets bored easily, requires constant challenges to keep his creative spark alive and his interest alert. Now that McGovern had written with Coltrane in mind, he couldn't imagine anyone else doing the part – not even if Robert Lindsay had suddenly changed his mind and agreed to do it.

It was therefore with some trepidation that Gub Neal and Jimmy McGovern travelled to Glasgow in the hope of finally persuading Coltrane to sign up for the part, as Neal recalled.

'I was convinced that our meeting was going to be a disaster. Jimmy and I were both extremely nervous, because we were desperate for Robbie to say yes, and Jimmy had started drinking well before lunch. By the time we sat down he was half pissed, and his first words to Robbie were, "I wrote the script and I want you to know that I see Fitz as a very thin man," I thought, "That's it, we're out of this restaurant." To Robbie's credit he hung on through lunch. I was willing Robbie to have a drink himself, but he stuck to Diet Coke, which made me even more anxious, and I drank too much myself. However, despite Jimmy's and my drunken ramblings, Robbie sensed that there was something in both Jimmy and the script to which he could respond, and he agreed to play Fitz.'

At least both Neal's and McGovern's subsequent hangovers were sweetened with the knowledge that they had got their Fitz. It was then up to Sally Head to take the script and Coltrane's commitment and sell the package for a proper series beyond the pilot stage.

'Armed with the first two-hour story and Robbie's commitment to Fitz, we submitted our proposals for five further hours of *Cracker* to Marcus Plantin, the Director of the ITV Network Centre. Although Marcus had only been in the job a short while, he clearly liked what he saw, because he gave us the go-ahead on 1 January.'

The next stage in the development of the scripts for the series involved long conversations between McGovern and Coltrane. The writer wanted to know what made Coltrane tick, the way he grew up, what he liked and disliked and all the constituent parts of his personality in order to create a character whom Coltrane could inhabit convincingly and with relative ease. So successfully did McGovern do this that the persona of Fitz was a glove that Coltrane slipped on whenever he was working on the series.

Not surprisingly, both actor and writer discovered they had several things in common. The similarities between Fitz and Coltrane are superficial: both smoke cigarettes, both have a liking for alcohol, both have a fondness and an extensive knowledge of jazz and films. Both are gamblers, fond of a flutter on the gee-gees, but while Coltrane is what is known as a 'smart gambler' – in other words he is not in the grip of an obsession and knows when to quit – Fitz is a 'degenerate gambler', a man for whom gambling is an addiction, a compulsive distraction that is exceptionally difficult to cure.

The principal differences between the two are that Coltrane is a very practical man, enjoys using his hands to make, build and mend things; his love of old cars and vintage machines is allied to a gift and skill for fixing them; in another life he would have made a great mechanic. Indeed, many of his friends who lack Coltrane's mechanical skills bring their cars to him for repair. Fitz, on the other hand, is someone who would make a complete hash of unscrewing a plug to change a fuse. Cars, for him, are simply vehicles to get you from A to B and back again.

Both Fitz and Coltrane share a similar sense of humour – they see the lighter side of dark places. It is a defence mechanism, often found among doctors, morticians, the police – any professional whose work brings them into frequent contact with death. It is the way they cope with a life that would otherwise become unbearable. Coltrane's own personal brand of sick humour may stem from his childhood, from his father's profession as a doctor and police pathologist, as well as the profoundly affecting tragedy of his younger sister's death. Humour is as much of a shield as a sword and can be used for defence as well as attack.

The most profound difference between the two is, I think, in their general attitude to life. Whereas Fitz is a cynical, almost bitter man who views the simple things in life as beneath contempt, Coltrane embraces many aspects of life with the joy of indefatigable curiosity.

'I get a great deal of pleasure out of the simple things in life [Coltrane told John Crace]. Last autumn I planted 200 bulbs in the garden because I wanted to see them coming up through the snow in spring.

Fitz would never bother with something like that. He's so intellectual, that he can't get any pleasure out of the predictable. Fitz is a cynic who spends his whole time quoting the price of things in the hope that he won't have to confront the value of them. Oscar Wilde once said, "If you scratch a cynic, you'll find a bruised romantic", and so at heart Fitz is a passionate man, but he subconsciously pushes away everything he really wants. He yearns for a close family, but despises himself for wanting it, and wouldn't be seen dead doing anything that smacked of domesticity, whereas I'm at my happiest when I'm at home with my wife and son, putting up shelves with a Black & Decker.'

The principal players who would forge *Cracker* into the ground-breaking, charismatic, award-winning series that it was to become were assembled; the quartet of Head and Neal, McGovern and Coltrane shared a common goal – to boldly go where no drama series had gone before. Coltrane himself later summed up their aims:

'We realized that there was a huge hunger for intelligent drama. And we were all committed to making something a bit different. We all need a dose of feel-good escapism like *The Darling Buds of May* from time to time, but we felt that too many TV programmes patronize their audience. So many police dramas are one-dimensional whodunits with a denouement at the end. In *Cracker* the interest isn't *who*, because the viewer often already knows, but *why*, and it makes people think about their own prejudices and fears. We all have some experience of sexism, racism, homophobia and religious persecution; we all have fears about loved ones dying, and so why should they not be challenged and explored on prime-time TV? It's not just the middle-class intellectuals who are capable of understanding and accepting difficult, unpalatable ideas.'

Chapter 10

COLTRANE PREPARES

One of the most conspicuous aspects of Coltrane's work is the amount of preparation he is willing to do. For *Cracker*, as with his role as Dr Johnson, Coltrane was not prepared simply to work from the script. Authenticity was important not just to the success of the series but to the actor himself. Without a thorough grounding in the finer points of the profession in which Fitz engaged, it would have been impossible for Coltrane to take the kind of risks with character and procedure that he did. It is not until you know the truth that you are able to stretch it and bend it without losing sight of credibility.

There are two areas of research that occupied Coltrane in his preparation for *Cracker*: gambling and forensic psychology. Although he had some experience of the former, he did not aspire to Fitz's hardcore addiction that found him as often in the casino, by a roulette wheel or a blackjack table, as in the local Ladbrokes.

Coltrane wanted to find out as much about the psychology of the gambling personality as the fundamentals and details of the actual business, and accordingly sought advice from an expert.

I spent a day with the manageress of a Manchester casino, who explained everything to me, from the nuts and bolts of blackjack and routlette to the psychology of winning and losing. I am the sort of bloke who can walk into a casino and leave when I'm ahead, and so, although I can see that gambling can be an addiction, I've never really understood the compulsion that can drive someone to lose everything he's just won. During my day at the casino I learnt a few home truths. By and large, gambling isn't about high-rollers winning and losing vast amounts of money. Casinos survive on regular customers who win or lose £100 a night. Gamblers fall into two groups – the sane and the degenerate. The sane gambler can win £1,000 in a night, pocket half and then spread the remainder over a number of tables to minimize any future loss. He will keep most of his winnings, because he sees it as his wages. If a degenerate wins £1,000, he will carry on until he has lost the lot, because the winnings were never real to him. The manageress told me that she could tell when someone has come into her casino to lose, because instead of covering bets with various permutations, he bets on single numbers. Losing is all part of the way the gambling addict confirms his self-hatred and punishes himself for it.'

Given Fitz's Catholic background and his rejection of the Church, this sense of guilt and self-flagellation is entirely appropriate.

'One of the saddest stories I was told was of a man who had been given £50 by his wife to buy sand-shoes for the kids as they were off on holiday the next day. He went to the betting shop and lost the lot. He then borrowed £150 from a loan shark in the bookies and lost that. He had to go back home to tell his family that not only were there no sand-shoes for the kids, but he'd also had to cancel the holiday to repay the money. When I heard this, the idea of Fitz forging Judith's signature on the bank details to increase the mortgage made perfect sense, and I came to terms with that part of his character.'

So much for the gambling aspect of Fitz's character. For Coltrane this was a relatively easy matter to research, since the betting shop and the casino were not entirely alien arenas to him. The science of forensic psychology, however, was another thing altogether.

Coltrane's background and his own morbid interest in cadavers and pathology as a child, an interest that arose as a result of his association with his father's profession, gave him a head's start on other actors in this particular field of research. He also knew that he needed to consult an expert who would be willing to answer each and every question he wanted to put to him.

As was his custom, Coltrane had already read voraciously on the subject of offender profiling, and he understood the conceptual aspects of forensic psychology; as an actor, of course, he would be familiar with the more basic aspects of applied psychology, which is an invaluable part of every actor's armoury. Before he began filming, however, he wanted to know how a forensic psychologist behaved, how he related to the police and to the criminal element. He wanted to pin down the details of dress, attitudes and stance in an attempt to create a sustainable and credible professional character.

'Even though it was a TV drama,' said Coltrane, 'nothing would have been worse than to have given a performance that alienated every trained criminal psychologist in the country.'

It did not take long for Coltrane to discover the perfect person: Ian Stephen, a forensic psychologist who was working at the time as the Director of Psychological Services at the State Hospital in Carstairs. Stephen had been in at the early stages of offender profiling in the late Sixties, when he was asked by Dr Robert Brittain, the psychiatrist in charge of the Forensic Psychiatry Unit in Glasgow, to help in the attempt to construct a profile of the serial killer known as Bible John.

Bible John had picked up three women in dance halls around the city and then strangled them. The police investigation had stalled, and they invited the two men to interview suspects being held on remand for other charges. Although they did not locate Bible John, Stephen is convinced he was among those they interviewed, as the killings stopped soon after one of the interviewees was placed in a secure hospital following another incident.

The 25th anniversary of the killings fell in February and the *Glasgow Evening Times* ran a centre-page spread about offender profiling, involving extensive quotes from Ian Stephen. Coltrane read the article and knew he had found his man. A week later he rang Stephen, explained about the part he was going to play and requested a meeting. Later that same month, Coltrane and Stephen sat down together in the bar of a Glasgow hotel to drink Diet Coke and discuss jazz and forensic psychology.

Stephen found Coltrane to be an astute interviewer. 'By the end of the evening I felt as if every bit of background and knowledge had been drawn out by an expert researching his work,' recalled Stephen.

Having established the parameters of the job, Coltrane went on to question him closely on how he went about it, the day-to-day details that would be invaluable to his performance.

'One of the first things Robbie asked me was where I would sit when conducting an interview with a prisoner,' said Stephen. 'This might seem like a small detail, but in fact it was a very intelligent question. A psychologist should always arrange the furniture in the room before a session. Ideally speaking, the most non-threatening set-up is to have no barriers between you and the prisoner, but sometimes you need them.'

Coltrane recorded everything that passed between them, taking the tapes home to study as assiduously as he had read his research books. Ian Stephen's information was invaluable to him, but only as far as it could be incorporated within the persona that Coltrane had already constructed for Fitz. Indeed, it was probably a good thing that, aside from their jobs, Stephen and Fitz were totally unalike; Coltrane could jettison any of Stephen's qualities that didn't suit Fitz. Coltrane then set about building a psychological profile for Fitz based on Stephen's information and his own extensive character research.

'The romantic in Fitz is interested in the pure motive – the why and how – but the cynic in him just loves to be right and rub people's noses in it, and psychology fulfils both needs for him perfectly. He has chosen forensic psychology because he likes the excitement of crime. Finding out why someone has committed a series of murders or rapes is fundamentally more attractive to him than why someone has nicked a pair of tights or has left his wife. He was probably something of an iconoclast twenty years ago; his friends would say that he just hasn't grown up, but he would say they were dull and boring. He likes to explain himself intellectually, but in fact it is often his gut instinct that gets to the heart of a case. Unlike, Ian, though, Fitz despises this intuition.'

Coltrane's primary objective was to create a believable and realistic character within the context of the fiction of *Cracker* rather than simply to ape reality. *Cracker* was never intended to be a documentary; it was, and remains, a drama, incorporating all the heightened elements and the reductions and torques of reality that go into making something that is entertaining, gripping and intelligent. Any lessons or morals that can be drawn from it arise out of conflicts within the episodes rather than being overlaid as clearly identifiable concepts. This is what has made *Cracker* so popular and so compulsive. Neither McGovern nor Coltrane has ever fallen into the pit of preachiness;

their aim, first and foremost, was always to fashion engaging entertainment that happened to be worthwhile.

Fitz is nothing like Stephen, physically or psychologically, but the professional ideology is similar, and Stephen was able to identify the elements in Coltrane's performance that arose from their conversations. 'The way in which Robbie incorporated what he had been able to extract from our discussions into his own forensic psychologist role within Fitz's personality without the joins being evident was remarkable. There was one scene in *To Say I Love You* where Fitz is called in from the next-door cell, where he was cooling off after his arrest, to help deal with Sean, who had been brought in for hijacking a bus. Sean had been interviewed by DS Beck, who had harassed him and made him confused and hysterical. Fitz manages to gain his trust and confidence and calm him down. He let Sean come to him and need him. It was a brilliant piece of acting, but I would be very surprised if Robbie had worked it all out for himself. If he had, he should have been a psychologist rather than an actor.'

Not everyone in the profession of forensic psychology thought *Cracker* was good, however. Aside from the police, women's groups and rape counsellors, who all objected to the series at one time or another, claiming it to be melodramatic and unrealistic, a number of forensic psychologists protested at the way their profession was being depicted.

'*Cracker* is total nonsense,' fumed Professor David Canter in the *Daily Mail* in December 1994. 'Viewers must understand that Robbie Coltrane is not portraying a psychologist in any sense at all.'

Professor Canter helped create the psychological profile of triple killer John Duffy, the so-called Railway Rapist, which led to his arrest in 1986. He now runs a 40-strong investigative psychology unit at Liverpool University. Canter was shocked at the liberties taken by McGovern's script and the extent to which Fitz was involved in investigation.

'It just does not happen,' he continued. 'It would be viewed as illegal, and defence counsel would have a field day when the case got to court.' As for Fitz's character, Professor Canter claimed that his personal conduct would automatically rule him out of working with the police. 'He would be seen as a professional outcast. His opinions would be worthless.'

Michael Berry, another profiling expert, said: 'Our job is to act as advisers. To see Fitz involved in case management is totally wrong.'

For Coltrane's own take on the character of Fitz and the background research to *Cracker*, one may turn to his self-penned piece which appeared in *The Guardian* on 27 September 1993 under the headline 'Crime Cracker'.

'How does a Scottish actor with a reputation for comedy get to play a clinical psychologist, solving violent and bizarre crimes for the Manchester police force, I hear you ask.

I get a phone call: it's Gub Neal, the producer. "We've got a terrific idea for a major drama series: the central character is a brilliant psychologist who helps the police solve crimes by understanding the true motives of the criminal mind. He sees other people's faults with blinding clarity, but he has no understanding of his own, which are enormous." He was right, of course, a terrific idea, but the road to good television is paved with great ideas, most of which remain just that: ideas. The ones that have legs also have two things: a committed producer and a good scriptwriter.

Next step? Lunch: who's paying? Are we kidding? So, we have lunch, we talk until we're blue in the cheese and biscuits, rarely about work (always a good sign), and I wonder, are more hip, likeable dudes becoming producers, or am I getting older? We agree that we'll outline the character, get Jimmy McGovern (always the choice writer) to write a pilot first episode, and take it from there. Our minds are racing: what sort of guy becomes a psychologist? What do they actually do? Can lunch be charged as a legit expense?

Psychologists try to predict how people will behave in any given situation. The good ones tend to be interested in "why". It was a psychologist, bless them, who advised the supermarkets to put the necessary at the furthest end of the shop, in order that we would be obliged to pass the tempting on the way back.

At the other end of the spectrum, the next time there is a hostage crisis it will be a psychologist who will be advising the cops about the terrorists' next likely move: are they serious about the getaway plane?

How long before they get trigger-happy? What tone do we use down the phone so as not to alienate them totally? It's inevitable, I suppose, that any science setting out to predict human behaviour will be used nowadays, from the ridiculous to something more purposeful – from deciding what colour packaging suggests "soft" for fabric conditioner, to which colour stripes on the road at pedestrian crossings will actually make us slow down.

Enter Eddie Fitzgerald, Jimmy McGovern's creation, the "Cracker" of the title. Fitz has a mission in life: to find the pure motive which is untainted by an expectation of peer group approval, of glory or self-righteous reward. A man who appears cynical, but is really just unsentimental. As an intellectual he would argue that none of us is fundamentally more purely motivated than any other; that most of us would rob banks, were we not afraid of the gaol.

Emotionally, he's a different animal entirely. Having worked out why someone perpetrates a murder, he's quite happy to see them "put away". He drinks too much, he smokes too much, and he's a compulsive gambler. He has just forged his wife's signature to raise cash for a mythical bathroom extension, so he can gamble some more. His wife leaves with their ten-year-old daughter; Fitz is left with their teenage son, who is very like his dad; they fight like dogs. The cops call him in to establish whether a prime suspect is faking amnesia, and away we go. In *Cracker*, as in real life, the police tend to be divided on the usefulness of psychologists. There are the old Plods, who regard any deviation from traditional police methods as voodoo, and the more progressive ones, who are not too proud to take advice from any informed source. A lot of their suspicion arises from the notion of the psychologist as outsider, not a team player etc. This makes him an ideal "hero", of course; on the side of good, but not an authority figure. Perfect for television drama.

There is no doubt that in many recent cases, psychological profiling has helped catch perpetrators and, in the early stages of investigation, helped eliminate hundreds of people from enquiries, in many ways just as important. A profile is used as a screen which may be placed over evidential patterns to give a good idea of "likelihood", a sort of rationalization of the old "hunch". A good psychologist may see patterns in the most irrational, even psychotic behaviour, which is why in the States the psychologist is often at the scene of the crime while the line is still being chalked round the body.

In the midst of this psychological mayhem, Fitz believes there is method in all madness and a pattern, no matter how subjective, to all human behaviour. With intuition and intelligence, once he has found the suspect's true motivation he can tell you the likelihood of their being guilty. He has no truck with external forces of good and evil. He is not impressed by the tabloids' delight in calling psychotics "maniacs", "beasts" or "monsters". He would argue that such tactics demonstrate nothing more than a desperate attempt to distance the rest of us from the "evil within". He would certainly argue that that was our motive for watching police dramas to begin with. Fitz would tell you we like to see a clear moral order in fiction that reality rarely achieves: that we like to see people behave atrociously, so long as capture and punishment are not far away. We identify with the bad guy, because he represents that part of ourselves which we repress; but we want to see him punished to confirm that we have done the right thing in not living our lives that way.

Cracker – and Fitz – challenge this. Fitz recognizes good inside the baddies. For him a "result" is the least important element of an investigation. The Truth is what matters most.'

That Coltrane has become synonymous with *Cracker* is indisputable. It is now hard to imagine a similar symbiosis of actor and role had the original concept been followed. Robert Lindsay as Fitz? It seems almost absurd – like Wally Whyton playing Doctor Who. McGovern has always been gracious enough to realize that he had made an error of judgement.

'I thought Robbie Coltrane was the wrong choice. The kind of anger I had inside was always a thin man's anger. But as soon as I saw the first rushes I knew Coltrane was right. He was perfect.'

So much so that the notion of a slim, wiry, conventionally attractive and weaselly Fitz is now difficult to swallow – in spite of the American version of *Cracker* which has cast Robert Pastorelli as a milder, toned-down kind of anti-hero who toys with cigarettes rather than smokes, whose alcohol intake is moderate as opposed to monstrous and whose worst vice is an addiction for gambling.

It is a measure of Coltrane's confidence that he is able to play the role of a villain in the American series, *Fitz*, which stars Pastorelli in the role that Coltrane made famous. Having gone through a series of complex negotiations to perform in an American version of the British *Cracker*, it was eventually decided to redo the series, with an American cast and crew and toned-down stories and characters more appropriate to the American television public.

The irony here is that *Cracker* in its undiluted British form had already been transmitted on Public Broadcasting (PBS) in America, allowing the more adventurous American viewers a chance to see what all the fuss was about. The winner of numerous television awards for its excellence in scriptwriting and the consistently high calibre of its acting, *Cracker* was not the usual material available to US audiences. The storylines, which dealt with sexually-orientated crimes, prostitution, psychosis and juvenile criminality, were alien enough to the great mass of viewers in the States. When such topics were dealt with, they were usually watered-down true-life sagas made anodyne in movie-of-the-week films. It was the abrasive and extreme tone of Jimmy McGovern's scripts that made *Cracker* different and, to some sections of the American media system, unpalatable.

In addition, the figure of Fitz, a leading man or series hero whose vices outweighed his virtues, was anathema to the networks. They were more accustomed to sympathetic leads, whose incipient recklessness was conspicuously countered by softening influences -strong family background, high moral values, or other character 'governors' – to make the bitter pill of reality easier to swallow. Such was Coltrane's commitment to the character of Fitz and the underlying truths of McGovern's scripts, however, that he never sacrificed the sense of reality for palatability. Given the fact that Coltrane has a vast repertoire of amusing voices and a deep fund of natural humour on which to draw, he had to rein in his tendency to play the funny man, allowing Fitz to live and breathe in all his awful glory.

The thing is, however wrong Fitz is in his personal life – and it is a blueprint of political incorrectness – his professional judgement is absolutely sound. In this I detect a strong link with a character played by Orson Welles, one of Coltrane's greatest acting heroes. Welles' creation of the overweight, monstrous Hank Quinlan in *Touch of Evil* might be regarded as a not-too-distant cousin of Fitz. In *Touch of Evil*, Welles created an extreme version of the edgy, massively corrupted and personally compromised detective, operating in a town on the US Mexican border, whose instinct for justice and nose for wrong-doers was rarely at fault, even if his methods were highly questionable. When confronted with a murder investigation that was a little light on evidence, Quinlan was the kind of cop who would think nothing of planting evidence on a suspect in order to achieve a conviction. Relying on nothing more than his cop's instinct, it was an horrendous practice and not one recommended in the rulebook. While Fitz would never resort to such nefarious practices, Coltrane ensured that his character was one who took the official rulebook lightly, and preferred to rely upon his own methods rather than be a 'by-the-book' inves-tigator. This, of course, often brought him into confrontation with his superiors, one of the great themes of conflict in modern police drama. In *Cracker*, this thematic conflict was explored to the hilt. Ultimately, *Cracker* revealed a rotten core of corruption within the police depart-ment itself, finally exposed by Fitz, that brought howls of outrage down upon McGovern's head from the Metropolitan Police. It may have been dramatic licence, but it was the cutting edge of television drama.

Like most big men, Coltrane sits uneasily on the small screen. And it is this aesthetic consideration that he used to his advantage when playing Fitz. His large, doughy face and his massive frame encased in a dark suit presented an unforgettable, slightly appalling figure whose occasional lapses into sickly humorous asides were delivered with a pointed finger invariably clutching a smouldering cigarette or a glass of whisky.

Fitz was never more comfortable than when making everyone in his vicinity – criminals and colleagues alike – feel ill at ease. Coltrane is gifted with a natural presence which has to do with more than just his size. He is the bad guy's nemesis, a bloated, balloon-like angel of vengeance, armed with a coruscating wit stropped to razor sharpness on his colleagues, friends and family, plus an analytical brain to match his bulk.

The threat implicit in Fitz is less to do with physical violence than the suspicion that he will discover your weakness, home in like a laser on your secrets, lies, hypocrisies and cover-ups – and expose them. For many, he is the criminal psychologist's criminal psychologist – an iconic, fretful and brilliant figure, a man whose sharpness of mind is constantly at odds with the slovenliness of his personal habits and life.

Few television dramas have attempted to create such an iconic figure. One that springs to mind is Hugh Burden in *The Mind of Mr J. G. Reeder* – the Victorian criminal psychologist whose investigative techniques and systems relied on the fact that this very meek and mild little Victorian clerk possessed a mind of criminal deviousness that allowed him to 'see' into the motives of his quarry with greater clarity than his superiors. *The Human Jungle*, with Herbert Lom as Dr Roger Corder, brought psychiatry to the small-screen drama series for the first time, but Lom's silky suave Middle European psychiatrist was light years away from Coltrane's sloppy and hedonistic Fitz.

To say that Coltrane grew into the character of Fitz would be to deny the initial research and the remarkable understanding he showed of McGovern's creation from the start. While there was considerable growth and development of all the characters in *Cracker*, it is significant that Fitz himself is the one who changes least in the three series. In spite of all that happens to him, both in his private life and in his professional career, Fitz ends the series as dark and troubled a character as he began, a man whose knowledge and understanding of the vagaries and nuances of human behaviour is equalled only by his own spectacular lack of self-knowledge – or rather, his inability to do anything about his own desperately anarchic nature.

Pastorelli's Fitz is more palatable to an American audience. The only slightly overweight New York actor plays him as a neurotic, wisecracking, roguish maverick. Pastorelli's preparation for the role did not, significantly, include a study of Coltrane's Fitz. He watched parts of an episode or two and concluded it was too dark, too dangerous. Set in Los Angeles, the American *Cracker* necessarily reflects the social climate – some aspects of the British version were simply taboo. Consequently, there is a veneer of glamour adhering to Pastorelli that Coltrane would never have tolerated, even if it had been suggested.

Then there is the smoking. Traditionally, only villains smoke in Hollywood films and television. Pastorelli is often depicted with a cigarette in his hand, but it is never actually alight. Incidentally, Pastorelli's excuse for not smoking is not that he bowed to the heady climate of political correctness and corporeal spirituality that pervades LA but that, having battled to give up smoking, he could not bring himself to do it again. Coltrane, of course, had no such worries. As a smoker who is constantly trying to give up, playing Fitz gave him a legitimate excuse to indulge.

'There isn't an actor in the country who wouldn't want to play Fitz,' said Coltrane. 'He's intelligent, perceptive, funny and women find him attractive. Plus you get to smoke!'

While it seems fair to point out that Coltrane actually gave up smoking during *Cracker* and substituted herbal cigarettes for those scenes in which he was seen puffing away, he slipped back to the real thing long before the series concluded.

Smoking aside, there is an extraordinarily convoluted cultural interchange at work here. As we have seen, all 23 hours of the British *Cracker* have been aired in the States by the minority Arts and Entertainment cable channel. Following the screenings, ABC, one of the four major networks, decided to gamble on an American version. In 1996 Granada set up an office in Los Angeles where they are co-producing the show – retitled *Fitz* – with American company Kushner Locke. The change of name was the least alarming thing about the American make-over of *Cracker*. For one thing, many observers felt it odd that Fitz should be set in Los Angeles rather than the more classic urban environments of New York or Chicago.

'We liked the concept of putting this guy who was politically incorrect and physically incorrect in this city of ultimate physical and political correctness,' said Jim Sadwith, executive producer of the series. 'We also liked the idea of this darkness, this exploration of the darkest corners of the psyche, in this bright, bright city, instead of the traditional grey.'

Robert Pastorelli, while not exactly a model example of the LA actor, is nonetheless a far cry from Robbie Coltrane. A New Jersey native, Pastorelli is a slimmer, less doughy figure. As well as not smoking, his Fitz doesn't drink with such sublime regularity as Coltrane's version, a fact explained away by the fact that the LA Fitz has to drive – a chore that Coltrane's version managed to avoid. Pastorelli's

Fitz therefore confines his drinking to outside working hours, relieving the character of the necessity of breaking the law every hour of the day he is at work.

Sadwith, however, defended the American version against the accusation that it was diluted for the American market.

'What they've bought is Eddie Fitzgerald and his world of dysfunctionality and darkness, so they're not gonna change that. We're going to be pushing it to the limit, because one of the things that grabbed me was watching this train-wreck of a marriage and this train-wreck of a character, teetering through life on the brink of complete meltdown. Anything less than that and he risks becoming Columbo.'

Gub Neal, who became Granada's Head of Drama, has defended the changes from McGovern's original concept.

'We were assured that the Americans absolutely got it. Fitz is an oxymoronic character. They have hung on to the heart of it. If they had wanted to change the character it wouldn't have worked. He is a monster. This is not *Baywatch*. You have to understand this is radically different by American standards. Fitz is not quite an anti-hero, but he has clear behavioural problems.'

Fine words from a man who stands to make a lot of money if *Fitz* takes off in the States. America is the Holy Grail for television executives, and it will only take one series to be successful for Granada to establish a strong foothold in the market.

Neal admits that they had to alter the pacing of the drama for the Americans and, in doing so, lose a lot of the background details that give *Cracker* its resonant reality. But he also offers the intriguing argument that, even in its original form, the series exhibited American characteristics more than English ones.

'*Cracker* was influenced by *NYPD Blue* and *Hill Street Blues*. It was not Anglo-Saxon like *Morse*. And it had a big central character: Americans like that. There is a degree of emotional expression. He is not repressed. He speaks his mind.'

Speaking his mind is something that Coltrane has never been afraid of doing. Which is just one of the reasons he was so perfectly cast as Fitz. *Cracker*'s success was due to several things. Clearly McGovern has an eye for accuracy and telling moments, and for the dramatic/humorous exchange that is slightly beyond reality – a romanticized version of the kind of spicy smart-ass dialogue we all like to think we'd be capable of, after reading a few Raymond Chandler novels and a few shots of bourbon. Of course, we rarely are, but that doesn't stop us enjoying the prospect of imitating those who make it appear effortless. Like Fitz.

But there is more. Attention to detail was paramount in *Cracker*. Actors and crew worked twelve hours a day for six months to produce an average of four minutes of film a day. Accuracy went as far as buying the paper boilersuits that adorn the forensic people at a crime scene from the same place that supplies the Metropolitan police force.

Accuracy was taken a tad too far during the filming of one of the last episodes of the final series, when a group of spectators watching a scene being filmed in Salford were asked to keep the noise down. The next moment one of the men returned waving a shotgun. In the absence of Coltrane, who was about half a mile away and therefore unable to perform one of his dextrous verbal miracles, the man was removed by the police.

But perhaps the best person to describe the background, the daily tensions and petty conflicts, the warp and weft of filming on a tight schedule, is Coltrane himself, as he did for the *Daily Express* on Christmas Eve, 1994.

'One day while making the latest series of *Cracker*, we filmed a stunt where a guy escaped over the rooftops of a three-storey house in Chorlton, Manchester. It took a crew of seventy to make that happen. The next day, we filmed a scene where a single woman cried into the mirror at her damaged reflection; it took seventy people to make that happen. If we shot a fly farting, it would take seventy people, and you have to get on rather well if you're planning a short prison sentence with a crowd that size. As it happens, the *Cracker* crew got on great, everyone respecting each other's contribution to the end product. We were all understandably neurotic about getting *Cracker II* right. Nine British and international awards tighten one's scrotum considerably; we were flying the flag for quality drama, so the slightest disappointment with a take and we had to go again. In fact, that was very much like the first series, except that we didn't have the accolades to mark its triumph, everyone just gleaned from the first-rate smell of

Jimmy McGovern's scripts that this was no sailing trip. Jimmy writes with such passion and poetry that no one wanted to let him down. it was a very powerful consensus. I often charged across Derbyshire to fly my plane. A model one that I built myself. I'd take it over Snake Pass into the Peak District where the hills become a plateau and the easterly breeze is nothing if not helpful. I crashed the plane as often as I flew it, so days like this were usually followed by 'engineering days' in my flat, with the thing in bits on my carpet. (And many thanks to Paul Carrington for his help.) All in all, I (like the *Cracker* crew) prefer to blend into places I'm not used to and scream through places I'm not wanted – fast or subtle. But on a six-month shoot, you have usually got to be adept at both. We have often been and gone before the city has clocked us, which suits me. I'm essentially shy and repressed, with a snappy and adroit alter ego, both of which I like to inhabit from time to time. I was lucky, I didn't have to run away to join the circus; the circus came with me.'

It is clear that it was Coltrane, more than anyone else associated with the series, who brought it to an end.

'It is my decision to let it go,' he admitted in America in August 1996. 'The network would quite happily see us doing *Cracker* until Penhaligon was drawing her pension, but I've seen other shows which have gone on and on and it hasn't helped them.'

Being so long engaged with one character also made Coltrane antsy about all the other characters lying dormant and unused inside him. In spite of a few forays into film during *Cracker*, like the Russian villain Valentin Zukovsky in the James Bond film, *GoldenEye*, he was not getting the rush of offers that he might have expected after a hit television series.

'I'm difficult to cast, I know that,' he once said. 'But producers always think I'm working on *Cracker* and don't ring up. I'm busy five months of the year on it, but I'd like to do other things in between.'

Nor does he want to become typecast, as so many of his contemporaries are following a successful run on television.

'He's not me. He's a character created by a writer, Jimmy McGovern. A great challenge to play. But I am not as brilliant, nor am I compulsive.'

Cracker was to yield dividends ultimately, in the shape of several

Hollywood movies, a proper full-blooded Bond villain and, potentially, another television series. Apart from money and international celebrity, *Cracker* gave Coltrane something else; an unexpected and quite welcome bonus.

'It's been good for my private life. When I was a comic everyone used to come up and slap me on the back. Now they tend to leave me alone.'

Chapter 11

COLTRANE, CARS, CADILLACS

Coltrane's obsession with cars spills into every aspect of his life. He has had many screen roles as a mechanic, allowing him to dress down in his favourite gear, an all-in-one boilersuit, and get down and dirty over the engine or underneath the chassis of a vintage American car. There are a few variations on this, and the abiding concern is that the car must be old and it must be American.

When Coltrane finally got the chance to drive across America in a Cadillac for a television series, it appeared to be the gig of a lifetime. But, as he explains in the accompanying book, things didn't turn out quite as he had expected.

Coltrane admits to having had a lifelong obsession with cars. And the ideal cars remain for him the great Detroit gas guzzlers of the 1940s and 1950s. From the moment he constructed the Coltrane Convertible (although it must have been called the Robbie Roadster as 'Coltrane' had yet to appear as a viable *nom de plume*) at the age of ten, Coltrane discovered a hobby which amounted to an obsession. 'The great advantage of rebuilding old cars,' he wrote, 'compared to, say, collecting stamps or making matchstick models of Chartres Cathedral is that you can't get on a Penny Black and cruise the Strip.'

American cars combined the twin obsessions of automobiles and America, which Coltrane has in approximately equal measure. As a Glaswegian, Coltrane admits to being brought up with the idea that 'New York was just like Glasgow, only more so'. And the American obsession with size and wide-open spaces and so on appealed to the man with the big suits, shoes and appetites. Coltrane and America were built for each other. In the USA, I believe, he feels less aware of his size, less self-conscious about his largeness; easier in his own skin.

Similarly, American cars are designed to show themselves and their drivers off in a way that is foreign to the more self-effacing Briton. And anyway, 'Coltrane in a Cadillac', as the series was entitled, is somehow more appropriate and appealing than, say, 'Robbie in a Rover'.

Coltrane's American obsession is the result of a steady diet of imported culture, from music to movies. It certainly hooked Coltrane from an early age, via Marlon Brando in *The Wild One* through his first experiences in New York during the years of punk and CBGBs. But to experience the drive from Los Angeles to New York in an American dream machine would, he confesses, 'tell me if any of my American dreams were near the mark'.

After a couple of false starts, Coltrane finally finds the car he wants to convey him the 3,500 miles across the country. It's a 1951 Series 62 Cadillac Coupe Convertible and it is housed in the warehouse of Cadillac collector extraordinaire Ed Sholokian. After enduring the high-pressure sales techniques of Cadillac salesmen in two or three other places, Coltrane is impressed as much by the genuine enthusiasm of Sholokian as by his vehicles.

'Ed Sholokian was a short, thickset man in his late fifties with a taste for Hawaiian shirts and a love of talking about cars. I liked him right away as he quickly introduced himself (with the kind of grip that has lifted a few transmissions in its time), then spent considerably more time introducing each of the cars around us ...'

And thus his description of the car he sets his heart, hopes and wallet on:

'If Rita Hayworth had been built in Detroit (and I've always had my suspicions), this is what she would have looked like. Curvaceous, naturally, but so well-proportioned that you could not imagine changing one detail without spoiling it. A 1951 Series 62 Cadillac Coupe Convertible, in glorious black with drop-dead gorgeous chrome-work and an ivory-white top over a burgundy Fleetwood interior, they did not get sweeter than this.'

You can feel the saliva of anticipation accumulating in his description, the mark of a true enthusiast and, it has to be said, no mean wordsmith. As he leaves the city for the beginning of the trip with the television crew in tow, Coltrane is clearly in a state of euphoria from where he can only descend. From that moment, indeed, both America and the car itself conspire to bring him down a notch or two, but the main thing is, he has had it, reached it, revelled in it, however briefly.

Driving a vintage American automobile across the United States has its disadvantages as well as its advantages, as Coltrane was to discover. Things are constantly going wrong on a car as old as the Cadillac, and parts are not always available, even if there is the expertise. While Coltrane himself is clearly an experienced and enthusiastic mechanic, there were many occasions when he needed assistance and some times when it was not forthcoming.

Like most city-dwellers, Coltrane's feelings about America develop and evolve to fit the actual environment and location. Most city people feel at home in New York, say, or San Francisco or Chicago. They have a harder time in the flatlands of Kansas or the museum towns of Dodge City or Salt Lake City. And thus it proved for Coltrane.

Following a brief and amazingly uneventful sojourn in Las Vegas, he drove to Utah, where he wanted to encounter the Mormons of Salt Lake City. It turns out to be a dispiriting experience, given that he gets a heavy sales pitch on the Latter Day Saints, as they prefer to call themselves. Needless to say, Coltrane failed to take up the offer of a late baptism and got the hell out of there. For one thing, it was incredibly difficult to get a drink in the place.

'All I wanted,' he concluded, 'was to get in the Cadillac and drive somewhere where people wore nylon shirts and sweated a lot.' Intriguingly, Coltrane's observation of the landscape as he passes through the extraordinary geographical sights of southern Utah and on into Colorado is clearly tempered and coloured by his observation of the inhabitants and the social, political and cultural geography he encounters. For him, it is not a separate issue; they are all bound up in one aesthetic. This is a man who has an all-encompassing mind, who cannot switch one part off in order to enjoy without distraction something else. He cannot, or will not, separate out various elements from society but will judge them, assess them as part of the whole. This is one of the things that make him such an amusing raconteur, such a grand observer, as he has a lateral rhythm to his thinking that can skip and jump and outfox many an opponent. It also explains his facility for dealing with tiresome interviewers and pesky journalists who persist in attempting to find out what makes him tick. Or focus too obviously on one or two facets of his personality. The chances are, he's got the broader picture, a kind of blueprint of reality, spread out in his mind and can travel faster across it than they can.

Take Coltrane's attitude to guns. The moment he arrives in Dodge City, Kansas, a place he has been wanting to visit since he heard of Wyatt Earp and Bat Masterson, he experiences that extraordinary push-me-pull-you feeling about American history and the political legacy of myth.

'Show me the man who hasn't felt a secret desire to put on a Stetson hat, saddle up a Palomino, spit a thin jet of tobacco juice into the dirt, then form a posse to catch the bad guys, and I'll show you a liar,' he writes, with the conviction of a man who thinks all men are equal when it comes to Wild West fantasies.

And yet, no sooner has he pronounced on his yearnings for the western experience than he is debunking the myth with the reality of history and describing the gunfights staged for the tourists in the main street. This leads him to expound on the dangers of handguns, and a trip to the local gun store does little to dent his argument. Having subjected himself to the argument from a representative of the pro-gun lobby, as any gun shop owner would be, Coltrane reaches the lamentably trite conclusion:

'I left Bob's Pawn and Gun Shop realizing that you can take the American out of the OK Corral, but you can't take the OK Corral out of the American.'

In other areas, a little less contentious than firearms, personal ownership of, Coltrane is more objective and amusing, scoring points by way of his observation rather than his opinion. This is when he is at his best, as the trajectory of his opinion can ruin even the most acute of observations.

Onwards through Kansas, he comments on the cattle and the beef market, juxtaposing the economic historical perspective with the present-day observation, and with a few wisecracks thrown in. As a meat-eater (it's well-nigh impossible to imagine Coltrane as a vegetarian, for some reason), he can only object to the process of raising and slaughtering, not the philosophy or the final product. Thus he sees beasts who appear well-fed and content because of their free-range lifestyle and diet; then adds the little coda that keeps you alert:

'They spend around four months being fattened up with a delicious mix of corn, alfalfa and molasses which helps them gain over three pounds a day. Just to make sure, they throw in a nice steroid cocktail as well. The final ingredient is now ominously causing major anxiety amongst food scientists. I kept thinking what life would be like here for a vegetarian.'

Shifting gear effortlessly from beef to politics, Coltrane reminds us of the precise period he is present in America; the day before the Presidential elections he discovers that the nation is divided over whether to re-elect George Bush or bring in the new boy, Bill Clinton.

'The Coltrane poll was saying George Bush was going to hobble back into the White House, but somehow I felt that I had not yet met on my travels what could be called a completely representative cross-section of the American people.'

What intrigues Coltrane in his travels across the US, as it does in much of his life, is the way in which people conceal their hypocrisies and double standards. If there is a guiding philosophy that drives Coltrane, that makes him angry, it is the hypocrisy of those who subscribe to one way of life and thought and behave in an entirely different, or opposite, way.

He is redeemed somewhat by his insatiable curiosity about people and his embrace of new things, new ideas. He may be opinionated and politically strident, but he is not closed; he is open to new experiences and, especially, people.

This is manifest in his comments about the Amish community, his next port of call in his Cadillac trip across the US. Coltrane admits to a certain curiosity about the Amish and, moreover, what sparked it. As with most of us, it was the Peter Weir film, *Witness*, with Harrison Ford. He wanted to find out more about them. 'Did they still wear seventeenth-century clothes and speak German,' and – he can't resist making fun of himself at this point – 'did all the girls look like Kelly McGillis?'

Having met up with a man who had been brought up in the Amish community but had managed to get out and build a life outside of the sect while retaining contact with the community and his family within it, Coltrane is confronted with a mass of contradictions and anachronisms. It is significant that he admits to being bewildered by it all without losing respect for the community as a whole. And, as always, he manages to put a comic spin on the list of contradictions in his description:

'But hey, excuse me, the Amish could use state-of-the-art medical treatment but they were not allowed to have electricity and phones in their houses. They could use tractors to farm with, but couldn't put air in the tractor tyres ... They have to wear seventeenth-century clothes, but as far as I know Nike Cross trainers were not worn in seventeenth-century Switzerland, and many Amish wore them now ... I found this concept of deciding when time had stopped for them all a bit farcical, but they seemed to lead a peaceful, productive life, so good luck to them.'

After whimsically commenting on their extraordinarily liberated attitude to teenage sexuality, Coltrane finally delivers his *coup de grâce*: '[I] just wished that they could all be big-hearted existentialists like me. Then the world would be lovely ...'

Aha. So that's the philosophy to which he adheres. Even if 'big-hearted existentialist' has the same kind of cracked ring about it as 'Benevolent dictatorship', at least we know where we stand with Coltrane. It's as good a summation of the contradictory forces churning within him as any.

One of the most bizarre and atmospheric stopovers enjoyed by Coltrane on this trip is at the Kansas salt mines, whose even temperature and climate are so unchanging that it is the perfect environment for storing unstable material like film negative or magnetic tape and sensitive material like secret files.

Fifty-four storeys (645 feet) beneath the surface of the earth lie the huge salt mines where, in a temperature of 65°F and a constant 50–60 per cent humidity, American cultural treasures like the master copy of *The Wizard of Oz* and *Taxi Driver* are kept alongside old television sitcoms.

'I spotted *Peyton Place*, *The Diary of Anne Frank*, *M*A*S*H*, and a host of Forties and Fifties bad movies. With some guilt I realized I had seen them all. And enjoyed them. It was almost like I had found the

Kansas equivalent of the Holy Grail, and I took the elevator back to the surface feeling a warm sense of pride and achievement. So, not yet half-way and I was already completely insane. Things were all going terribly well.'

Things got even better when Coltrane fetched up at an all-women feminist dude ranch in Matfield Green in the Flint Hills. Run by Jane Kroger, whose family had farmed the land for four generations, it was a typical Coltrane stopover, quirky and eccentric – a place that might fuel his exasperation or enthusiasm. Either way, it was going to make good copy for a seasoned and garrulous observer like Coltrane.

He was, of course, on relatively safe ground. Kroger turned out to be a terrific human being, full of integrity, ingenuity and a good heart – the kind of person who endears herself to Coltrane and finds him endearing too. Just to cement the relationship, they all sat down and watched the television coverage of the Presidential election. Much to everyone's delight, though to nobody's surprise, Bill Clinton won.

'I had also been right in my prediction of Jane Kroger's politics,' wrote Coltrane, with just a trace of smug self-satisfaction. 'She was overjoyed Clinton was to be President, and we both looked forward to his victory speech. When it came it was a little disappointing, lacking in the rhetorical power you would want from the most power-ful man on earth. In fact, it was Vice President Al Gore who made the best speech, filled with passion and enthusiasm for the future. I went to bed that night filled with new hope and confidence about tomorrow. Tomorrow we had to look forward to a new America, a better America, an America which did not have Presidential campaign commercials every five minutes.'

Shifting gear from the vaguely sublime to the patently ridiculous, Coltrane drove through Kansas City and out the other side, where he came across a character called Ted Bliel. Lured by the sound of Bliel's voice issuing from the Cadillac's ancient radio, Coltrane made a detour to Boonville, Missouri, home of KWRT 'Hometown Radio'.

It was a less than happy meeting. Coltrane has never been shy of telling people what he really thinks of them, but in this case there was a delayed reaction to his response, which was just as well as he would probably never have got out of Missouri alive had he told Bliel his reactions over the radio. But the encounter gave Coltrane the opportunity to deliver one of his trenchant critical arias on a local area through the conduit of one of its most archetypal individuals.

'Ted Bliel was a twitchy, bespectacled man in his mid-forties, and it was his flat, monotone voice which had led me to the station. Ted, it turned out, had been a broadcaster at KWRT for 21 years, in which time he had become by far the most famous person in the area. It was said he could run for any job in the country and win, if he chose to. There was no doubt, Ted Bliel was Mr Boonville.'

Coltrane then conducts a character assassination of the unfortunate Mr Bliel with almost surgical precision. And in doing so, he manages to damn the entire population of Boonville to boot.

'I have been interviewed by many different journalists and broadcasters over the years but never by anyone so devoid of response to my words. Ted had no sense of humour; in fact, he had no sense of anything. His interview style reminded me of the man who did the Speaking Clock, but without his sparkle. After half an hour Ted threw the interview open to the people of Boonville to see if they could do any better. As I listened to a lady caller bring her singing dog to the phone, I decided the answer was they couldn't.'

Coltrane may, of course, have simply selected an easy target for his volleys of contemptuous wit. While it is clear that Mr Bliel may not be the most professional or slickest of radio presenters, Coltrane's own words suggest that he savages him more because he didn't laugh at his jokes than for being a poor interviewer. In Coltrane's terms, the two things are inextricably linked. During a recent Michael Parkinson interview, while he was telling a story which he deemed to be funny, he suddenly stopped and waved his hands in front of Parky's eyes, as if to wake him up. Parkinson was simply listening without making any kind of flamboyant response.

Coltrane seems to demand, even need, a conspicuous response to his torrential verbals; it's almost as if he cannot bear the silence of humanity. He has to be talking and entertaining and creating atmosphere and prodding responses – even if it is only laughter – from his surrounding fellow beings. He simply cannot stop himself. If this is indicative of a huge ego which is constantly screaming, 'Look at me! Look at me!' it is equally suggestive of a man suffering from a deep insecurity.

While Coltrane himself would no doubt regard this kind of comment as a glib, superficial attempt at a psychological profile, it is worth bearing in mind when confronted with the remaining evidence. On that Parkinson programme, Eddie Izzard and Dame Diana Rigg were fellow guests, and the air was thick with competitiveness. Coltrane and Izzard were circling and testing each other like pitbulls. There was no out-right winner, but the skirmish illustrated the huge differences in comic technique, timing and attitude between Coltrane and Izzard.

Coltrane's next stop in his American jaunt was St Louis, Missouri, where he encountered yet more fodder to fuel his formidable sense of injustice. While residing temporarily in an hotel on the safe side of the city, Coltrane recites the statistics relating to East St Louis, on the other side of the Mississippi, in the state of Illinois.

'... of a population of 40,000, ninety-eight per cent of whom are black, around seventy per cent are on Welfare; the city has the highest per capita murder rate in the US, and an infant mortality rate five times worse than the national figure.'

Sniffing a story, Coltrane was sensible enough to realize that it would be very unwise to go strolling through that part of the city alone, and enlisted the help of a local journalist – a species of human not normally held in high regard by the actor.

'In America the word journalist is not a dirty one and the trade is respected in a way that seems a distant memory to a British person. Unlike the UK with its huge selection of national papers, America relies on an army of local papers to do the noble work of the press in a quiet, businesslike way, free from the excesses I was used to.'

The trouble is, Coltrane wants his cake and he wants to eat it too. Then again, what's the point in having cake and not eating it? Having just lambasted poor old Ted Bliel for not displaying the spark and snap of a professional radio interviewer, Coltrane is now praising newspapers for being quiet and discreet – which is hardly the role of newspapers at all. The thing is, Coltrane prefers American newspapers and journalists to the British equivalent because they are polite, so polite they wouldn't dream of asking him questions which he wouldn't want to answer. And that is the kind of journalism Coltrane really likes. An adjunct to his own publicity.

And with his natural propensity for romantic mythologizing, Coltrane mourns the passing of the old-fashioned glamour of newspapers and laments the advent of technology in the newsroom. Coltrane would be happier stepping into the offices of a newspaper that looked like something out of *The Front Page*, where the sound of the presses rolling could be heard by the City Desk water-cooler. At heart, he is a nostalgia junkie, preferring the glamour, style, engineering and hydraulics of the past to the laminated, transistorized, byte-sized, digitalized present. Hence his love of old gas guzzlers; hence his love of rock and roll over techno.

'I'm always disappointed when I visit newsrooms these days, because new technology has ripped the romance out of them, and this one was no different. There was just a faint clicking of computer keyboards and a polite hum of discussion stirring the intellectually charged silence as I walked to the Editor's office. Nobody asked loudly for the front page to be held and there was not a single green eyeshade in sight.'

More disappointment was in store for Coltrane when he made a special detour to Hannibal, home town of Mark Twain. Here, he was confronted with small-town exploitation in its most extreme form. From the moment he claps eyes on a sign proclaiming 'The Mark Twain Dinette', an establishment that is apparently the 'Home of Mark Twain's Fried Chicken', he fears the worst.

Sure enough his fears prove well-founded. On a tour of the town, Coltrane encounters the Mark Twain hotel, the Mark Twain Wax Museum, Mark Twain Antiques, the Mark Twain Bookshop, the Mark Twain Riverboat, the Mark Twain Cave, the Mark Twain Supermarket, Tom Sawyer's Snac Attack, the Huck Finn Shopping Centre, the Injun Joe Campground, the Becky Thatcher Bookshop and Tom and Huck's Go Karts. None of these, to be sure, help Coltrane get over the feeling that Americans – especially small-town Americans – are shameless when it comes to exploiting every and any angle of whatever intrinsic merit and cheapening it for profit.

Coltrane delivers his *coup de grâce* on Hannibal after he has been delivered to a cobbled lane with early nineteenth-century houses. Here he finds the boyhood home of Mark Twain (completely restored in 1990), and nearby the house of Twain's childhood sweetheart, Laura Hawkins. But it is the home of Twain's father, J. M. Clemens, that really takes the biscuit; the entire house, which had originally stood in another part of town altogether, had been taken apart, moved piece by piece and rebuilt in this convenient new location. Coltrane can barely contain his wrath at this example of pandering to the worst excesses of tourism.

'Another illustration of something I had discovered in my travels about the strange American attitude to their own history: what they prefer is a theme-park version of the past in which historical locations are clean, accessible, and have all the necessary facilities. If a location fails on any of these requirements then the solution is to knock it down and rebuild it correctly. The American people are very proud of their heritage and they like it to be as modern as possible.'

Coltrane's bile rises towards the end of his journey, which is hardly surprising, though he keeps a large reserve of optimism in store for his final destination, New York. New York, he is fond of saying, is his second home; it is the American equivalent of Glasgow, where he grew up, and he has an enduring affinity for the city in all its hellish, gorgeous, aggressive glory. Having spent a couple of years hanging out in New York City at the end of the 1970s, Coltrane regards it with the affection of an old flame. After a long separation, the occasional reunion can fan the embers of passion into a fire for a short time.

Coltrane suits New York; they both share a sense of scale and cynicism – a positive negativism that seems to sneer at the world while secretly remaining excited by every new development.

The city brings out the best in him, too. Here he drives down 46th Street in the gleaming black Cadillac in a state of near euphoria. And like all true city-dwellers, Coltrane loves to hear and tell stories about the inherent dangers of the city. It is part of the urban machismo, designed to warn off faint-hearts and country bumpkins while simultaneously fuelling the city-dwelling ego. New Yorkers, like Londoners, spend a great deal of time and energy complaining about their city. But they wouldn't have it any other way.

'I lived here off and on for a couple of years back around 1980 and loved the experience,' he writes, 'but the city had got darker since then.

It used to be that there were few bad parts of town, but now it seemed that every part of town was a bad part of town. The gun culture which I had seen right across America combined with the craziness of New York made for an explosive mixture which tended to go off in the faces of innocent passers-by. So whaddaya gonna do? Spend all your life in Des Moines?'

Before finally taking leave of Jezebel, Coltrane finds time to catch up with his old New York buddies, including the film-maker Amos Poe, who had made Coltrane's first ever movie, *Subway Rider*. Intriguingly, although Coltrane describes several characters he meets in New York, including the extraordinary John Manniel – The Ninja Assassin, and the closest thing to Batman the real-life Gotham actually has – he somehow fails to describe his best pal, Poe, who remains a shadowy figure throughout the final chapter. Poe is a notoriously reclusive guy, in spite of having made several films, and it is highly likely that he insisted that Coltrane avoid describing him in detail or relate much of their conversation. There are certainly no pictures of him in the book. Odd, that.

Chapter 12

THE LATER MOVIES

1986 was a turning point for Coltrane. Having played variations on a comic theme in films for many years, his advent as a serious actor was due to his relationship with Stephen Woolley, who had watched his work in *Chinese Boxes* with interest.

In spite of protestations, Woolley insisted on casting Coltrane in *Mona Lisa* (1986), Neil Jordan's comedy thriller about a no-account criminal (Bob Hoskins) who is given the job of chauffeuring a black prostitute (Cathy Tyson) by his ruthless boss Michael Caine. It was to provide Coltrane with his first truly memorable film role.

Where in *The Supergrass* he was playing a dangerous, if comical, brute with fascist tendencies, Coltrane's role as Thomas in *Mona Lisa* is gently eccentric; the loyal friend to Bob Hoskins's ex-convict George.

Reverting to his natural Scottish accent and dressed throughout in the familiar motor mechanic's gear of a dark green boilersuit, Coltrane is the epitome of a modest-minded man with deep reserves of loyalty and a simple but muscular sense of justice and morality. The comic element is provided by Thomas's increasingly bizarre schemes to make money by dealing in strange artefacts like decorative plastic spaghetti and illuminated statues of the Virgin Mary.

We don't have to wait too long for Coltrane to appear in *Mona Lisa*. When George loses his temper outside his estranged wife's house and is set upon by locals, Thomas comes wading in to the rescue, gently but firmly extricating his friend from the flying fists and feet with mollifying words: 'Can't you see he's upset? That's the word, isn't it, George? Upset.'

He walks George back up the street to his garage where, much to his pal's surprise, he has kept his pride and joy during his incarceration, a gleaming yellow Jaguar. George can hardly believe his eyes. Thomas may not be too bright and his sexuality may be mysterious, but he's a good solid friend. When George complains about his treatment by his wife when he went to see his daughter, Thomas observes: 'You can never tell with women, George. They're different. When they go to Heaven they get wings.'

George's reply that angels are men completely flummoxes the simple Thomas. 'Men? Men? Nobody told me that.'

Right from the start, Thomas is presented as one of life's innocents, and it is greatly to Coltrane's credit that he never once allows his natural cynicism to peep through. Much of their conversation revolves around books, exclusively whodunits and thrillers, with which Thomas is obsessed and which he has been lending George throughout his prison term.

Thomas takes George back to his place, which involves clambering along gangplanks and through piles of junk and old cars, and it is understood that George will stay here until he is back on his feet. Thomas appears to live in an old warehouse down by the river and here we see his library of books and the detritus of his schemes. Holding a plate of ornamental spaghetti, George dubiously says: 'Fancy a fibreglass fruit flan? Or a polystyrene tutti-frutti?' This exchange defines the difference between the two friends. George is a criminal with a strong streak of romantic naïvety, Thomas is an innocent without a criminal bone in his body. It is a nice distinction and it reverberates throughout the film.

The relationship is cemented by Jordan's visual linking gags. Following the plastic spaghetti scene, George and Thomas are next seen eating real spaghetti at Thomas's place – causing a pertinent comment from George ('It *is* real, isn't it?') – while they peruse Thomas's library of crime and pulp fiction. There is an air of comfortable friendship here, of unspoken male bonding without any of the overtones of homosexuality that might have crept in.

As the film progresses, and George becomes increasingly entangled with his former gangster associates through the black prostitute whom he chauffeurs from client to client, he is unwittingly estranging himself from Thomas, though it takes Thomas to finally voice his fears. Each of the scenes between the two men, which punctuate the narrative proper and provide as it were a little respite from the story, illustrates the distance that is growing between the two, and consequently between George and reality. Thomas is in this way a kind of Jiminy Cricket, George's conscience, whose role is to keep bringing him back to reality.

When next we see the two friends alone, Thomas has exchanged his stacks of plastic pasta for crates of light-up Virgin Marys. 'What happened to the plastic spaghetti?' enquires George, somewhat aghast. 'They went like hot cakes,' replies Thomas with insouciance.

As an epilogue to the scene in which George loses his temper and swears blue murder, Thomas turns to the tacky statues and whispers, 'Sorry about the language' before switching them off.

The next time we see Thomas it is classic Coltrane: head bent over a car engine, cigarette dangling from his mouth, sparking battery wires off the engine block. When Thomas comes inside to wash for supper, he finds George watching a pornographic video on his television set. Thomas watches the screen very briefly and sneers, 'Channel 4, is it?' before walking away.

It is at this point that the two friends have reached a crisis. George is in too deep to extricate himself, and Thomas is fearful of the outcome.

'You used to be my hero, George,' says Coltrane with real puzzlement. 'What's happening?'

As events head on towards a bloody climax, it seems that we have seen the last of Thomas. Luckily, we haven't. He turns up at the last moment to rescue George and his daughter in what looks suspiciously like a 1959 Cadillac – probably one of Coltrane's own vehicles. The final shot is pure fairytale: Coltrane, Hoskins and his daughter walking arm-in-arm away from the camera, allowing themselves the occasional little skip. The future is uncertain but they have endured and survived the vicissitudes of the present. It is a strangely optimistic and wholly appropriate ending. What we have here is some kind of remodelled nuclear family – two guys and a girl. All of them innocents in a bad world.

Coltrane's role as Thomas in *Mona Lisa* – encouraged by Woolley upon seeing his work in *Chinese Boxes* – is a rare case of Coltrane actually making himself vulnerable. The combination of daring, gratitude and possibly Neil Jordan's direction (plus whatever assistance and encouragement he was afforded by co-star Bob Hoskins) – in short, the entire environment of *Mona Lisa* – made Coltrane feel safe; safe enough to risk stepping out of his customary role as consummate entertainer, performer, man of many voices, to actually be someone else. But it did not continue like that. He did not find another opportunity, or combination of opportunities, to break out until *Cracker*.

Derek Jarman was at the height of his creative powers when he made *Caravaggio* (1986), an imagined life of the sixteenth-century Italian painter. Considering the ludicrously low budget, the screen is awash with transcendent filmic ideas – chiaroscuro lighting, terrific production design and truly inventive costumes. By making deliberate use of anachronism – although 'set' in the 'period' some characters wear double-breasted suits, smoke cigarettes and even use a typewriter – Jarman's sense of 'found' materials and imagery serves his concept well. By concentrating on the faces of his characters he captures something of the spirit of Caravaggio's paintings, peopled as they were with real characters from the streets and taverns of his locality.

The dying Caravaggio (Nigel Terry) lies on a bed in his studio, cared for by the mute youth he bought from a family as a child. His memories turn to his youth as a street painter and rent boy – or the sixteenth-century equivalent – which establishes the sexual nature of his transactions. Soon, he is living in a precarious *ménage à trois* with his model Ranuccio Thomasoni (Sean Bean) and his mistress Lena (Tilda Swinton).

At the unveiling party for one of his works commissioned by the Church, Caravaggio encounters Cardinal Scipione Borghese (Coltrane), the libertine nephew of the Pope. Just to make the point clear about Borghese's massiveness, he is introduced by a dwarf, which accentuates Coltrane's size and, incidentally, hints at his decadent tastes.

Flamboyantly moustachio'd and swathed in the scarlet of a cardinal, Coltrane makes an impressive entrance, but it is not long before he is allowed to guy the figure he presents when he attempts to seduce Lena by first removing his moustache, revealing it as false. 'The agony of fashion,' groans Coltrane, as a preliminary to removing Swinton's shoe and paying homage to the exquisite foot revealed. 'Madonna. Queen of Heaven.'

Coltrane makes a good cardinal, even in this venal, bloated caricature, and sets the right tone in a very brief scene or two until the crisis of Lena's murder. When she is discovered floating in the river, Thomasoni lays the blame with Borghese, and soon tongues are wagging.

Thus, when Caravaggio is finally granted an audience with the Pope, his encounter with Borghese *en route* is fuelled with menace and threat. Having airily thrust his hand before the painter for him to kiss his ring, Coltrane issues his official warning in declamatory tones: 'The Holy Father and myself are prepared to turn a blind eye to Sodom provided you bring the riff raff back to the Church and place in them the awe of the Holy Father who is, of course, the sole interpreter of Jesus Christ here on Earth.'

Having delivered the official line, Coltrane leans in to Nigel Terry and hisses: 'And Michaelangeli. I must advise you that these slanders against my personal life must stop.'

It's a chilling threat and Coltrane is equal to it. But there is also just a hint of injured innocence behind the warning. For, as we discover, Borghese, for all his decadent and libidinous ways, had nothing to do with the death of Lena. Her murderer was, it transpires, far closer to home: Thomasoni, her lover, killed her for love of Caravaggio. A fatal mistake, as it happens, because Caravaggio then cuts his throat.

Jarman's casting of Coltrane in a relatively minor but significant role is important. It established that Coltrane worked in two ways – as a physical presence and as a clever actor. In just a few short scenes and a few lines of dialogue, Coltrane sets up the paradox, the guessing game about his character that has become almost his trademark. He can be funny at the beginning of a sentence and sinister by the end of it. It's a great trick and one that he uses to terrific effect.

From the divine to the ridiculous, Coltrane's next film was the woefully inadequate *Absolute Beginners*, Julien Temple's attempt to film Colin MacInnes's 1959 novel about the teenage scene in postwar Britain. Coltrane plays Mario. This was an ambitious movie that flopped like a dying whale. Perhaps the results and consequences of these frequent incursions into failure led him to the safer territory of comedy and *The Comic Strip*.

But it was Richardson's next *Comic Strip* film that really landed him in trouble. *Eat the Rich* (1987) was a black comedy of class war and cannibalism, a subject that suited Coltrane down to the ground. Unfortunately, he had not reckoned with the fastidious and finicky Lanah Pellay, the fey young actor playing the restaurant worker whose sacking from a posh London restaurant inspired him to return with a band of terrorists. They reopen the restaurant and run it their way, feeding their new customers with the former ones, who have been slaughtered in the takeover. Some heavy-duty friends turn up on screen to be killed and eaten, including Paul McCartney, Bill Wyman, Sandie Shaw and Koo Stark. As a satire it was pretty crude, but Coltrane (as Jeremy) provided as much entertainment as anyone else. The real problem was Pellay, who took an instant dislike to Coltrane and sold his story to the tabloids. It was one of the few truly anti-Coltrane pieces that had been run. And it cut him deeply.

It is an intriguing speculation that his experiences with the flamboyant Pellay on *Eat the Rich* may have prompted his next role, that of the transvestite Annabelle in Philip Saville's *The Fruit Machine* (1989), later retitled *Wonderland*. This was a serious departure for Coltrane, a raging heterosexual, who hadn't even so much as dragged up for a pantomime dame, let alone played a bona fide cross-dressing character. It was, by several accounts, not a particularly comfortable experience for Coltrane or those around him.

He had to go through two hours of make-up every morning, plus having double shaves to make his face as smooth as possible. Huge false nails were glued to his own considerable fingernails, which made it virtually impossible for him to go to the loo. 'Have you ever tried going for a leak with nails that length?' he said to Alasdair Buchan. 'You can't undo your zip or get your tights down.'

'I'm not a closet transvestite,' he told Lucy Robinson. 'So I didn't object to dressing in women's clothes. But it did become exhausting after a while. All that oohing and aahing and camping it up. There were 120 queens in the extras – all those red slashed lips and tongues never stopped moving. It wears you out, love, it really does.'

It was also a relatively minor role, although it does provide the fulcrum for the plot. When two young gay boys from Liverpool – one black, one white – witness the brutal slaying of a nightclub owner – Coltrane, whose club is The Fruit Machine – they find themselves on the run from exceedingly unpleasant gangsters. Saville's unusual, shape-shifting movie isn't entirely successful, as it keeps changing its mind about how seriously it should take its subject. Is it a sensitive if off-the-wall study of young gay life in a world ill-equipped to deal with it? Or a cartoonish, gay Donald McGill-like farce of sex and violence with a bit of social observation on the side? Given that the script was the work of Frank Clarke (brother of Margi), it seems more likely to be the first, though Saville's direction, confident though it is in individual scenes, cannot quite convey the sense of the thing as a whole.

And Coltrane was difficult to handle, according to Saville. He admired him tremendously as an actor but he remembers the trouble they had finding a dress and shoes to fit him. Also, the long hours standing around in high heels took its toll on Coltrane's back and he suffered severe back pain for much of the shoot. This also made him somewhat bad-tempered and there were days when it wasn't easy to get the shot they wanted.

Nevertheless, Coltrane took the research for *The Fruit Machine* seriously. Given that he wasn't just dressing up in women's clothing for a laugh or two, he decided to hang out with genuine transvestites (if that's not an oxymoron) to find out what makes them tick.

'I went up to Manchester and went round all the TV clubs up there. It was fascinating, a real eye-opener. They accepted me once they realized I hadn't gone there to laugh at them. They are, quite naturally, quite defensive because they are always getting beaten up. But once I got to know them they talked openly. When you're standing in a bar where everybody else is dressed as a woman, the back chat and the banter is fantastically funny and very wicked. There's a tremendous amount of self-hatred. Some of them are very sad, but by no means all. And a lot of them were vitriolically bitchy. In a way, it's a bit pretentious because the vast majority of the audience aren't going to know if I've got it right or not. But I don't want every transvestite who sees it throwing things at the screen. And I didn't want to take the easy way out and say, "Hey I'm pretending to be a drag queen but actually, ha ha, I'm butch," à la Benny Hill.'

No, no. That would never do. If there is one thing Coltrane is terrified of, it is of being considered politically incorrect.

This is where Coltrane's career starts to hot up. Having played a succession of caricatural or overloaded characters, he was offered the part of the villainous Victor Hazell in Gavin Millar's *Danny, the Champion of the World* (1989), based on the book by Roald Dahl.

Set in rural England, it is a sort of Home Counties *Jean De Florette*, with villainous, grasping landowner Victor Hazell, a *nouveau riche* exploiter who owns one half of the land in question, plotting and scheming to acquire his neighbour's half by fair means or, preferably, foul. As Jeremy Irons and his real-life son, Samuel, play the owners of the neighbouring land, where they run a garage, it is clear that they are the good guys and that their brilliant relationship will serve them in good stead to outwit Robbie Coltrane's Hazell.

Taking a few visual clues from George Cole's spiv character in the St Trinian's films, Coltrane wore a moustache, slicked-down hair and a checked suit and delivered a fully-rounded portrait of cowardly villainy perfectly attuned to the film's sensibilities. It was a challenge and Coltrane was equal to it.

The film opens on a typical pheasant shoot, with birds plummeting from the sky and gun dogs picking them up gently and depositing them in a pile. It is Somewhere in England, Autumn 1955. We see a large, impressive estate and the house.

From the moment we first see Coltrane, waddling forth from his grand pile, it is clear that this is a man lamentably out of his depth, with aspirations that he hopes to buy his way into. He is wearing the townie's idea of a country squire's attire – plus-fours, cap, mustard yellow waistcoat. He has a truly ghastly Hitlerite moustache and greased-back hair which is a little too long for comfort, style, fashion or hygiene. He is an arriviste, bogus gentry.

He gets into his Roller – which is precisely what he'd call it – and checks his pheasants on the way. The evil glint in his eye leaves us in no doubt that he is a machiavellian son-of-a-bitch. He lights up a big cigar, which cannot but look obscene between his babyish pouting lips.

Stopping on the boundary of Hazell Estates Ltd, he takes out a pair of binoculars to spy on the garage where Danny (Samuel Irons) and his father (Jeremy Irons) live and work. Shortly thereafter, we see Hazell driving furiously towards the garage.

As Danny is backing a car out of the garage, Hazell comes careering up in his Rolls Royce. Danny just stops in time.

'Why don't you watch where you're ...?' begins Hazell, before realizing it's a child he is dealing with.

Following an exchange with Danny's father, Hazell attempts to introduce himself; Irons butts in and says he knows he is Victor Hazell.

'Correct,' replies Coltrane. 'Already famous around here, am I?'

'Notorious,' says Irons.

'That's what I like about the country. Everybody knows everybody ...' says Coltrane, revealing at once that he is a townie, an outsider. Intriguingly, Coltrane pitches his accent somewhere between Roy Kinnear and George Cole. There is a whiny, wheedling, patronizing, aggressive, spiteful, cowardly, nasty tone to whatever he says. He attempts to persuade Irons to sell his land, as it is right in the middle of his estate, which he is hoping to turn into one of the best pheasant shoots in the country. Coltrane is in his element here, playing the 'shyster' character to which he so often alludes.

'Business is business and I do happen to be a very rich man,' Coltrane leans into Irons' face and rolls his eyes. 'I'll offer you £2,000 for this place.'

Turning to Danny, he slides into his most patronizing and oleaginous tones: 'Yes. That is a lot of money.'

When Irons tells him in no uncertain terms that the place is not for sale, Hazell tries a different tactic.

'How much do you make in this place?' he sneers. 'Ten, maybe twelve quid a week, if you're lucky. I'm offering you a small fortune, the opportunity of a lifetime. And what about the boy there, eh? Shouldn't you be thinking about his future?'

Irons does the calm and sensible thing and simply asks his son whether he should sell or not. Danny is not fooled by Hazell's slippery tongue and shakes his head, no.

'I think I should warn you. I always get what I want. One way or the other.'

Coltrane now moves into threat mode, and it's not a pretty sight. When Irons and his son state that they don't want to move because they are happy where they are, Coltrane ripostes:

'Happy here, are you? We'll see about that.' He lights a cigar and throws the lit match down on to the garage floor to express his contempt: the oils, petrol fumes, no smoking signs and so on contribute to the element of menace in his action.

Soon after this encounter, Hazell begins his war of attrition. His first action is to send down two men from the ministry to check the grades of Irons' petrol. After the war it was not uncommon for unscrupulous garage owners to try to pass off low-grade petrol as the high-grade stuff. Irons, needless to say, is an utterly honest man. When he challenges the two inspectors on why they are there, just two weeks after he has already been inspected, they deny all knowledge of Hazell or any dealings with him.

When Coltrane is on the phone later that evening to the pissed-off inspectors, who reveal to him that Irons knew exactly what was occurring, he turns the tables with the aggressive clumsiness of the truly cowardly bully: 'Yeah, well, of course he knew it was a put-up job. That was the idea.'

Like all rich bullies, Hazell has friends in relatively high places. He puts in a call to a local councillor – love the white telephone – and sends in two District Council Child Welfare Department and Housing Inspectors.

1989 was to prove an important year for Coltrane in his film acting career, if only because of the variety of roles in which he was seen. Having successfully made the transition from transvestite victim to snarling villain, he turned to The Bard in Kenneth Branagh's screen version of *Henry V.*

Branagh, who had reached the position of being able to call on any and all of his friends in the business – both theatre and film – to join him in his enterprises, gathered a cast to die for. The one thing he wasn't going to do, it was clear, for his revisionist version of Shakespeare's most popular history play, was create a movie that might in any way be compared with Olivier's super-heroic version. On the contrary, Branagh went in the other direction, and where Olivier had taken his cue from Eisenstein (especially *Alexander Nevsky*), Branagh took his from Kurosawa – particularly the battle scenes in *The Seven Samurai*. This was muddy, bloody, thuggish and violent stuff – probably closer to the reality of fifteenth-century warfare than Olivier's shining, heroic version of events.

It was, for me, a film of great parts rather than a great film; but what great parts. Derek Jacobi as Chorus, Ian Holm as Fluellen, Judi Dench as Mistress Quickly, Robert Stephens as Pistol, Emma Thompson as Princess Katherine – and, of course, Robbie Coltrane as Sir John Falstaff, a role that he was clearly designed to play.

Perhaps the most impressive thing about Coltrane is not that he should be so good as Falstaff, but that he should be so good in such company. We first sight him lying in bed, a nightcap on his head and a candle burning on the table; grey whiskers and a huge bulk. He is, it is clear, dying, probably as a result of the rejection by young Henry. By the simple device of using a flashback – which Robert Stephens' Pistol sees in a vision of the past – we see the actual rejection.

Sir John is holding court at the tavern, surrounded by Nym, Bardolph, Mistress Quickly and Pistol, among others.

'But do I not dwindle? My skin hangs about me like an old lady's loose gown,' he says, to roars of laughter from the company. 'Company, villainous company hath been the spoil of me.'

When Branagh's Henry enters the tavern, Coltrane's face lights up and he goes to embrace the boy king. In close-up we see him plead for mercy from Henry.

'If to be old and merry is a sin. If to be fat is hated. Now my good lord, when thou art king, banish Pistol, banish Bardolph, banish Nym. But sweet Jack Falstaff, valiant Jack Falstaff and therefore more valiant being as he is old Jack Falstaff, banish him not from Harry's company. Banish plump Jack and banish all the world.'

In voice-over Branagh replies: 'I do. I will.'

Coltrane's eyes widen momentarily in disbelief, then close in sadness. 'But we have heard the chimes of midnight, master Harry. (Jesus. Days that we have seen.)'

Still Henry is adamant. 'I know thee not, old man.'

It is the *coup de grâce* for Falstaff. He steps back and closes his eyes. It is very touching.

Coltrane is clearly too young to play Falstaff, and his voice, devoid of any regional accents or Shakespearean enunciation, seems strangely high. But it's a youthful high, not an ageing one. Even so, it is a fine contribution to Branagh's movie.

Considering his paucity of Shakespearean experience, it is a tribute to his facility with language of all kinds and his understanding and expression of character that he creates a truly memorable figure, shifting effortlessly from the grandstanding, come-all-ye humour of Shakespeare's most lovable hedonist to the pathos of a dying fat man betrayed by his best friend. Branagh and Coltrane play brilliantly off each other, and it is as much a tribute to Branagh's sympathetic direction and inventive casting as to Coltrane's skill that the whole thing works. This, more than anything previously, established Coltrane as an actor of note.

It was a busy year. 1989 also saw him in what might have been a terrific introduction to Hollywood, Carl Reiner's affectionate comedy, *Bert Rigby, You're a Fool*. Sadly, things did not turn out that way. Having seen Robert Lindsay in the musical *Me and My Girl* on Broadway, Reiner wrote this whimsical saga of a Northern England coal miner who wants to get into showbusiness and arrives in America, where his impersonations of Buster Keaton and Gene Kelly do not get him very far. Undaunted, he heads for Hollywood, where he gets a job as a butler in the household of movie mogul Corbin Bernsen, only to find he must fend off the advances of the mogul's libidinous wife, Anne Bancroft. Coltrane plays a character by the name of Sid Trample, which goes some way to illustrating the calibre of humour on display. It's an absolute mess from start to finish, poorly written, ill-conceived, badly directed and woefully performed. Considering the talents involved, from Bancroft to Lindsay and Liz Smith to Coltrane, it is a shameful waste. The cinematographer, incidentally, was Jan de Bont, who went on to rather more successful things when he directed *Speed*, with Sandra Bullock and Keanu Reeves.

Remaining in 1989 yet shifting into the future, Coltrane popped up in *Slipstream*, a British attempt to cash in on the science fiction craze begun by *Star Wars* over a decade earlier. Produced by the Quaker Gary

Kurtz (who also produced *Star Wars*), it also starred Mark Hamill, who was perhaps the one actor in the *Star Wars* films who had failed to become a star as a result. Ageing badly (maybe it was the beard) and saddled with a serious-minded but not very interesting or cinematic script, Hamill could make very little headway in this movie.

The ecologically-inclined script follows the fortunes of a futuristic bounty hunter as he pursues his quarry, a psychopathic android who has escaped from police custody, into the ferocious and lethal winds known as the 'slipstream'. Coltrane plays a character called Madeleine.

Same year, another movie. In America in 1989 Coltrane picked up a role in director Joe Pykta's debut movie, *Let It Ride*, featuring a cast of quirky Americans including Richard Dreyfuss, former New York Dolls' singer David Johansen, the impressively constructed Jennifer Tilly, Teri Garr and Michelle Phillips. Described as a modern-day Damon Runyon-style comedy, it tells of a cab driver who gets a tip on a horse that's ready for the glue factory and finds himself on the gambling hot streak of his life. A modest and likeable urban fairytale, well played by Dreyfuss and Coltrane as a pestered and increasingly frustrated bookie, it is peppered with intriguing cameos and almost-famous faces which keep the thing watchable even when the script fails to rise to the occasion. Worth a look for another of Coltrane's impeccable American accents. And it must have been fun for him, hanging out with several characters he would have known in his New York days in the Seventies – including Johansen and Warhol actress Mary Woronov.

Having established a working rhythm throughout 1989, Coltrane finally returned to England to star in the 1990 Jonathan Lynn/Eric Idle comedy *Nuns on the Run* (see Chapter 6). Loosely based on the idea of *We're No Angels*, in which convicts escape and hide out in a monastery posing as monks, and the Jake Thackray song, 'Sister Josephine', which touts a similar idea. This gets a little extra mileage from the old cross-dressing routine, with Coltrane and Idle as a brace of bank robbers who nab a million then have to hide out in a religious order when their getaway car breaks down outside the walls of a convent. Unfortunately for them, though hilariously for us, this forces them to pass themselves off as nuns to avoid detection, which they do with predictable but nonetheless amusing results.

The script displays no great wit, but the laughs are present if only because of the practised ease with which the two stars mug and pratfall their way through the farcical proceedings. Much like a *Carry On* movie with a few good jokes and several more naked females (there's the obligatory nuns in the communal shower scene – all of whom seem to be distressingly young and pretty), it's an enjoyable romp that was more successful than it truly merited.

As Charlie McManus, the less intellectually able of the two thieves, Coltrane is frequently hilarious, often outshining Idle as a master of the double take. And, however obvious it may be, the sight of Coltrane in a nun's habit attempting to act 'girlie' is so ludicrous that it never fails to get a laugh.

Coltrane's next film was a real weirdie. In *Where the Heart Is* (1990), veteran director John Boorman returned to the genre with which he had experimented in his youth with *Leo the Last* – that of whimsical urban fantasy. Boorman and his wife co-wrote the screenplay, and I believe that several of the characters are loosely based on their own children, so there isn't anyone else around who can take the blame.

Set in New York, it tells of a well-heeled family whose head (Dabney Coleman) is a self-made man, having built up his demolition company from scratch. But his children, who have never wanted for anything, suddenly seem to him to be ungrateful layabouts. To teach them a lesson in self-sufficiency and personal motivation, he sends the three of them (Uma Thurman, Suzy Amis and David Hewlett) to live in an inner-city tenement.

Allegedly inspired by *King Lear*, this is rambling, arty, precious, 'message' movie-making, which promotes the idea that the artist can survive the businessman when the motivation is pure. It is incredibly soppy, quite sexy and, on occasion, staggeringly beautiful to watch. Coltrane appears in it fleetingly but doesn't even have a named credit. Definitely an indulgence from Boorman, and Coltrane must just have been passing the location at the time and got roped in.

Taking a break from Britain, Coltrane was lured across the water to Canada for two films, both of which offered him opportunities to expand his repertoire and to have fun without too much risk of over-exposure in the case of failure.

Oh What A Night (1992) is one of those post-war rites of passage movies beloved by Americans and Canadians as they hark back to an era when everything was changing, when people still had an innocence to lose, and rock and roll was stirring the nation's loins and hearts.

Set in a small town called Carlisle in Ontario in the 1950s, the film tells the story of an adolescent boy (Corey Haim) and his infatuation with an older, ostensibly married woman. It begins on a beach (as they are wont to) with Haim and a Staffordshire bull-terrier being cooed over by several girls. His voice-over indicates that he has borrowed the dog specifically to woo the girls, who like nothing better than a spectacularly ugly dog.

Picked up by his best friend and his girlfriend, they drive recklessly back home in a borrowed car, which they crash and accidentally blow up. Emerging unhurt, they return to their respective homes. Here we learn that Haim is an embryonic writer and he keeps a diary addressed to his dead mother. In it he admits to borrowing one of Todd's pups for the purposes of seduction, though quite what he's going to do once he's got a girl isn't entirely certain.

Todd turns out to be Robbie Coltrane, who has reverted to type by playing the local garage owner and auto mechanic. Thus we first see him – as we see him in many other films – in a XXXL boilersuit, with his head bent over an engine, and wielding a greasy spanner. Interestingly, when he goes to pump gas for a customer we see that beneath the grease and the boilersuit he is wearing a shirt and tie, a subtle indication of the era.

Todd, it emerges, is the local sex guru for adolescent boys. While changing a carburettor he can dispense advice on engines and girls. Coltrane speaks in the soft burr of a Scots-Canadian, a tone which suits him very well.

'There's nothing like pups for attracting the girls,' he says, giving us an idea about the set-up. Basically, Todd lends his pups to the young, hormonally challenged boys and expects to be regaled with the details should the ploy succeed.

'Still not getting any, I suppose?' he enquires, loosening a nut. 'Don't worry, son, you will. There's plenty out there. Plenty.' As Coltrane repeats this, he gazes up for a moment, looking into a kind of imagined world of willing young girls. But the rueful look in his eye reveals that it will never be a world that he can enter, pups or no. He is destined to be a kind of sexual Moses, leading frustrated adolescent boys to the Promised Land while not, himself, being able to enter.

The next scene reveals a shade more about Todd. As well as the garage, he also runs the general store attached to it, a cornucopia of stuff that is irresistible to the light fingers of young boys. But Todd keeps a smart eye open. Having spotted a young shoplifter attempting to liberate some apples – 'And the rest' – he settles down to give Haim a lesson in sales technique. He's one of those founts of all knowledge who has just enough originality of expression to give credence to his endless stream of clichés and homilies.

Coltrane here does a remarkable thing; he captures the loneliness of Todd without ever making him seem sentimental. He even risks delivering his talk about selling and understanding human psychology with the suggestion of camp flamboyance, as if he were trying to bottle up his true nature. It's an intriguing performance.

The other thing that is immediately evident is how good Coltrane is with kids. Not little tiny kids but adolescents – boys and girls – who are, in fact, the hardest people with whom to act. Coltrane appears to gain their trust to a greater extent than many other actors on the screen, allowing him to achieve something like a real relationship.

And he never loses sight of the value of intelligence. In the middle of a speech about the need to think, he suddenly digresses: 'Farmers in particular don't think, except possibly about farming . . . Sit yourself down and think about what people – actually – want.'

Then, through the agency of an erotic novel – *Forbidden Flesh* – he deconstructs the art of selling and business technique. Todd, you realize, is more than just your average blue-collar worker, but he hasn't got much farther than impressing young men.

Then there are the cars. How Coltrane must relish delivering 'auto' lines. 'That's a Studebaker, all right. Nice and low to the ground like they say . . .' Well, it would be, wouldn't it? Stuck fast in the mud and needing a tow from Todd's service truck.

Todd is one of those local guys who is verging on an asshole but doesn't quite make it; he manages to stay on the right side of eccentricity through sheer force of personality and humanity. This is particularly evident when he is caught asleep in a wheelbarrow, one of his dogs curled up asleep in his lap. Rising suddenly, he clambers out of the wheelbarrow, and undoes his flies to relieve himself in his yard, unaware that a local farmer's wife has just driven up to see him.

Very embarrassed, Todd zips himself up with profound apologies. 'Nonsense, Mr Todd,' replies the woman. 'I'm a farmer's wife. I've seen a horse urinate.'

Coltrane does a funny little ducking bow and says, 'Thank you.'

His humanity comes out in the scene during the travelling carnival in which Haim finally gets to dance with the woman of his dreams while her 'husband' gets drunk in the cab of his truck. As Todd walks by and they exchange greetings, he notices that the boy and the woman are clearly visible in the trucks's wing mirror, so he subtly shifts the position of the mirror out of alignment. It's one of those small moments on screen that register perfectly.

Coltrane's final scene in the film sums up his character and gives him a terrific pay-off. We see him playing with his pups when the boy walks in. Todd sniffs the air.

'Aqua Velva! Turning into a regular Elvis, aren't you?'

He then embarks on a story about mating a male and a female dog and the expressions they go through; one of which he tried on the woman owner of the bitch in question. It doesn't go down at all well.

'The point is, do not mix humour with sexual passion. Because it doesn't work.'

It's not bad at all. And Coltrane proves the exception to the rule that an actor should never work with animals or children by working very nicely with both.

Coltrane's other Canadian movie is a different prospect altogether. In *Perfectly Normal* (1991) he is presented as the star, in a grand-standing performance of operatic eccentricity. Coltrane plays Alonso Turner, a figure of mystery as the film opens, who arrives to take over the life of a diffident, ineffectual young man who has just come into a surprise inheritance.

Michael Riley is Renzo, who works in a beer-bottling factory by day and drives a cab by night. His unadventurous routine is interrupted by the occasional game of ice hockey in which he participates. He is a dreamy, nice, unambitious layabout whom most of his colleagues – especially the boss – regard as dull; and whom one in particular, the psychopathically resentful Hopeless (Eugene Lipinski, who wrote the script), regards as his mortal enemy.

As in *The Supergrass*, Coltrane arrives in an Ontario town at night, embarking from a bus and emerging on to the street through a cloud of mythologizing steam. Turner wears a white panama and a cream linen suit, not exactly the right costume for wintry Canada. The suggestion is that he has come from somewhere much warmer – probably in a hurry. Turner is a chancer, a vaguely notional busi-nessman and a facilitator who might, or might not, hail from New York. He certainly has a New York accent and attitude.

He gets into Renzo's cab and says with typical flamboyance: 'Take me to a place of food.'

In the course of their conversation, Turner reveals to Renzo that he is 'in the people pleasing business'. He is certainly a take-charge kind of guy; or a royal pain in the ass, depending on your point of view or proximity to him. When Renzo invites him to sleep on the couch, he doesn't know what he is letting himself in for. Returning home after a day in the beer-bottling plant, he finds Turner still there, swaddled in an apron, preparing Pasta Alonso for them.

In a somewhat stretched sequence, Alonso and Renzo drink wine in the kitchen and get drunk. Alonso sings snatches of *La Bohème* to Renzo, establishing the operatic theme that runs right through the film like a river. Renzo simply goes along with it. In spite of his discomfiture, Renzo finds the food delicious. But he has to leave again for his ice hockey game. Alonso is intrigued.

But Alonso isn't finished with Renzo. When he discovers that the young man has inherited money, he lures him into a scheme which is a dream project combining his two great obsessions – opera and food. Thus he persuades Renzo to invest in an Italian restaurant complete with opera-singing waiters.

The remainder of the movie is constructed out of two strands, the pursuit of Alonso and Renzo's dream restaurant and the machinations of Renzo's workmate to wreak revenge on him for some imagined slight. How these two resolve themselves is the narrative trick of the movie, even if the actual denouement leaves a lot to be desired. At least it's a wild trip *en route* to the destination.

The Adventures of Huck Finn (1993), the Disney version of Mark Twain's classic novel, was something of a landmark for Coltrane, who plays one of the two scallywag villains, the Duke, opposite Jason Robards as the King. It is also a strong addition to the half dozen or so earlier screen versions of Mark Twain's visionary American novel about a young boy's gradual enlightenment concerning the perils of racial prejudice.

When the semi-literate young Huck escapes from his drunken, abusive father, he encounters a runaway slave, Jim, with whom he teams up to travel down the Mississippi to 'freedom'. In the course of their eventful journey, Jim educates Huck in the ways of tolerance, and Huck, although steeped in the prejudice of the South, finally comes to realize that all men are equal, regardless of race or colour.

The first third of the film concerns their flight and a variety of hairsbreadth escapes from Jim's pursuers; as there is a reward of $500 on his head, dead or alive, Huck is courting real danger by associating with him. But the real fun and meat of the tale begins with the arrival of the King and the Duke.

When Huck and Jim are camping on the riverbank, their well-stocked raft moored close by, we see two pairs of legs running through the undergrowth and hear the distinctive tones of Coltrane and Robards arguing.

'Why are you always stealing chickens?'

'I love chickens. They're succulent.'

They burst on to the bank near Jim and Huck, who make hurried preparations to leave before they can be caught by the intruders. Too late. The two strangers come scurrying on to the raft, their hands filled with sacks of swag. Their dress – tattered fol-de-rols of ersatz Southern gentlemen – and their preceding dialogue mark them out immediately as rapscallions, rogues and ne'er-do-wells. Crowding on to the raft, they immediately accost Huck and Jim.

From the outset, it is clear that Robards is the more devious of the two, while Coltrane is the more aggressive and volatile. While Robards introduces them as the King and Duke of Bilgewater, affecting a preposterous gentleman front, Coltrane grasps Huck by the throat and accuses him of trying to elude them before they had a chance to get on to the raft.

It is a terrific double act. American critic Roger Eberts lauded the film and especially the performances of the two villains: 'The supporting cast is uniformly splendid, especially Jason Robards and Robbie Coltrane, as the King and the Duke, who impersonate visitors from England in an attempt to swindle two innocent sisters out of their inheritance.'

He refers to the scam they perpetrate when, having stopped to replenish supplies at a landing post, the two villains are mistaken for the long-lost brothers of a recently deceased member of a wealthy Southern family. By this time, Coltrane has already blackmailed Huck into assisting them by threatening to expose Jim as an escaped slave, having found the wanted poster while rifling Huck's possessions on the raft. Huck has no option but to remain silent and play along with them.

The real comedy kicks in at this point. Upon hearing that the Wilkes brothers have been sequestered in England for twenty years, and that the older one is a preacher and the younger, larger one is deaf and dumb, they embark on a brace of impersonations that are little short of hysterical. In a bar, they exchange views.

'How are you at playing preacher?' asks Coltrane of his ally.

'How are you at playing deaf and dumb?' responds Robards.

'Pardon?!?' bellows Coltrane as the two collapse in gales of laughter.

They pressgang Jim and Huck into their elaborate scam, dressing up Jim as a Swahili chieftain and Huck as an English valet. As this motley and extremely unlikely crew, they arrive at Phelps' Landing in time to encounter the grieving members of the family Wilkes, who have just laid their brother to rest. The ensuing opening gambit, with Robards posing as a pious preacher with an English accent to equal anything by Dick Van Dyke in *Mary Poppins*, and Coltrane doing a ludicrous deaf and dumb act, including preposterous sign language, is one of the funniest moments in the film or, indeed, that Coltrane has ever achieved.

Somehow, they achieve their objective and are welcomed into the family home, where they are treated to a grand dinner at which Robards regales them with increasingly tall tales. Only the youngest daughter suspects they may be frauds. When they read the will and discover they have been left a chest of gold, which they locate in the barn, Coltrane delivers a warning speech to Huck about the effects of tarring and feathering (his fate if he should give the game away) with lip-smacking relish.

When the local doctor voices his suspicion that they are imposters, Robards hits on the breathtaking psychological ploy of giving the money to the two sisters, who promptly give it back in recognition of their honesty and chivalry.

Huck returns to the craft to find that Jim has been arrested. The villains have sold him down the river for the reward. As he wanders through town, Coltrane leaps out of nowhere and nabs him: 'Now where have you been, you little turd pie?'

It is at this point that the two villains show their true colours. Coltrane just wants to take their ill-gotten gains and run; Robards, a visionary scallywag, sees a way of acquiring more. By claiming he wants to take the two sisters back to England, which would entail selling the house and all its contents, he proposes to relieve them of every asset, which, converted into cash, will make them rich beyond their wildest dreams. In spite of Coltrane's protestations, Robards persuades his companion to pursue the scam to its bitter end.

And bitter it is. When the two (apparently real) Wilkes brothers arrive in town, the situation becomes more complicated than they can handle. Robards and Coltrane are revealed as the imposters they are, and we last see them being trundled along the street covered from head to foot in tar. It is a suitable end for a brace of the most shameless, devious and unscrupulous villains ever to walk the pages of literature.

For Coltrane, it is a personal triumph. His accent is perfect and he plays off the veteran Robards to perfection. Once again, too, he works brilliantly with children – in this case Elijah Wood's Huck – offering no quarter or sentimentality. He is the archetypal coward and bully, bigger than his opponents, who cowers in the face of equal opposition. The flamboyance of his clothes and his manner – especially in the deaf and dumb act – indicate a roguish actor, a part that Coltrane plays to the life. For Coltrane is, like the Duke, a man of many parts; so many, in fact, that it is often very difficult to determine the true person who lurks beneath.

The boy Macmillan and his father Ian.

The boy MacMillan on a family holiday.

Teenage MacMillan and his sister Jane.

Coltrane delivers his most authentic Orson Welles impersonation as the mysterious Harwood in Chris Petit's *Chinese Boxes*. U.S. actor Will Patton looks appropriately bemused.

Coltrane as a somewhat larger than life Ken Livingstone in *The Comic Strip* episode *GLC*. Rumours that Livingstone went on a crash diet after seeing it remain unfounded.

Quite possibly Coltrane's most dangerous moment – as Det Sgt Troy in *The Comic Strip* episode *The Supergrass* – carrying the cello case (containing a chainsaw) along a sea wall with the waves crashing all around him.

Coltrane holds forth in the pub to fellow newspapermen Jack McLeod (Bill Paterson) and Nick Mullen (Gabriel Byrne). A small but credible role in *Defence of the Realm*.

Coltrane wigging out as *The Master of Dundreich* in *Laugh? I Nearly Paid My Licence Fee.*

Mean and moody as the simmering Det Sgt Troy in *The Comic Strip* episode *The Supergrass.*

Coltrane's rock and roll years as Danny McGlone in John Byrne's
television series *Tutti Frutti*.

Fine and dandy: Coltrane in flamboyant mood attends the 1988 BAFTA Awards ceremony with Rhona Gemmell and his close friend Emma Thompson.

Darling, I was wonderful. Coltrane as the drag queen Annabelle in *The Fruit Machine*.

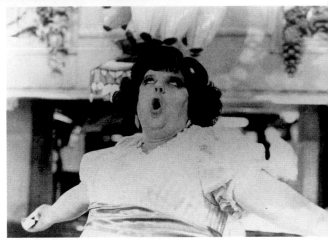

A tad too young to play Falstaff, Coltrane nevertheless gave it his best shot in Kenneth Branagh's film of *Henry V*.

Chapter 13

AMERICAN MOVIES

Coltrane's attempt to break into American movies has been erratic. He is, it seems, more comfortable in quirky little independent films or well-polished cameos in studio pictures than in large parts in studio films. Maybe the right part has yet to present itself. Clearly, he falls somewhere between the big comic status of John Goodman and John Candy and the class act of *Cracker*. His own attitude to the business may make it difficult for casting directors and Hollywood studio executives – not renowned for their imagination or their grasp of anything but the simplest concepts – to position him in a movie successfully.

This can be the only reason he was cast in *Buddy*, a curiously unsuccessful attempt at a children's movie with an environmental conscience.

Buddy was made in 1997, a joint venture between Columbia Pictures and Jim Henson Pictures. It was released in the USA on 6 June but never reached the cinema screens in the UK. It went straight to video and it is not hard to see why. In spite of a fine Anglo-American cast which included Rene Russo, Coltrane and Alan Cumming, an entire menagerie of animals and some state-of-the-art animatronics, courtesy of the Jim Henson Creature Workshop, it is a singularly lifeless movie.

Set in the late 1920s, the film is based on the life of eccentric New York socialite Gertrude Lintz (played by Russo), who used her wealth and position to create a haven for a variety of animals, from championship Briard dogs, Rex rabbits, guinea pigs, schools of tropical fish,

121

flocks of geese, a stable of horses, two horned owls, three snakes and a kitten to a quartet of mischievous chimpanzees.

She treats all her charges like children, dressing them (where possible) in specially tailored clothes and generally allowing them the run of the house. The chimps' clothes are tailor-made at Bergdorf-Goodman; she teaches them table manners, how to play croquet, mix Martinis, do light housework and say their prayers.

The film opens with her taking two chimpanzees, dressed to the nines in little sailor suits, to the cinema where, unsurprisingly, they create a near riot. After the opening credits, she receives a call summoning her to Philadelphia, where she rescues a baby gorilla who is clearly near to death.

Coltrane plays Dr Bill Lintz, a physician who is seen from the outset to be a doting husband. While he may not actively encourage his wife's eccentricities, he indulges her and does what he can to support her. The Lintzs are childless, and it does not take a quantum leap of the imagination to infer that the animals represent a substitute family. Dressed in elegant period clothes and sporting a soft and impeccable upper-class New York accent (which is closer to New England and Bostonian than contemporary New York dialect), Coltrane certainly looks and sounds the part, even down to the elegantly greying hair at his temples.

But it is a passive role, and too often he is employed simply to react to Russo's antics, or those of her animals. Our first proper sight of him, after a few establishing shots early on, is when Russo returns from Philadelphia with the sick baby gorilla and we see Coltrane listening to the animal's heartbeat through his stethoscope. Yet even in the short scenes between the two of them, Coltrane and Russo establish a believable husband and wife bond which is remarkable. It is what's left unsaid between them that resonates.

When Russo calls the gorilla by name, Coltrane brings gentle concern to his response: 'You've named him? Why did you do that? You know it'll only make it harder when you . . .' This line, plus the big meaty paw (complete with one or two chunky rings) gently drifting across Russo's shoulder-blades, speaks volumes about the level of protection that husband feels for wife, as well as his understanding of her need for independence.

Sadly, it is the actors who have to do all the work, with very little help from the script and almost none at all from the director, Caroline Thompson. (I find it difficult to believe that this is the same Caroline Thompson credited with the authorship of *Edward Scissorhands*.) She opts, instead, for the strictly sentimental approach, layering the already mushy script with even softer visuals, effectively losing the laughs and undermining the drama.

When Coltrane finally gets to deliver a proper speech, as he does to Russo in a sun-dappled garden – 'You know, I've finally figured out what it is, Trudy. You have to save this gorilla. So we finally have somebody in the house who can wear my hand-me-downs' – the only reaction Russo can give is to laugh (and it's not that funny). Somehow, they pull it off, as Coltrane leans in to embrace her with: 'I can still make you laugh.' What a pity he doesn't have the material to make the audience laugh, too.

The next scene involving Coltrane *is* funny, however, and I strongly suspect he contributed it himself. He is depicted on the telephone to the mother of a small boy who has got his hand trapped in one of his own orifices. The concept is pure Coltrane and, coming as it does, out of nowhere, and being at odds with the banal humour of the rest of the script, leads me to believe he wrote it himself to liven things up a bit. 'Keep yourself calm,' he says. 'Well, where is his hand now, exactly? Really? . . . Plenty of butter and a gentle pull should fix that.'

The other line of humour that is pursued relentlessly throughout the film is the comparison between Coltrane's bulk (and he is very big in *Buddy*) and the rapidly growing gorilla. While Coltrane deals well with the real animals around him, especially the chimpanzees who are natural camera-hogs, he doesn't fare quite so well with the animatronic, man-in-a-gorilla-suit Buddy, played as a full-grown gorilla by ape specialist Peter Elliott, who had earlier simian experience in *Greystoke* and *Gorillas in the Mist*. The sight of the impeccably dressed and distinguished Bill Lintz awaiting his wife at the dinner table while surrounded by mischievous chimps ('Trudy, do you think you'll be here by dessert?') is amusing enough, but it is not helped by the dialogue.

Bill: Darling, I hate to be the one to tell you, but before we know it he is going to be huge.

Trudy: Well, I imagine you know how I feel about that.

Bill: Yea, well, I'm not a gorilla.

Trudy: Don't underestimate yourself, darling. You know you're capable of almost anything.

Bill: Sweetheart, do you know anyone, offhand, who has a full-grown gorilla in their house?

Trudy: No. But I have my suspicions about that new fellow who works down at the drugstore.

Cue gales of rather forced laughter. Not even kids would find this kind of pap funny.

The mood changes when Trudy Lintz is invited to the World's Fair in Chicago with her entourage of apes, in spite of the fact that Buddy is becoming dangerously big. At one point, he even appears to be dressed in identical clothes to Bill Lintz, giving rather more credence to his earlier remark about hand-me-downs than we had previously suspected. During a late-night snack session in the kitchen in which Coltrane, tellingly, is making the sandwiches, he shifts into serious mode:

'Do me a favour, Trudy,' he says about the impending visit to Chicago. 'Don't take Buddy.'

When Russo responds airily that he is worrying about nothing, Coltrane simply breathes, 'Gertrude!' – as good a way as any of expressing his displeasure. 'I don't think it's safe. Not for him, not for you, not for anybody.'

His wife, wilful and whimsical as she is, ignores him, and Buddy causes chaos at the World's Fair when he escapes from his cage and runs amok through the crowds.

When Russo returns with Buddy to the Lintz mansion, she rather ruefully says to Coltrane: 'Thanks for not saying "I told you so."' Coltrane replies: 'Oh did I forget? I told you so.'

In spite of the fact that Buddy is now the simian simulacrum of Coltrane, wearing his clothes, affecting a gentle style, genteel behaviour, it is blindingly obvious that he is beyond their control. The inevitable happens and he is delivered to the zoo, where there is a painful farewell between Trudy and Buddy and a pained one between Buddy and Bill. Indeed, Coltrane looks so uncomfortable in this concluding scene, trying to keep a straight face as a man in a gorilla suit lopes off into the trees clutching one of his wife's dresses (with all that implies), that the camera shifts away from him at the earliest opportunity to study Russo's tearful face.

I hope they were well paid.

Coltrane aimed for a different kind of role in *Montana* (1998), first-time director Jennifer Lietzes' low-key thriller in which he plays a gangster chief called simply The Boss. It is a one-dimensional role which Coltrane strives to make at least two-dimensional, but in which he is hamstrung by a duff script and lacklustre direction. There is the faintest suggestion that the stereotyped characters are meant to be more iconic than real, and that the film itself should act like a fable; but Lietzes is not yet the director to pull off this kind of dangerous stunt.

She certainly assembled a good cast which, Coltrane aside, includes Kyra Sedgwick, Stanley Tucci, Philip Seymour Hoffman and John Ritter. Sedgwick is Claire, a low-level criminal who works for The Boss. From the beginning, it is clear that Claire's main problem lies in the fact that she is a lousy judge of character. When she brings in a bagman to see The Boss, without the expected bag of money, The Boss is none too pleased. He is even less pleased when the bagman pulls a gun on him. As a punishment for her mistake, Claire is demoted in the organization and dispatched to track down Kitty (Robin Tunney), The Boss's errant and erratic girlfriend.

The situation is further complicated when The Boss's right-hand man, Duncan makes plans to take over the outfit by bringing down his employer. Worse is to come when The Boss's beloved and stupid son attempts to rape Kitty and she shoots him dead for his pains. Aware that this is the opportunity he needs to outmanoeuvre The Boss and his associates, Duncan manipulates the situation and puts the blame for the boy's killing on Claire and her boyfriend, Nick (Tucci), a hit-man with a terminal illness.

The plotting is so loose that it looks as if they made it up as they went along, and the random elements never begin to cohere. There is some good work, admittedly, from Sedgwick and Tucci who, in spite of the preposterousness of their characters and motivation, manage to convey the sense of a real relationship. Coltrane, however, is utterly wasted.

While there are some sequences which have an abrasive energy, the scenes involving Coltrane are oddly static, as if the director were filming a series of playlets. Whenever we enter The Boss's head-quarters, the film dies on the screen; everybody just sits around talking. There is little movement from the actors and none from the camera. Even Quentin Tarantino, when filming *Reservoir Dogs* on what was virtually a single set, realized that something had to move on screen in order to create tension and drama. And, of course, his characters had terrific dialogue to deliver, something that is sorely lacking in this film.

It is difficult to blame Coltrane for this wasted effort but it is equally hard to see what attracted him to the project in the first place. Maybe he just wanted a change of pace; maybe it was a favour for a friend. Or maybe he just wanted to play a villain. Whatever the reason, it was a poor choice.

Having played a garrulous hack in *Defence of the Realm*, Coltrane finally came back to playing a journalist in a more exalted capacity in *Message in a Bottle* (1999). This is a major Hollywood romance, star-ring Kevin Costner and Sean Wright Penn, who plays a researcher on the *Chicago Tribune*. She is one of a team who works for the news-paper's leading columnist, Charlie Toschi (Coltrane), supplying leads and checking facts. As Charlie, in a succession of exciting ties and expensive suits, Coltrane is well-nigh perfect, his Chicago accent impeccably honed and his general demeanour unswervingly authen-tic. He is one of the few genuine things in a movie peopled by frauds.

Penn has secret dreams of becoming a journalist herself and is encouraged to do so by the waspishly cynical Charlie. A young divorcee with a young son, she has suffered a blow to her confidence and her self-esteem, to the extent that she cannot bear to make herself vulnerable in the field of journalism, preferring the backstage role of a researcher. Charlie, it is clear from the outset, harbours amorous thoughts about her, but covers them with a barrage of bawdy banter directed at all the girls on his team.

'Woof Woof! Ruff Ruff!' are virtually the first 'words' he speaks, an unusual dialogue for an apparently literate columnist, to say the least.

When he follows it up with an observation on 'lonely women', we are getting semaphored in the least subtle way possible about Charlie's character. The amazing thing is that Coltrane manages to salvage some vestigial reality if not dignity from this inauspicious – if not offensive – beginning.

When Penn discovers a bottle buried in the sand on a beach where she has gone to collect her thoughts after dropping off her son with her ex-husband and his nubile new wife, she is astonished to find inside it an immensely romantic and heartbreaking letter written by a man to a woman who has evidently left him.

Unwisely, she takes it back to the newspaper and reads it to her girlfriends. Before long, Charlie gets wind of it and – unbeknown to her – prints it in his column. Among the oceans of letters that flood in as a result is one from a correspondent claiming to have another letter by the same person, also found in a bottle. Finally, a third letter turns up, allowing Penn, with all the resources of a large newspaper at her disposal, to trace the source of the letters and pin him down to a small seaside town in Cape Cod.

When she begs Charlie to be allowed to track down the writer of the letters, Charlie correctly surmises that she is entertaining the possibility of some kind of romance with the mystery man whose love is so honestly expressed. The jibes he offers are far from offensive, rather those of an affectionate and lovelorn man who worships the girl from afar.

'You're thinking Heathcliffe,' he says. 'You're thinking Hamlet. What you might get is Captain Ahab.'

Penn goes off to Cape Cod and finds – lo and behold – that Kevin Costner is the melancholy man and that the letters were written to his dead wife. He lives in splendid, proud and useless isolation with his old, former alcoholic father for company. As the dad is played by Paul Newman, you can imagine the surfeit of strong jaws and blue eyes around the place. It's like a graveyard for handsome people. Poor Charlie doesn't stand a chance.

There are a few twists and turns before true romance finds its way home, notably when Costner accidentally comes across the letters and, worse, the article by Charlie in Penn's drawer, and leaves her just as romance was blossoming. Luckily, Charlie is on hand to dispense sound advice through gritted teeth.

In a sorely underwritten part, Coltrane shines with a verisimilitude usually associated with American character actors. His Charlie is not only a totally believable newspaperman, but also an entirely convincing lovelorn sap, hopelessly longing for the unattainable Penn. It's a tricky act to pull off as, tilted too far one way or the other, it would have looked awkward and stupid, a big soft mush puppy who could never have been responsible for a hard-hitting column.

Coltrane never strikes a false note, which has much more to do with his acting (and his occasional ad lib grace notes) than anything in the original script. Espying Costner in the office, Charlie comments: 'That's him. That's Ahab. She's going to smell of haddock for the rest of her life.' Apart from being funny, Coltrane twists the line to reveal the fact that this might be true love after all, and that he must retire gracefully from the fray.

The girls, especially Ileanna Douglas and Robin Wright Penn, respond to him warmly, making the scenes in the *Chicago Tribune* offices the most comfortable, authentic and enjoyable in the movie.

Chapter 14

TELEVISION AND RADIO HIGHLIGHTS

Blackadder's Christmas Carol (BBC, 1988)

This is one of those seasonal compilations that are loosely framed by a general context before flashing back to selected parts of previous episodes. It's an old television trick and a very cheap way of exploiting existing material while appearing to make a 'new' programme.

As exploitations go, this isn't at all bad, thanks largely to the quality of the series it draws upon and also the script of the actual special, which cleverly reverses the Scrooge tale of *A Christmas Carol*. The Blackadder of this Dickensian Christmas is an old softie, a man who gives away everything he has whenever anyone comes knocking at his door with the begging bowl. He is not just generous to a fault but a totally gullible idiot. When he goes to bed on Christmas Eve, he has given away everything he had put together for Christmas, leaving his servant Baldrick (Tony Robinson) and himself with nothing for Christmas Day.

In the night, he is visited by the Spirit of Christmas, played by Robbie Coltrane. He enters through the bedroom window in a blue light and clouds of smoke. Dressed in a variation on the red, fur-trimmed tunic of a Victorian Father Christmas, with a wild gingery-grey wig and beard, Coltrane hams up the role for all he is worth, speaking in a slightly exaggerated form of his own accent, he greets Blackadder, who is cowering under the sheets.

'Just popped in to say hello. Spirit of Christmas. How d'ye do? Just doing my usual rounds; a wee bit of haunting. Getting misers to change their evil ways. But you're obviously such a good chap there'll be no need for any of that nonsense. So, I'll just say cheeribye. Cheeribye.'

Blackadder (Rowan Atkinson) lures him into staying by offering him a cup of tea. Typically, Coltrane responds by asking him if he has anything a wee bit stronger. Blackadder thinks a moment and says: 'Nurse MacReady's surgical bruise lotion' – which Coltrane accepts like the fancifully garbed Meths drinker that he resembles. 'Oh, nothing but the best in this house,' he says, uncorking the bottle and taking a swig.

After a bit of chitchat, Coltrane introduces the concept of the past, recalling Blackadder's ancestors as 'stinkers to a man'. Nice Blackadder is intrigued, however, and wants to know more about his evil heritage. Feigning reluctance, Coltrane wiggles his fingers and conjures up a flashback.

Following a sequence from an early episode, in which 'the Blackadder' outmanoeuvres a rival at the court of Elizabeth I over a Christmas gift, Coltrane remarks to Nice Blackadder: 'What a pig.'

Nice Blackadder, however, is clearly hooked. He wants to see more. 'Aye, you're an improvement on them all. You're a guid boy. Have a shufti at this.' More waggling of fingers in a kind of postmodern ironic gesture that sends up the flashback cliché, and we're off to the Regency period Blackadder, behaving just as badly as his Elizabethan ancestor. When we arrive at the final sequence, we can see exactly what is going to happen. On Coltrane's final appearance, as he makes himself comfortable on Blackadder's bed and swigs the last of the bruise lotion, he is beginning to realize he may have overplayed his hand, as Blackadder now sees the advantages of being bad as opposed to being good which, as displayed by Coltrane, has very few advantages at all. By the time Coltrane leaves, slipping backwards through the window in billowing clouds of smoke and more blue light – a film reversal of his entrance – he has unwittingly persuaded Blackadder to imitate the evil ways of his ancestors.

For Coltrane, this is little more than a camp cameo in a silly costume. It is pretty funny, but it doesn't stretch him as an actor or a comic. As part of a linking process, it looks as if his sequences were filmed in about ten minutes. Money for old rope.

The Ebb-Tide (ITV, 1997)

Based on a short story by Robert Louis Stevenson and his stepson, Lloyd Osbourne, this two-hour television drama was adapted by Simon Fraser and directed by Nick Renton. Coltrane starred as the washed-up and disgraced Captain Chisholm, who had been drunk in charge of his ship when it grounded on the Humboldt Reef with the loss of 27 lives. Stuck on a French Caribbean island, he survives by begging and stealing, in the company of two ne'er-do-wells, a petty thief, Billy Bunch, and a psychopathic murderer, Ludwig Swanson.

Their only way off the island is to volunteer to crew a plague ship bound for Australia with a cargo of vintage champagne. Their first task is to get rid of the rotting corpses of the former captain and first mate. Thereafter, further disasters beckon as they sail the unseaworthy hulk into the high seas, discovering *en route* that most of the champagne bottles are empty.

Eventually, they come across an uncharted island inhabited solely by the deranged Ellstrom and his female servant. As Ellstrom has a hoard of pearls worth millions, it is not long before Chisholm and his crew are plotting to relieve him of them and take flight. Ellstrom, however, is not so easy to outwit.

Coltrane is beguilingly ghastly as Chisholm, like an unholy combination of Cracker and Long John Silver. It's a return to the rollicking rogue he played to tremendous effect in *The Adventures of Huckleberry Finn*, but the drama is an overstretched mess, and Coltrane's performance cannot save the thing from drifting into oblivion. Even his co-stars, Nigel Terry, Steven Mackintosh and Chris Barnes, aren't enough to support Coltrane in this failed endeavour.

Cinderella (BBC Radio 4, Dec 1998)

Among the star-studded cast of Stewart Permutt's topically made-over pantomime was Robbie Coltrane as Thelma, one of Cinderella's two ugly stepsisters. It is intriguing to hear Coltrane delivering lines while not actually seeing him, as it provides ample evidence of his comic timing and vocal depth. As one of the 'facially-challenged, calorifically-advantaged' daughters of Baron Hardup (John Bird) and

Lady Susan Hardup (Maureen Lipman), Coltrane shares stepsisterly duties with Peter Capaldi, who plays Louise to Coltrane's Thelma.

Often they are called upon to speak in unison, and it helps enormously that they are both Scottish. When Maureen Lipman returns home from a shopping trip to Paris and summons her daughters, their joint reply is: 'We're busy! We're on the toilet!'

Throughout the banter that follows, it is clear that Thelma is the more brutalist, controlling stepsister, which gives Coltrane great latitude in his characterization. He broadens his Scottish accent and makes little attempt to feminize his voice – rather, at some times he roughens and deepens it even further, making it funnier.

Louise: 'I'll have you know I have the figure of Kate Moss.'

Thelma: 'Well, give it back to her, you're stretching it.'

Best of the opening lines is Coltrane's throwaway remark that 'We don't get out of bed for anything less than ten thousand calories' establishing the running gag that the two ugly sisters have aspirations towards modelling.

As the panto progresses, it becomes ever more clear that Thelma is the real bully of the two; she is the one who slaps Ruthie Henshall's Cinderella and the one who elicits the most boos and hisses. Coltrane plays up to this perfectly, occasionally indulging himself in an outrageously camp and over-the-top laugh of delighted malevolence.

But best of all is his way with the pay-off line. When they are discussing what they will wear to the Prince's ball, and Louise says she will wear her Partick Thistle bra, Coltrane's rejoinder is: 'Very little support and no cups.'

He also has a wonderful moment of extended malice when he gives Cinderella her invitation to the ball, only to insist that she then tears it up. Even when called upon to deliver some of the more groanworthy and clichéd lines in the panto, Coltrane gives it plenty of spin. Just listen to the way he gets his tongue around a line as predictable as the following: 'I do declare, Louise, the Prince's balls get bigger every year.'

During the final sequence, when each of the sisters attempts to squeeze her huge feet into the glass slipper, Coltrane has a couple more good lines.

Louise: 'I'm the one who'll get my foot in the crystal slipper.'

Thelma: 'You couldn't get your foot in the Crystal Palace.'

Upon utterly failing to get anything more than his big toe into the slipper in question, Thelma says: 'Typical man. I thought size wasn't important these days.'

They exit, following Buttons, who has gone to pursue a career as a photographer, with Thelma and Louise hoping for a career as fashion models in the style of the larger girls: 'Sophie Dahl, eat your heart out.'

Cinderella offers a rare opportunity to savour exclusively one of Coltrane's greatest assets: his voice. Without the distraction of his presence, which is a powerful entity and often overwhelms his actual interpretive ability, it is evident that Coltrane not only has the vocal gifts of a great comedian in his timing and timbre, but also the actor's facility for finding a character and sticking to it; which is, frankly, more than Maureen Lipman can manage as Lady Susan Hardup in this pantomime.

In addition, there is a sense of generosity in his performance, especially in his exchanges with fellow Ugly Sister Peter Capaldi, which confirms that he is a terrific ensemble player. As witnessed in many of his screen performances, Coltrane – in spite of his powerful presence, or maybe because of it – is not a screen hog. He works well with fellow actors, keeping a check on his flamboyant demeanour to remain in character and serve the material. Little wonder is it that the majority of actors with whom he has worked have nothing but praise for the big man. His spurs may have been hard won but he can wear them with pride.

Best of all, Coltrane is as funny on radio as he is on screen when he wants to be. Given the vibrant and witty script which successfully mixes traditional pantomime style, music-hall japery, vigorous topical jokes and cultural references, Coltrane embraces the role with gusto and professional ease, making the most of the material at his disposal. There are times when his vocal inflections are reminiscent of the vocal pyrotechnics of Spike Milligan and Peter Sellers in *The Goon Show*. There is no higher compliment.

Chapter 15

CRACKER: BLOW BY BLOW

Cracker remains the most comprehensive example of Coltrane's developed talent. Throughout the course of ten stories, he established not only his popularity as a leading man in a ground-breaking television series but also a level of playing which had previously been unguessed at. The trajectory of his performance is worthy of study as it reveals the strengths and weaknesses of Coltrane's acting skill. It also contributes to our understanding of how quickly Coltrane can get bored; there are occasions, admittedly rare, when he seems to be sleepwalking through the role. And the intrusion of his American impersonations – which are usually justified by the scripts, especially the early ones by Jimmy McGovern – veer from amusing to tiresome. Frankly, Coltrane is a much better actor when he is verbally 'naked', not employing one of his three hundred accents. These seem increasingly to be distractions from his real talent as an actor. Fitz doesn't employ any particularly amusing or oddball accent in his normal speech. The way is clear to get right to the heart of Fitz without the flashy, admirable, egotistical smokescreen of the accents.

Two things are certain: Coltrane began *Cracker* as a popular performer and emerged as a star; and he moved from a reasonably good actor to a comprehensively great one. In other words, all of Coltrane's potential, which I have attempted to explore throughout this book so far, finally bore fruit in *Cracker*. It is the watershed of his career.

It is this growth, this gradually augmented confidence that prompts me to launch into a close study of each *Cracker* story. If, in describing the stories in detail, I ignore essential plot points it is simply because they are not relevant to the study of Coltrane himself. And as I am convinced that Coltrane has never elsewhere scaled the heights of acting in the way that he does in *Cracker*, I beg leave to indulge myself in the minutiae of the screen performance; the nuance of language, the reaction shots, the increasingly intimate close-ups. All of this builds a picture of an actor stretching his talents, plumbing depths of his own psyche and braving the emotional nudity that is 'essential for the role'.

As Fitz, Coltrane takes risks that he has never taken before. And his performance, his capacity as an actor is all the better for taking them. It is entirely possible that he will never again have the opportunity – might never wish to take the opportunity – of forging such a complete, authentic wholly believable and dangerous character. It would be a pity if this proved to be the case. But the fact that he once did dare enough in a role that was as sustained as it was multifaceted is perhaps enough. In *Cracker*, Coltrane finally delivered on his promise of the years before. And delivered in spades.

STORY I (SEASON 1) 1993
The Madwoman in the Attic

It may be pushing it to say that the inaugural episode of *Cracker* changed the face of British television, but it certainly gave it a good nutting. The combination of Jimmy McGovern's powerful script, Michael Winterbottom's restless, Americanized direction and a fistful of terrific performances ensured that *The Madwoman in the Attic* grabbed its audience by the throat and shook it like a rag doll. As a statement of intent, it could not have been more perfect.

All the essential *Cracker* elements are contained within the story: the extraordinarily violent deaths, the sexual motifs (and motives); both the discrepancies and the similarities between Fitz's private life and his professional career; the attention to gruesome pathological detail and the morbid, professional humour that accompanies things like autopsies and crime scenes; Fitz's vices and his egotistical show-manship; his son Jake's slacker ways; the red herrings that eventually add up, the blind alley that doesn't. All of these elements are not only present and correct in *The Madwoman in the Attic*, but they are virtually all present and correct in the first half-hour. Whichever way you cut it, it is an extraordinary accomplishment, a brilliant feat of narrative distillation.

The mood is set even before the opening titles, with a racetrack commentary relayed over a black screen. Then we see parts of a large, twitchy face listening to the commentary as he smokes a cigarette. The song 'Stormy Weather' drifts in across the soundtrack, heralding what is to come. We see Coltrane as Fitz, very short hair and very big suit well to the fore, reacting angrily to the result of the race. Clearly, he has lost a bet. How much, we won't find out until later.

He is summoned away by a respectable-looking man and Fitz reappears at the lectern of a large lecture hall where he proceeds to hurl copies of books by philosophers and psychoanalysts into the audience. It is pure confrontational theatre – academic showtime.

Cut with this scene – almost subliminally – are scenes of a blood-spattered railway carriage, parts of a body. The cops, headed by DCI Bilborough (Christopher Eccleston) are gathering around the train. Meanwhile, Fitz has concluded his lecture and is trying to get paid in cash by the man who hired him, who is not terribly happy about Fitz's unorthodox approach to lecturing.

'Yeah, well you know,' says Fitz. 'A little controversy, a bit of faked passion. They lap it up.'

When the man refuses to give him cash Fitz storms away muttering, 'Bastard, bastard!'

After a slightly wobbly start, Coltrane gets Fitz into gear and soars through these first crucial scenes. He establishes everything we need to know about his character: his recklessness, his irresponsibility, his cynicism, his arrogance and his insecurities. Coltrane presents us with a character who is unstable and dangerous but whom we would trust to do the right thing in his professional capacity.

Humiliation is heaped upon humiliation. Returning home, Fitz asks his layabout son if he has any cash and then tries to borrow money from his young daughter. Back outside we see him writing a cheque to the cab driver who has brought him home. Fitz and the cabbie do not part amicably.

Fitz then picks up a bottle of whisky and glares accusingly at his son.

'Have you been at this?'

When his wife Judith (Barbara Flynn) arrives she reminds him sharply that they are going out. Fitz says, 'I know.'

'Sober' is Judith's pithy rejoinder.

At dinner in a crowded restaurant, Fitz gets drunk and begins hectoring his 'friends' over issues of exploitation – they have just hired a nanny and a cleaner at what he regards as a scandalously low wage. Of course, it is Fitz's own guilt about money and his gambling debts that drives this particular outburst, though we don't quite know that as yet. When one of the other couple throws a drink in his face, Fitz splutters and employs the good old standby, a quote from a movie. 'What we have here is a failure to communicate.' It's a direct lift from *Cool Hand Luke*, the Paul Newman film, and it is typical of both McGovern and Coltrane to include a line like that.

When Fitz attempts to pay the bill, he finds that both credit cards are maxed out and waffles on about there being something wrong with the restaurant's computer. On the way home in the car, Judith simply asks how bad it is this time, and Fitz tells her the catalogue of debts he has run up through his gambling losses. To cap it all, he has just borrowed (and lost) £5,000 against the mortgage taken out ostensibly to build a new bathroom. 'I forged your signature,' he says, like a naughty boy. When they get home, Judith tells the kids to pack their bags. They are going to stay with their grandmother. Mark stays behind, simply because he is too lazy to leave.

It is an extraordinary way to introduce the hero of a series. From the beginning, Fitz is a desperate man, clinging to the last vestiges of dignity while still attempting to feed his addiction. Coltrane gets absolutely right the air of suppressed panic coupled with a festering resentment against the world that must, perforce, be responsible for his own lack of responsibility. He is courageous enough to appear pathetic – and a man that big blundering and muttering his way down the cul-de-sac of his life is a fairly terrifying prospect. One wonders just where he is going from here and how bad it is going to get.

Fitz sleeps on the sofa and awakens to see a news report of the train murder with the volume turned down. Catching sight of the face of the victim (a dark, attractive girl), he struggles to turn up the volume and manages to do so just as the item ends. He asks Mark if there is a paper anywhere and sits on the loo to read it. He starts to weep and moans: 'No, oh no.' When Mark looks in on him, Fitz simply shuts the door in his face.

What has happened? What is the connection between Fitz and the girl? We don't have long to wait. The next scene shows Fitz turning up at the house of the dead girl's parents, where he struggles to make himself understood and sympathetic.

'I'm a psychologist. I'll do anything I can to help. She was a student of mine.'

The parents are too distraught and send him away with hurried thanks.

Fitz is then seen distractedly holding an analysis session with a pathetic Welshman who is blathering on about his low self-esteem. Fitz is staring into space, completely oblivious to the guy's meanderings or, perhaps, finding the guy's problems rather too close a reflection of his own feelings of low self-worth.

The parents finally come to him and, after questioning him as to how he might help, they ask him to get involved. By this stage, Fitz has almost changed his mind.

'I thought the police were coping.'

He just needs reassurance that he can be useful in the case rather than run the risk of failing. This is Fitz all over, and Coltrane evolves an acting style that can suggest the various emotional levels occurring which are nothing short of brilliant. The occasional volley of humour, the volcanic anger, the addictive compulsive puffing on a cigarette, all the signs and signals of an actor well versed in the semaphoring of body language and the semiotics of acting.

Fitz has to introduce the idea of himself – i.e. a behavioural psychologists, a profiler – to the police, and to DCI Bilborough in particular. He has a head's start on the case – or at least the profile of the killer – and tries to persuade Bilborough he can't do without him.

'Look, homicide and amnesia are . . . heavy. You need to know what you're doing. And I do know what I'm doing. I've forgotten more about amnesia than they'll ever know.'

Having tried unsuccessfully to see his wife at work, Fitz returns home to find his son Mark in bed and goes completely ballistic, playing the heavy father because he is himself full of guilt and he has become an almost redundant human being.

Salvation of some kind arrives when Bilborough finally relents and summons Fitz to talk to the suspect in the hope that he'll get a confession. This is our first opportunity to see Fitz in action within a police environment. We have seen how he behaves with his students and his private patients; is he going to be able to cut it with a suspected murderer?

Coltrane sits down opposite Adrian Dunbar, the amnesiac man suspected of being The Sweeny serial killer.

'They call me Fitz,' he says, by way of introduction. 'What do they call you? Bloodthirsty murdering bastard?'

Not only is it the least likely introduction, it is very funny and entirely logical. From this moment on, Coltrane (like McGovern) never puts a foot wrong. Fitz is in his element. He delivers a long speech on sex crimes and the idea of the fact that for men it is entirely natural as the camera closes in on him. He pushes the elements as far as he can while Dunbar sits quizzically silent.

Finally, Dunbar says: 'There's a great sadness in your life.'

Coltrane's look at DS Jane Penhaligon (Geraldine Somerville) at this remark is priceless; he can't believe that this worm before him can have the effrontery to try and psychoanalyse him, The Mighty Fitz. And so he continues the interrogation.

In some lubricious detail he describes the feelings of Dunbar when he sees the girl in the train carriage; he puts himself inside the mind of the 'murderer' and gives an empathetic description of what he was thinking. Fitz's refrain – part of his methodology – is 'I understand.' As a man, he knows what it is like to want someone, something that you cannot have – the frustration of desiring the unattainable. McGovern deploys this as a motif right the way through, and while it is clear that this is part of Fitz's professional approach to psychological profiling, it is equally clear that he is trading off elements within his own psyche, his own neurosis. As a police psychologist, Fitz finally finds the right conduit for his own almost pathological frustrations. This is very clever, as it brings a tension into the relationship between Fitz and the job – which is ultimately conveyed to the audience – that is entirely truthful and unresolvable; it is literally only the job that is keeping Fitz from going over the brink – physically, emotionally, psychologically. It is the one aspect of his life that gives him the self-respect he has forfeited everywhere else. When the job goes, it will be the end for Fitz.

This first interrogation scene is crucial as it sets the standard for Fitz's approach. And Coltrane handles it like a virtuoso, concluding with the now infamous train-rhythm refrain: 'Kill-the-bitch, kill-the-bitch, kill-the-bitch.'

Afterwards, Fitz goes into the betting shop where the manager refuses him credit, much to his disgust. High on a combination of humiliation and professional adrenalin, Fitz wanders aimlessly around Manchester, a walking pile of festering, volcanic resentment. When the ticket inspector on the tube challenges him over the fact that he doesn't have a ticket (he is also smoking) and asks Fitz where he got on, Coltrane points to the side of the carriage: 'That door.'

Driven partly by the fact that he has nothing else to do and partly because he believes it might help, he goes to the dead girl's house, where he asks to see her room in the hope that it might yield some clues. Looking around, he finds a home video she has made and watches it. Even Fitz himself is on it – visual proof of the fact that he was close to the student, if not actually intimate. Back with Dunbar, Fitz cranks up the interrogation using word association and a series of photographs of the dead girl to try to crack the guy into confessing. He even throws in a Latin and a Greek declension which Dunbar continues without hesitation. Fitz's last-ditch attempt is to make a direct appeal to the man's humanity.

'It's the last decent thing you can do. Please ...' he begs, and Coltrane's eyes melt into the man. 'Please ...'

It's a terrific act. Stepping outside the interrogation room, Fitz snaps back to his normal, abrasive self like an india rubber man. This is just one of the subtle agendas that run throughout *Cracker*; it is as much about role-playing, about the business of acting as it is about police work. Fitz is acting all the time, developing different faces for different circumstances, and Coltrane understands precisely the playing levels of the character. The interesting thing is to see this evolve and develop as the series progresses and to study Coltrane's reactions as his own level of interest in Fitz shifts, matures and finally begins to evaporate.

It is almost as if through a process of professional osmosis, Fitz's boredom infects Coltrane and he becomes a victim of his character's ennui. But we're getting ahead of ourselves.

Outside the interrogation room, Bilborough quizzes Fitz about the 'Amo amas amat' dialogue. Fitz tells him its Latin for 'I love, you love, he loves' and adds: 'Catholic grammar school boy. Like me. God help him.'

This is a brilliant line: it sketches in the educative and background influence of Fitz and Dunbar, it illustrates an empathy between the two of them and it suggests a trenchant ambiguity. Does Fitz pity him because he was a Catholic grammar school boy or because he is 'like me'? It is a terrifically poised piece of dialogue.

So far, we have seen what Coltrane can do with Fitz's verbal dexterity. The following scene – during the alarmingly graphic post mortem of the dead girl – shows what he can do without dialogue. In a scene during which Coltrane has virtually nothing to do but react to the post mortem surgery and the pathologist's running commentary about God and the human body, he displays a sound camera technique, and conveys everything we need to know about what Fitz is thinking.

Clearly, Fitz is not quite used to seeing this kind of operation close up; nor is he inclined to avert his eyes; Fitz is far too macho for that and, anyway, Penhaligon (Geraldine Somerville) is standing right next to him. There are several emotions and reactions that pass across his face as he watches. Equally clearly, he is appreciative of a consummate professional at work but at the same time disagreeing violently with his philosophical stance on religion, God and the flesh.

It is around this point in the proceedings that we see a few tentative sparks fly between Fitz and Penhaligon – whom Fitz insists on calling 'Panhandle'. He also gives her a free psychological profile, referring to her need to be competitive in a male-dominated environment, her unsmiling toughness. 'It's penis envy,' he says. 'Penis envy.' Whether Fitz is serious or not is irrelevant; he just wants to wind her up, to get her going. It is obvious that he is very attracted to her.

Dunbar is released into Fitz's care who immediately takes him off to the dog races. While there, Dunbar sees a man he recognizes, confronts him and is nutted in the nose. When Fitz realizes he has lost his patient he puts in a call to Bilborough, but spots Dunbar coming towards him before he is put through.

On a train together, Fitz is indulging in his usual orgy of smoking and drinking, watched quietly by Dunbar.

'Why do you drink so much?' enquires Dunbar.

'Because I like it,' says Fitz.

'Why do you smoke so much?'

'Because I like it.'

'Do you gamble too?'

'Yes.'

Dunbar immediately makes the association and offers Fitz his own psychological deduction. It must be hard to fill in such a void in his life, he says. Not surprisingly, having been played at his own game, and rather successfully, Fitz blusters his way out of it.

'Void in my life? Void in my life? Ha ha.'

Later, as Fitz reveals his feelings about women in their relationships/attraction with convicted murderers, Dunbar quietly says: 'I'm sure she'll come back to you.'

This completely floors Fitz. Coltrane's strength here is that he has mastered the look of complex reaction. If ever there was a reaction shot that suggested several things at once it is this one. Bilborough takes Fitz off the case when another body is discovered following a phone call from a man describing himself as a catholic priest. He had apparently heard the killer's confession and tells them where the body is. Fitz, who is convinced that Dunbar is not the murderer, is devastated. He needs to stay on the case as much to solve it as for his own self-respect.

Accordingly, when he finds himself in a lift alone with Penhaligon, he stops it between floors to beg her to help him. She thinks he intends to attack her and starts screaming in a kind of role-playing, perfunctory manner. Fitz keeps talking through her performance to try to convince her he is the only one who can sort this out. When they finally emerge from the lift and Fitz walks through a small crowd of puzzled policemen, he remarks: 'Multiple orgasms.'

This is the funniest scene in this episode. It's positioning is vital as it plays off the characteristics of both Fitz and Penhaligon – if we didn't know these people as well as we do at this stage, it would not have worked. It also sets up the sexual frisson that will develop throughout the series, reflecting much of the nature of the crimes they are dealing with but also the competitive elements and envy at work between the characters – especially Fitz, Penhaligon and Lorcan Cranitch's DI Beck.

When Penhaligon turns up at Fitz's house and states: 'You've got me for one week,' there is a suggestion of something more than professional support in the air. Fitz immediately picks up on that and uses it to his advantage.

'I've had pleurisy once, for two. Drink? Right. No sex. Strictly platonic. I know it's going to be hard but that's the way it is. Hands off. OK?'

Fitz is using Penhaligon's own reactions against her and he isn't finished yet. When he goes in to interrogate Dunbar for the last time, Penhaligon sits in. Fitz uses Penhaligon as his image of a female victim, a conduit for an exposé of her own childhood, psychological profile and emotional development ostensibly to get Dunbar to admit something but also to nail Penhaligon to the wall which he effectively does. It is brutally unfair, and Penhaligon takes her revenge in a high-speed car drive which scares the shit out of Fitz. Coltrane does alarm very well – he can put a comic spin on it without losing the credibility of his response. Clearly, having gone through this period of mutual testing, they have formed a kind of bond.

Together they pursue the murderer via his father and on to a train, where Fitz manages to restrain him by jumping off with him. This is a classic Coltrane action scene: not a lot of running around but an unlikely and therefore alarming burst of physical violence that illustrates an unforeseen depth of courage. He and Penhaligon are heroes of the hour.

The last scene shows Fitz dropping off Dunbar at the catholic seminary where he intends to return to take up the priesthood – his former occupation. Fitz, as usual, is gruffly empathetic but attempts to dissuade him.

'If you want to be banged up for life why don't you do a bank robbery? Do something to deserve it.'

The final scene is of Fitz and Panhandle driving off in her car, sparring and spitting at each other. The start of a beautiful friendship.

Or not, as the case may be.

STORY 2 (SEASON 1) 1993
To Say I Love You

This is to *Cracker* what *From Russia with Love* was to the James Bond movies; the second and, in many ways, the most audacious and confident. The ground rules, the human geography of the characters and the tone have all been established with the brilliant opening episode, and now there is a general sense of creative assurance and mastery of the material.

This was one of Jimmy McGovern's greatest triumphs of plotting and character narrative. It is also one of the wildest and most down-right dirty of all the *Cracker* episodes, thanks to the eternal theme of a pair of misfit outsiders who can only find true fulfilment by getting together on a killing spree. The relationship between Susan Lynch's remarkable Tina and Andrew Tiernan's Sean is reminiscent of every bad boy/bad girl combo since *Gun Crazy*; check out *Badlands*, *Bonnie and Clyde*, *Murder in the Heartland* (the Chalkie Starkweather Story) and *Natural Born Killers* for additional comparisons.

McGovern takes the basic theme and adds his own contemporary, idiosyncratic wrinkles to it to make it appear like a hugely topical tale while remaining classical at core. It is an amazing script, and all involved respond with the confidence and gusto of a group who know – with one episode under their belts – that they are working on something truly special, truly ground-breaking.

The episode opens in a karaoke pub where a lad (it turns out to be Sean) is singing 'I Who Have Nothing' with some style and dramatic flair. He is watched closely by Tina, a dark, very sexy girl who introduces herself to him at the bar. Sean has a big problem, however – a catastrophic speech impediment and chronic stammer that means he can hardly get any words out at all. The only time he can talk with any fluency is while singing or when he is really angry.

The next scene finds Fitz sitting alone at a table for two in a restaurant, waiting impatiently. Judith eventually arrives accompanied by a balding, moustachioed man whom she introduces as Graham, her therapist. The look of disgust that passes across Coltrane's face is priceless, a vintage Fitz double take, and he sneers: 'You don't need crap like that.'

'Twenty years married to you, I need more than therapy,' ripostes Judith. 'I need a trip to Lourdes.'

Fitz, who recognizes a wanker when he sees one (and probably rather more quickly than most), sips his drink ('Diet Coke,' he says with feeling), ignores Graham and speaks directly to his wife.

'I'm not discussing anything in front of that talking bloody text-book.'

As Judith and Graham get up to leave, Fitz relents and waits to hear their proposal. Judith wants Fitz to go to Gamblers Anonymous (the local group is run by Graham himself), put the house in her name and arrange their joint bank account so that cheques can only be cashed with two signatures. Which tells us everything we need to know about Fitz's handling of their finances and Judith's faith in him.

Fitz's response is to retreat into humour with an edge. 'Waiter! Could I have a very sharp knife, please? My wife would like to cut off my balls!' This is not just typical Fitz, it is typical Coltrane. In lines like this, Coltrane and his character are one and the same, the perfect synthesis of written character and interpretive actor.

Fitz takes the interview over as only he can – he can't actually help himself, knowing the best form of defence is attack. 'Life needs a bit of risk, Judith, a bit of Bogart and Hepburn on the *African Queen*.'

Herein lies the thread of their relationship, continually conducted as if they were a brace of great film pairings. It is a theme, a game, that Fitz and Judith will continue throughout the series. Classic American movies are Fitz's great reference points, his totems for extrapolating his relationship with people, with his wife, with the world.

He takes Graham and Judith back to his house to prove a point. Opening a wardrobe, he switches into a hugely effective Lloyd Grossman impersonation.

'Well,' he drawls in a perfect facsimile of Grossman's strangulated vowels, 'whoever lives in this house obviously has extremely expensive taste in clothes.'

He lists the dresses he has bought for Judith as a result of his racetrack winnings. But Judith is ahead of him.

'I shared in your winnings, is that it?' she asks. 'Then why do you think I left them all behind?' She has bested Fitz. He has no answer.

While Tina and Sean steal a bus during the night, Fitz is seen ringing the doorbell of Judith's parents, where she is hiding out from Fitz with her daughter. He simply cannot let it lie, in spite of remonstrations by his father-in-law.

We see police cars in hot pursuit of the stolen bus. And also outside the house where Fitz is still ringing the bell. A light shines in his face.

'Look,' he says to the cop with the torch. 'All I want to do is to talk to my wife, OK?'

'If you don't leave these people in peace I am going to have to arrest you,' says the cop.

Fitz cannot believe his ears. 'You're kidding,' he says.

Having been wound up mercilessly by DI Beck in the interrogation room, Sean loses control entirely and starts bouncing off the walls of his cell, screaming and shouting.

The Judas door of a cell is opened to reveal Fitz sitting on a cell bunk, smoking as usual. Beck opens the door and looks at him. 'He's throwing fits, Fitz.'

'I'm in custody, custody,' ripostes Fitz. Fitz's razor-sharp tongue is at its most active and humorous in this episode.

Coltrane is particularly fine in the scene that follows, where he is led into Sean's cell to try to quieten the raging young man down and talk to him. The cynical façade drops for a moment or two as he faces the deeply disturbed individual and he repeats over and over 'Calm down, calm down, calm down' until he can get close to him. Coltrane then does a remarkable and unexpected thing: he grabs Sean in a bear hug and holds him against him. Fitz looks him straight in the eye and, anticipating Sean's next action, says: 'You butt me, I'll butt you right back. Harder.'

This is Fitz at his most persuasive and dangerous, for there is never any doubt at all that – unethical as it may be – Fitz is prepared to carry out the threat.

Fitz sits down, lights a fag. He has understood a great deal about Sean in the space of a very short time and sees immediately that he is in desperate need of help, that he is, in effect, a human time bomb and the clock is ticking.

Coltrane invests this scene and much of the subsequent material with naked, vulnerable humanity. For most of the time we are happy to watch Coltrane as Fitz the sneering, cynical, romantic, over-the-top gambler, drinker, smoker and so on; a man who is smarter than the average hero, yet more fallibly human also. Having suckered us into this character identification, Coltrane is then at liberty to show us from time to time an aspect beneath the veneer which is quite shocking – a human empathy that he rarely displays with his colleagues or family but is usually on show with strangers, victims, patients, murderers – in other words, people with whom he will have only a temporary relationship.

'You don't stutter when you're angry,' says Fitz. 'Do you mind if I help?'

Sean is released on probation in spite of Fitz's recommendation that he should be the subject of a psychiatric report before being freed. Nobody listens to him.

Faced with the overworked, uncaring bureaucracy that wishes to wash its hands of anything that smacks of responsibility – care in the community means not having to deal with people like Sean in an official capacity – Fitz himself forgets about him as he takes his daughter out for the day.

They go to the park, where Fitz sails her in a pedalo across a park lake and they talk of monsters. When Fitz delivers her back to the house, Judith's father won't let him in.

That evening, Fitz gets drunk in his garden while playing his blues records very loudly. Neighbours complain, and he falls over while attempting to make his motion sensor outdoor light work.

The following morning, Fitz is in the cop shop with a massive hangover that he is trying to douse with a can of Diet Coke. There has been a murder in the night – Sean and Tina have bashed the brains out of a loanshark who has been hassling Tina.

But Fitz hung over is a better detective than most cops sober. He studies the walls and angles of the alley in which the murder was committed, bleary-eyed but with the deductive powers of a somewhat Rabelaisian Sherlock Holmes. He tells Bilborough there were two killers, a man and a woman, and sketches the scenario.

'The female leads him up here for sex. The male is hiding behind there. He's strong, thinks he can kill him with his bare hands. Has second thoughts. Pulls the brick out . . .'

It is a very professional and authoritative assessment, and Coltrane is in no mood to be disagreed with. Bilborough, however, has other ideas.

'Absolute bollocks,' he says of Fitz's speculation.

Fitz simply stares at him, reaches into his pocket and pulls out a wad of notes which he counts quickly.

'Forty-five quid,' he says, offering a wager.

Bilborough accepts and Fitz re-enacts the murder, much to the amusement of the onlookers, among whom is a researcher for a local television programme, hosted by Lenny Lyon, in which Bilborough is scheduled to appear.

Fitz speculates that at the moment after the murder the couple made love against the wall, and uses Penhaligon to help him demonstrate the events.

' "What is death, Panhandle?" sayeth Fitz.'

'The finest aphrodisiac in the world, Dr Fitzgerald,' responds Penhaligon, right on cue. Both Fitz and Penhaligon are now operating as a double act and are clearly playing to the crowd.

After appearing on the *Lenny Lyon Show* in place of Bilborough and revealing his profile of the murderers – having been specifically told not to by DCI Bilborough – Fitz then goes off to visit his mother (Beryl Reid), with whom he has an amusing and, of course, revealing discussion about horse racing.

There is absolutely no point in this scene except to introduce the motivational element behind Fitz's gambling addiction: like mother, like son. Also, of course, to provide the possibility of another domestic plot strand. More of which later.

Fitz then is depicted talking to Judith through the door of her parents' house; the chain is on. He asks her if she saw him on the *Lenny Lyon Show*, hoping that she will have been impressed with his 'performance'. She replies that she didn't see it as she was out with 'a friend'.

'What kind of friend?' asks Fitz.

'A friendly friend,' says Judith.

'A male friend?'

'Yes.'

'Graham?'

'Yes.'

This news is, of course, devastating to Fitz, who possesses an ego the size of a tower block. Coltrane, smoking nervously in the doorway, captures perfectly the exquisite agony of a man caught between the rock of guilt and the hard place of jealousy.

Unable to take it out on Judith, Fitz lets rip at Bilborough the next morning when the DCI berates him for revealing too much on the television programme.

'I don't have time to hang around and stroke your ego. Your bloody publicity-seeking ego,' roars Fitz.

To rub salt into Bilborough's wounded pride, Penhaligon enters with the forensic report proving Fitz's assessment of the crime scene to be accurate. In his mind there is no greater high than being proved right, and Fitz just cannot help himself. 'Ninety quid,' he says to Bilborough. He's won the bet.

Fitz is next seen in a session of Gamblers Anonymous, sitting in front of the gathering, alongside Graham.

'I was born 19 September 1949. Do you know who else was born that day? Twiggy.'

Fitz is holding court, turning the potential humiliation of the situation to his advantage, as usual with humour. Having warmed them up, he tells a tale about the discovery of an ancient entombed mummy whose face – once it has been unwrapped – shows signs of conspicuous unhappiness. The archaeologists are puzzled until they open the clenched fingers of his hand and discover a betting slip: 'Two hundred quid to win. Goliath.' Naturally, he brings the house down. Shaking his head, Fitz gets up. 'I'm sorry, this isn't for me.'

Graham tries to stop him but makes two fatal errors when he says: 'Eddie, you're a fool.' Being called a fool by someone Fitz regards as a completely worthless human being is bad enough; being called 'Eddie' is worse still. Fitz turns at the door and stares at him. It is a classic Coltrane moment. What's he going to do? Kill him? Walk out? Make some venomous comment?

Fitz does none of these. He's got something far more destructive up his sleeve. He starts laying out cards on the green baize table and delivers a passionate speech about the joy, the excitement, the sheer bloody terrificness of gambling. And he equates the winning of money with the deployment of grey matter; to his way of thinking, an unbeatable combination. 'I used this [taps his head] and I was right!'

Having incited what amounts to a small betting riot in the room, he leaves triumphant.

But their encounter is far from over. Outside in the street, Fitz waits like a mugger waiting for a victim. When Graham comes out, Fitz asks him for a drink. Following a very intimate tête-à-tête in the pub, Fitz loses control and Graham walks out as Fitz yells after him: 'You believe in safe sex, Graham? Screwing my wife could be extremely dangerous.'

For once, Fitz has lost the battle of wills and is reduced to voicing threats.

A great deal of the central part of this episode is taken up with Fitz and his evolving relationships with Penhaligon, Judith, his son Mark, and the cops Beck and Bilborough. The lucidity with which this complex pattern of relationships is presented is quite remarkable, given that we are only in the second full-length tale. A scene in which Fitz consoles Penhaligon in the pub after she's been turned down for promotion is quickly followed by Fitz at home quarrelling with his son over suspected dope smoking.

'Oh yeah, says the man who's pissed out of his head every night,' spits Mark. 'Who's pickled his brain in booze.'

Coltrane moves through a spectrum of emotions very quickly, changing gear with consummate ease. Encountering Judith in a supermarket car park he is absolutely desperate to talk to her – talk, for Fitz, is the currency of humanity, it's what he does best. Take that away from him and he is helpless. Judith simply gets into the car and drives away as Fitz shouts after her: 'I love you! I love you!' flinging his arms around in utter despair and helplessness. This is epic stuff from Coltrane, signs of truly epic talent at work and the possibility of a great screen tragedian.

When Fitz takes Penhaligon out for dinner, there is something in the air. No sooner have they sat down than Judith and Graham enter and sit at an adjoining table. Fitz starts to heckle them and create a scene until Penhaligon tips a jug of iced water over his head. Even then, Fitz retains a degree of sang-froid by picking up the ice cubes and putting them in his whisky.

But the crunch doesn't come until the next scene. Fitz turns up at Penhaligon's flat to apologize and there is an awkward, adolescent sexual frisson between them. Fitz, as usual, asks to borrow a fiver for a taxi; Penhaligon tells him he's welcome to stay.

Coltrane's double take is swift and subtle; he simply cannot believe his ears. Penhaligon coyly says she's known all along she fancied him but didn't want to make a move until she was sure that Fitz and Judith had burnt their bridges.

'We haven't,' says Fitz – one of the most unwittingly brutal lines McGovern has given him so far. It's a bad call. Fitz has accidentally humiliated Penhaligon very badly and she knows it.

'You just can't see it, can you?' she says.

'What?' asks Fitz, now completely bewildered.

'Fitz, you've driven her into bed with him.'

The following scene, with Fitz and Penhaligon carrying on their post-non-coital discussion on the telephone, is redundant. Both are destined to meet the following morning at a murder scene.

This time it is a policeman, Penhaligon's partner, killed by Sean. In searching the cop's belongings, they come across a packet of condoms. Penhaligon is brought in and questioned about her partner by Fitz and Bilborough. Fitz here is at his most diplomatic, subtle and forceful. But trouble is brewing.

Spotting Sean Kerrigan signing in at the police station – a condition of his probation – Fitz starts putting two and two together. Unfortunately, he is now caught in the crossfire between Beck, who hates him, and Bilborough, who reluctantly trusts him. When Penhaligon is called in to substantiate Fitz's claim that Beck ignored his recommendation that Kerrigan be sent for psychiatric evaluation, Penhaligon supports Beck, knowing Fitz is right.

'A woman scorned,' scoffs Fitz as he leaves in disgust.

Fitz is making enemies inside and outside the law now. He has made himself an outsider by virtue of the fact of being right. Worryingly, Fitz is followed to the pub by Sean and Tina. Sean knows Fitz is on to him and Tina attempts to vamp him. Fitz plays along but something in his eyes gives the game away to us. This is one of Coltrane's double whammies – saying one thing while conveying something completely different; it is a smart trick and he uses it sparingly.

As usual in McGovern's scripts (doubtless encouraged by Coltrane), movie references abound. Fitz entertains Tina with Peter Falk impersonations – a classic in the Coltrane repertoire – until Penhaligon (whom he has secretly phoned) enters to arrest her. Fitz claims his ninety pounds, the bet that had been held by the murdered cop, which even gets a smile from Penhaligon.

The next scene is one of the best jokes in the entire episode. Fitz is sitting at a desk being interviewed by a man who is attempting to tell him he is sacked. Our question is: who is sacking him? Is it his university superior? A member of his psychology practice? Fitz is taking it badly. After all, he needs the money. Suddenly he pulls out a gun and points it at his head, then at the guy, then back at his own head, and pulls the trigger. A flag pops out of the barrel with the word 'Bang!' on it. The camera pulls back to reveal a small audience. Clearly, it is a lecture/lesson.

'Comments?' says Fitz, turning to his audience. 'He didn't handle that very well, did he?' This has been a typically flamboyant piece of Fitz theatre.

Its placing here is crucial to the balance of the episode. After the heavy-duty activity of the crimes and the two perpetrators which permeate the episode, plus the sensitive domestic crises, this short but highly effective scene lightens the burden in a way that is positively Shakespearean. Somehow, we know that everything else that occurs from now on is going to be pitch black.

Sure enough, Fitz begins questioning Tina in her cell. He refers to age and aspiration, using Penhaligon (who is sitting in) as an example of a young woman who has made a commendable effort to advance herself through the ranks of a male-dominated concern. It is a compliment – the exact reverse of the earlier interrogation in episode one during which he reduced Penhaligon to the level of victim – and he can't resist topping it off with a joke.

Once again, Fitz uses film references to get inside Tina's mind; in this case, *Bonnie and Clyde*. He leads her on, suggesting that he empathizes with them (and therefore her) before brutally reversing his opinion. Having thus weakened her defences, he goes for the jugular.

'Tell me what makes you tick. I'm sure it'll take all of fifteen seconds.' Fitz here is visibly angry, and it is a testament to Coltrane's performance that we can't quite decide whether it is genuine or still part of the act. There is something thrilling and dangerous about a big man losing control and Coltrane knows it; but it is an aspect of his performance that he reserves for special occasions. While there are often similar events, set-ups and situations throughout *Cracker*, they rarely descend to the level of formula.

More drama of a domestic nature awaits Fitz at home. Mark falls out of the bathroom with blood running from his mouth. Our natural assumption is that somehow Sean has got into Fitz's house and attacked his son. This is almost too smart of McGovern, but it turns out that Mark has a ruptured appendix and is immediately rushed to hospital, where Fitz and Judith have some kind of *rapprochement*. But Judith won't allow Fitz to take advantage of the situation, even though she unwittingly catches him weeping at Mark's bedside. It is a delicately balanced dramatic scene, and both Coltrane and the superb Barbara Flynn handle it with uncluttered brilliance.

Fitz returns to the station to break down Tina and to destroy the bond between her and Sean. But he is interrupted by the arrival of Judith, who tells Fitz that she wants to come home after confessing that she had sex with Graham. In one of the most remarkably written monologues of the series, Fitz runs through the gamut of his emotional responses to the news, numbering them and effectively psychoanalysing himself in front of her. It is an unsparing and painful performance and Coltrane gives it the full welly.

Returning to Tina, he keeps going at her until she tells him that Sean is going to kill her sister, who is blind and lives with her parents. Almost at the same time, through a series of coincidences and accidental encounters, a cop radios in with the address of Tina's parents. Bilborough doesn't even thank him for the effort he has put into the interrogation which has achieved the same results.

'Ungrateful bastards!' he shouts after them and slumps down in a chair.

But it's not over for Fitz yet. Sean, who is holding Tina's sister hostage in the house and has soaked the place in petrol and opened all the gas taps, will speak to nobody but Fitz. In spite of the presence of the parents, Fitz is not inclined to be a have-a-go hero.

'I'm not going in there,' he says. 'Rule number one about hostage negotiation is you do not put yourself at risk.'

Bilborough looks bewildered. 'That's not rule number one,' he replies.

'That's *my* rule number one,' ripostes Fitz, lighting a cigarette. He tries to talk to Sean on the phone, but the boy's speech impediment makes it impossible. Finally, Fitz shames himself into going in, after first finishing his cigarette.

Once inside, Fitz challenges Sean directly by eating the confession Sean has laboriously written out, claiming Tina had nothing to do with the murders. This is tricky stuff and Coltrane and Tiernan handle it well; Coltrane is under no illusions about fear and cowardice and knows exactly how to register the rising panic while at the same time attempting to maintain control of the situation. Fitz is not a natural born hero; he may not even be a brave man. But he is resilient and resourceful, and his alert mind keeps ticking over under any circumstances.

He manages to get the girl out, but events are getting out of control: Fitz is informed by phone that the gas central heating is on a time switch and is due to fire up in three minutes, which will effectively blow the house and everyone in it to smithereens. He tries to persuade Sean to leave, but clearly it's no use. Fitz walks out and strolls up the road as the timer kicks in and the house explodes, blowing him to the ground.

Penhaligon rushes over to him, sure that he is dead or badly injured. She slaps his huge body as it lies immobile on the ground: 'You stupid bastard! You stupid bastard!'

Fitz stirs. 'I think you'll find there's some activity further down,' he says, still face down in the road. But he's pushed it too far and Penhaligon falls against him weeping. Gently, Fitz embraces her and says: 'I'm sorry. I'm sorry.'

It is very difficult to separate the elements of this episode and single them out for praise as every single aspect is saturated in brilliance. McGovern's script is the finest of the series, juggling plotlines and human causes and reactions, humour and horror with deceptive ease. The direction by Michael Winterbottom is equally superb, capturing the streets and environs of Manchester with fluidity and grace. And the performances are incomparable, both from stalwarts like Barbara Flynn, Christopher Eccleston, Geraldine Somerville, Lorcan Cranitch and Beryl Reid and especially from the two newcomers, Susan Lynch and Andrew Tiernan – both of whom have forged successful careers following this ultra-impressive work.

STORY 3 (SEASON 1) 1993
One Day a Lemming Will Fly

Rock and roll music plays over the opening credits. Above the sound-track we hear Fitz and Judith having a discussion. But this is not a marital argument. They are having an amicable disagreement over old movies – a key component of McGovern's scripts and Fitz's char-acter. The difference between Bogart and Cagney having been estab-lished, they continue arguing at a fairly fundamental level about Cagney's walk to the gas chamber in *Angels with Dirty Faces*. Does Cagney really break down in terror and beg forgiveness? Or is he just acting out the role of penitent so that the street boys won't regard him as a hero and emulate his life of crime? Fitz and Judith agree to differ, but Fitz, as always, has the last word.

'I tell you, if Cagney's in Hell, he's watching British movies,' he slips into a Cagney accent: '*Room with a View*, you dirty rat.'

Film references abound in this episode and there is a great deal of humour to lighten the load between the previous episode and the one to come. Also, there is a major development between Fitz, Judith and Penhaligon which puts the landscape of their relationship in a new light.

At home Judith asks Fitz to return to the marital bed, which he does. But he goes out in the middle of the night to a gambling club where, after catching the female dealer cheating, he wins £1,000. As he walks away from the club he is set upon and mugged severely, given a couple of kicks in the head. It is a painfully realistic scene and Coltrane plays it straight down the line; no wisecracks, no funny business and no heroics. He goes down and stays down. He arrives back home, bloody, battered and without the money he had hoped to give gloatingly to Judith and shuts himself in the bathroom to tidy himself up.

Meanwhile, later in the night, the female croupier and a man sneak into the woods by the club for some illicit sex. They are rather distracted, however, by the sight of someone hanging from one of the trees.

News comes in from the police station that a teenage boy is missing. Fitz and Penhaligon are summoned to the station. Penhaligon drives, as usual, Fitz pops a sherbert lemon into her mouth. In the space of about fifteen seconds' screen time, we can see clearly the sexual frisson between Fitz and Penhaligon – the sexual innuendoes that have become part of their private language, the Laurel and Hardy double act that occasionally manifests itself before an audience. It is at times like these that Coltrane reveals the different strata of his ability: the arrogant, jokey, would-be knavery and the deeply vulnerable, uncertain man beneath; the two concepts of honesty and hypocrisy collide in Fitz like planets and it takes an actor as 'big' as Coltrane to accommodate the explosion, contain it and make proper use of the energy released.

Having been briefed by Bilborough, Fitz quizzes the family; the mother and father are separated and the other son seems strangely upset. Having spotted a rather unusual book of poetry in the boy's bedroom which he brought home from school, Fitz asks: 'Who's his English teacher?'

Rather surprisingly, the English teacher, Nigel Cassidy, is found beating the shit out of a punch bag in the school gym. 'Saves me taking it out of the kids,' he says, by way of a joke.

Coltrane's reaction is priceless. He sort of laughs but doesn't quite get it out; his eyes flick hard on to Cassidy before skimming away as if he has just seen inside the man's soul and doesn't much care for what he sees.

Later, following a television appeal by the parents organized by Beck, the dead boy (Tim) is found and taken to the mortuary.

There is a brief and biting exchange between Fitz and Judith in the kitchen as she comes in and drops a letter on the side while Fitz is preparing the evening meal. 'It's from the bank,' she says. Fitz fends off the inevitable conversation about money and finances by saying that he can't get the thought of Judith sleeping with Graham out of his head. Clearly, Fitz (whether he knows it or not) is going to use this as an excuse to lay a guilt trip on Judith and give himself some leeway in exploring the possibilities opened up by Penhaligon.

A very brief scene in which the police pathologist arrives, having been summoned from a grand fancy dress ball, is extremely funny. He turns up as Napoleon and is extremely pissed off. Fitz takes one look at him and leans in close: 'I'm a psychologist. I can help' – which even gets a laugh from Beck.

As the pathologist delivers his assessment of the cause of death – it's murder, of course – Coltrane stands with his right hand tucked into his jacket in a kind of little visual pun about Napoleon. No one notices. As he leaves, he can't resist another dig: 'What are you going as?' – which gets another laugh from Beck.

This is the only harmonious moment between the two, however. Much of the remaining time Beck and Fitz are at each other's throats. Back at the police station, Beck is suggesting they get to grips with the parents straight away. Knowing Beck's unsubtle and clodhopping interrogation methods, Fitz interjects: 'I'd like to talk to them first.'

Beck is furious at being interrupted: 'I'm talking.'

Nonetheless, Fitz and Penhaligon go to interview the parents in depth. Director Simon Cellan Jones makes an interesting decision here. He cuts up the interviews so that the questions and answers between Fitz and the father and Fitz and the mother have a cumulative effect.

'You want the truth? You'll despise the truth,' says the father.

'You would have preferred it to be suicide,' says Fitz. Cut to the mother.

'I knew it wouldn't be suicide.'

'Because,' says Fitz, 'suicide is a bomb under the kitchen table. Every member of the family cut to pieces. He wouldn't do that to you.' Cut to the father.

'You got a son?'

'Yeah,' says Fitz. 'Eighteen. Eighteen years old. Not eighteen sons.'

This is the kind of juxtaposition that makes Coltrane so daring; the collision between humour and horror. And the combination of

McGovern's dialogue and Coltrane's delivery ensures that it seems totally realistic. In the McGovern-written episodes, Coltrane never gets a bum line, never has to force the language to work.

The interview with the parents is beautifully modulated. This is Coltrane at his most subtle – quiet, caring but always teasing out the truth from his subjects by empathizing with them, showing them he understands. Gradually, bit by bit, he gets it; unlocks the family's secrets. The murdered boy was gay.

What is remarkable about this episode is not that Fitz spends the entire time with his face stitched and wounded from the mugging – but that nobody mentions it. It's as if they have come to expect Fitz to get into trouble one way or another and therefore choose to ignore the fact that he has been beaten up again. Also, it invites the possible thought that Fitz's wounds arise from a domestic fight.

It is a very useful device, however. Just like Jack Nicholson in *Chinatown*, in which as private detective Jake Gittes, Nicholson had his nostril slashed open by Roman Polanski's switchblade-wielding bad guy and spent the rest of the film with a plaster across his nose, Fitz's wounds suggest a fallibility beyond the norm. And yet, even while sitting bruised, stitched, bothered and beaten up he is never bewildered, never loses the authority of his position or his personality.

Having interviewed the parents with great tact and skill. Fitz is rather more abrasive with Tim's brother Andy, who has attacked a couple of his brother's schoolmates brought in for questioning. Clearly, Tim has been the victim of some bullying at school.

Fitz and Penhaligon are then called to the scene where the English teacher, Cassidy, who has already tried unsuccessfully to gas himself in his flat (his meter ran out of money), is threatening to jump from the top of a very tall building. Bilborough wants Fitz to talk him down.

The drive over gives Penhaligon and Fitz a further chance to develop their relationship.

'This morning with Mr and Mrs Lang.'

'Yeah?'

'I thought you were brilliant.'

'You should hear my pillow talk.'

When they arrive at the scene, Fitz delivers a great speech to

Penhaligon across the top of the car. Having told her he is afraid of heights, he recants:

'Afraid of heights? That's a lie. Nobody's afraid of heights. They're afraid of themselves, of what they might do. Listen, if I do survive this, will you let me take you out and get you pissed and make a pathetic attempt to seduce you?'

Penhaligon doesn't answer. She doesn't have to. Fitz has already shown his willingness to forge a relationship with Penhaligon but also his vulnerability and fear of 'what he might do'. It is this that makes Fitz – and, I suspect, Coltrane – so attractive to women. Underneath the great covering of jovial cynicism, of politically committed, empathizing, smart-ass wisdom, there lurks a wounded romantic. The other aspect that is drawn out and examined in this episode in particular is Fitz's inability to take action unless he initiates it. He is a control freak – Judith is right. Whenever Penhaligon makes a move on him, he backs off. At the top of the building Fitz finds Cassidy standing on the edge. In a remarkable bit of acting and camerawork, Coltrane lies down flat on the parapet, looking straight down at the street below. The camera rises above the building over the two men to reveal that they are really there. It's not faked.

'Forty or fifty feet's enough, you know,' says Fitz. 'Why so high? Too much time to think. Might change your mind half-way down. Lemmings. We laugh at lemmings, you know, for throwing themselves off cliffs. But I have a suspicion that the lemmings will have the last laugh. Because one day ... what's your name by the way?'

'Nigel.'

'Nigel – God, I'd be suicidal – one day, Nigel, a lemming will fly.'

Coltrane delivers this speech lying flat on his stomach staring straight down into space. He shifts gear into humour with ease, inserts the 'God, I'd be suicidal' joke brilliantly into what is a remarkable sequence. Having delivered his speech about instinct he gets up and makes as if he is going to jump. He can't resist doing another Cagney impersonation, this time from the final scene of *White Heat*: 'Top of the world, Ma!' Intriguingly, for such a film buff/pedant, Fitz gets the quote wrong. As with the apocryphal line 'Play it again, Sam' from *Casablanca*, which Bogart never said, Cagney never delivers the line as repeated. What he actually says is: 'Made it, Ma! Top of the world!'

Not that any of this bothers Cassidy, who has other problems on his mind.

Cassidy, of course, tries to stop him and they both come down from the parapet. Fitz and Penhaligon then cruise the shopping mall with Cassidy quizzing him all the way.

'You think I'm gay,' says the troubled teacher.

'No,' says Fitz, ever ready to split hairs. 'You think you're gay.'

Back at the station the homophobic Beck has been whipping up a crowd gathered outside with some agitation tactics. When Fitz, Penhaligon and Cassidy arrive, the car is attacked by the crowd and they just manage to escape from danger.

Cassidy's girlfriend comes in to provide an alibi for Cassidy on the night of the murder. Fitz sees straight through the ploy and understands that she has been his 'alibi' for some time. Beck, as usual, makes a hash of things by trying to question the girl in his own crass manner.

'What would you say if I told you he was queer?' says Beck to the girl.

Turning to him, with great sang-froid, she says: 'I'd say that you were the one with the moustache.' Even Fitz – a man not given to laughing at jokes other than his own – has a good laugh at that.

Fitz then goes in to interrogate Cassidy, believing that he has got the whole thing sewn up in his mind. He tells Cassidy how he thinks it all might have happened, with great sensitivity, great empathy for the teacher's plight.

'But that night he came to you, didn't he? In that tee-shirt. A blonde, beautiful, teenage boy. Those arms, those eyes, that smile. I don't blame you for weeping. Nobody does.'

This is a superbly played scene. Coltrane retains enormous authority even with stitches in his face, grazes on his head and cheek and the beginnings of a black eye.

When Fitz and Penhaligon take Cassidy back to his flat they are attacked by Tim's father and another man who destroy the walls with a mechanical digger. Fitz and Penhaligon take Cassidy to a hotel, where he will be guarded by Beck and Fitz. Penhaligon decides she is going on a two-week holiday and asks Fitz to go with her. Briefly interrupted by Bilborough, Fitz says yes.

In the hotel room, Beck gets to work on Cassidy, attempting to get him to break down and confess. Beck throws around homophobic jibes and comments, prompting Fitz to try to parry Beck's abuse.

'You can tell he reads *The Guardian*, can't you?'

But Beck won't shut up and soon the room is knotted with tension. Fitz then gives Beck a thorough verbal mauling, probing him psychoanalytically about his youth, his schoolfriends and his incipient homosexuality, and generally trying to get Beck to back off. Lorcan Cranitch's Beck is easily the most detestable character in *Cracker*, and it is a major tribute to his ability and lack of ego that he never attempts to be anything else. He and Coltrane work particularly well together, and this game of sparring cat and mouse – which continues throughout the series – is at its best in the early episodes. Having humiliated Beck, Fitz turns back to Cassidy and tries to break him down.

'You've killed a child, Nigel. That's a terrible, terrible burden. You want to share it. I'm here, Nigel. I'm willing to share your burden.'

'You're willing to share my burden?' says Cassidy.

'Yes,' says Fitz, suddenly hopeful of a breakthrough.

'I won't forget you said that.'

'I won't forget it.'

'I killed Timothy Lang,' says Cassidy, finally.

The camera stays on Coltrane. He stares at Cassidy, lets the information soak into him, then takes a deep breath and leans back. Like Father Karas in *The Exorcist*, Fitz has taken on board the diabolical burden of his subject.

It seems like the end, a satisfactory conclusion. The cops are already celebrating. But, of course, it is not as simple as all that. Fitz tells Judith in the garden that he is thinking of going away for a bit. Judith, who can see through Fitz like glass, knows there is something up.

'I've loved you for 25 years and I've never wanted anything else.'

This, of course, has absolutely the desired effect. It is guaranteed to make Fitz feel guilty about whatever it is he is planning on doing.

Penhaligon goes off, expecting Fitz to follow her and meet her at the airport. Beck and the boys are celebrating the confession of a 'pervert'. Fitz goes to talk to Cassidy in his holding cell. Cassidy psychs him out. He's got Fitz's number. In a common McGovern device, Fitz finds himself being psychoanalysed by his own subject (one thinks of Adrian Dunbar's amnesia victim in the first episode). He calls Fitz a hypocrite, to which Fitz can only weakly riposte: 'There are worse things in life, Nigel.'

But Fitz is really flummoxed by Cassidy, who tells him that he didn't kill the boy after all. And Fitz finds it difficult to cope with when Cassidy says he hopes the murderer will kill again. Because then, and only then, will Fitz be able to share his burden; to be responsible for the death of a child. It is a psychological gambit of unbelievable cunning. And it is Cassidy's revenge on Fitz for saving his life; for preventing his suicide.

Fitz leaves the cell really worried. This is the first time we have seen Fitz professionally undermined and it is truly unnerving. Coltrane strikes just the right note of moral panic and damaged ego when he confronts Bilborough and tells him that Cassidy didn't do it after all. Bilborough is about to go into a press conference to say they have their man, and Fitz's news distracts him.

'It's the truth that matters, not the result,' pleads Fitz.

Fitz goes home, where Judith, Kate and Mark are lounging around in the garden; a happy family scene. He hears the phone ring and listens as Penhaligon leaves a message from the airport. 'I think you've forgotten our appointment.'

Suffused with guilt, Fitz is unable to respond and certainly cannot pursue Penhaligon. He is in a kind of low-key crisis of the soul and he knows he is on the edge looking down; he decides not to jump. He turns and goes out into the garden to join his wife and children.

STORY 4 (SEASON 2) 1994
To Be a Somebody

Written by McGovern and directed by Tina Fywell (the first *Cracker* story to be directed by a woman), this stars Robert Carlyle in the role of Liverpool football supporter, Albie, which became one of the most notorious television roles any actor had played in recent years. The scale and scope of Albie's crimes, the motivation for his actions and the results of the murders he committed reached deep in the public consciousness – as McGovern intended – and stirred things up a bit.

It begins with a funeral; the funeral of Albie's dad. Fitz first appears speaking on the telephone (a customary image for Fitz at an early stage in the episode) to Judith, trying to cover up his whereabouts.

'Just gone for a quick drink,' he says, as a loud voice comes over the roulette table: 'No more bets please', which sort of gives the game away.

Much to Fitz's surprise, Judith tells him it's OK. Fitz just can't help it; he just fits into the scene. 'A hundred cash,' he says as money goes down on the table. This is him, Fitz the gambler, smoking, lying, gambling.

For a few moments we are treated to a dialogue-less series of shots as we watch Fitz gamble through the night. Through a series of reaction shots from Coltrane, we can chart his progress, or certainly his psychological condition. His lips and mouth are constantly moving, as if he were talking to himself or praying; the eyes are watchful, a combination of hope and distrust, pleading and malice.

Elsewhere, we see Albie becoming increasingly agitated. In the middle of feeding his cat he shaves his head – a sure sign that something fantastically nasty is going to happen. It's what we might now call That *Taxi Driver* Moment: the moment in Martin Scorsese's film when disenchanted Vietnam veteran Travis Bickle (Robert De Niro) shaves his head into a Mohican plume and starts buying guns.

In the morning Fitz turns up back at his house in a taxi. '*How* much?' he gasps. 'Did you have the meter on fast forward?' From this we deduce that he probably hasn't had a successful night.

Mark catches him coming into the house and starts questioning him as if their roles were reversed; as if Fitz were the teenager and Mark his father.

'Where've you been?'

'Out. Every time I come home it's the same. What time do you call this? Where have you been? Who have you been with? Well now you know how it feels, right?' Fitz uses his superior psychology skills in a particularly juvenile way to score points off his pissed-off son.

Upstairs in the bedroom, Fitz is rather taken aback by Judith's changed attitude towards him. She seems very tolerant, more able to accept his addiction and up-all-night lifestyle. This bothers Fitz, who hates having the one part of his life that he can predict becoming suddenly unpredictable.

'This isn't going according to script,' he says. 'You're supposed to bollock me, Judith. And then in the middle of a particularly insulting sentence, I go . . .' and he throws great fistfuls of money at her which land on the bed with a satisfying thwack. Judith all but ignores them and pulls the covers back, indicating that Fitz should join her.

'Please . . .' she says. This is the worst thing she could say to him, as it gives Fitz the opportunity to play the guilt card all over again – reminding her that she was the one who was unfaithful and that he hasn't yet forgiven her.

'I can't,' he says. The way Coltrane plays it there is an ambiguity about the line that is entirely appropriate: does he mean that he is really hurt by her lapse, or is he just exercising his moral superiority by making her suffer? It is probably both, Fitz being the complex cove that he is.

Albie has had a complete makeover: he has gone from respectable, suited chap to shaven-headed, combat-geared skinhead, and he walks into the Pakistani corner shop where the owner had previously been rude to him. After a further exchange of views, Albie stabs the owner to death with a long bayonet.

The cops are worried: is this a racially motivated crime? Fitz is awoken by a sawing noise. There are men in the bathroom, plumbers and builders come to do the bathroom extension (at last). But there are clearly problems. Fitz goes in and out singing: 'Oh give me a home/Where the buffalo roam', which eventually gets a reaction from one of the apologetic builder/plumbers: 'Look. We are not cowboys. We're not cowboys.'

While Fitz is having problems with plumbers, the cops raid a local neo-Nazi club where a pro-fascist gig is taking place. This is a tremendously scary encounter with a whole heap of what look like very convincing and authentic neo-Nazi skinheads (and I've encountered a few myself).

The cops are trying to play down and keep the lid on the racist element in the slaying of the Pakistani shopkeeper, but new cop Harriman leaks the information to the *Manchester Evening Post*. Their next headline is 'Skinhead Sought'.

Judith is seen in a class full of students when Fitz sheepishly puts his head round the door.

'Can I speak to you for a minute?' he says.

Judith dismisses him: 'I'm busy.'

Fitz doesn't take the hint. Putting on his very best sheepish look (which by now Coltrane has perfected, a sort of ageing and not very seemly little boy lost look), he whines: 'Please.' Judith plays Fitz at his own game – after all she's had the best teacher. She pulls a wad of cash from her bag (the wad Fitz had given her the night before) and waves it at him, inviting him to come and get it.

Seeing he can't win, Fitz immediately goes into performance mode and addresses the class as he walks across. 'How to handle an addict, Chapter 3, Verse 12. Public humiliation.' He takes the money and vamooses.

He goes straight into the betting shop and puts down £3,000 to win on a horse which falls as it comes out of the traps. Brim full of self-disgust, Fitz deliberately picks a fight with a pair of skinheads in the toilet by winding them up something rotten.

'You trying to get your nose broken, pal?' asks one.

'Yeah,' says Fitz. 'You know anyone who could do it, pal?'

The next scene, inevitably, is of Fitz mopping blood from his nose. He has assuaged the need to punish himself and then goes on to stage two of self-mortification: getting drunk in a pub.

Later that night, as Penhaligon arrives at her place, Fitz comes up behind her.

'I'm not wearing any underwear' says Fitz, in a pathetic attempt at humour. 'Look. Let me explain.'

Penhaligon is unimpressed by his appearance, dishevelled and bloodstained as it is.

'You owe me £972. That's the flights and the hotel.'

There is a terrific exchange between the two. Fitz is losing it desperately, becoming pathetic in his need to communicate.

'Can I come in?'

'I'd let Oliver Reed in before you, Fitz,' says Penhaligon. The line was written, of course, before Ollie himself died.

But Fitz knows they need him. He's seen the television, read the papers about the murder.

'You need a profile,' he pleads. Penhaligon stitches him up.

'If we need a profile we will get one. Psychologists are two a penny.'

This is too much for Fitz. His professionalism has been impugned.

It doesn't matter how pathetic he becomes as a human being, as a husband and an errant lover – his professional acumen is unassailable; it's the last shred of dignity he can cling to. He tells Penhaligon exactly the kind of profile they might expect from another psychologist. If this is what they come up with, he says, it's wrong.

Penhaligon slams the door in his face, causing his nose to bleed again.

On his return home, Fitz finds his house being used for a massive party, teenagers everywhere, music blasting out. When he locates Judith in the kitchen she simply says: 'Did you lose it all?'

Fitz is ready. 'Ah, the row. At last the row. We could skip it if you like. Just don't speak to me for a week.' Fitz may be a lapsed Catholic, but he still thinks that he can find some kind of absolution, do some kind of penance and it will make everything all right again and he can go back to his wicked ways.

But this time he has miscalculated, and Judith gives him both barrels. It is Mark's birthday, which is the reason for the party, and Fitz has completely forgotten.

'You selfish, arrogant sod.'

Fitz is in a bad way. Racked with guilt, he makes his way upstairs to find an unoccupied bathroom, passing scenes of teenage debauchery which only serve to heighten his feelings of inadequacy and the onset of age until he comes across a bathroom that is more or less empty. But something is wrong. Fitz starts to have trouble breathing, and even to pass out. He just manages to grab the whisky bottle. This is truly alarming. Coltrane makes us believe that Fitz is having some kind of seizure in a most authentic manner. We even suspect he may be dying.

When Mark tries to open the door and finds it locked, he kicks it in. Fitz is panting heavily over the loo. Finally he is brought out by the paramedics with an oxygen mask over his face. He mumbles to Judith, 'Heart attack.'

In hospital, awaiting tests, he starts to moan, for no apparent reason, about the media perception of psychologists and psychiatrists, including Herbert Lom as Dr Roger Corder in *The Human Jungle* (as we have determined, one of the very few prototypes and precedents for

Cracker). Fitz is wired up for tests and gets the interrogation from the doctor.

'How much do you drink?'

'Six, maybe seven a week.'

'Pints?'

'Bottles.'

'Of beer?'

'Of whisky.'

'And you smoke?'

'Fifty, sixty.'

'Please say a week.'

Judith interrupts with 'a day'.

Fitz cannot help himself, however. Not content with being the centre of attention, he wants to be the centre of attention. Now that he has a captive audience, he bloody well intends to capitalize on it, especially if his contract is running out.

'Give it to me straight, Doctor. I've always wanted to read *War and Peace*. Is it worth me starting?'

'There is nothing wrong with you,' says the doctor, to everyone's surprise. 'Nothing physical.' Then he delivers the *coup de grâce*. 'But I would like you to see a psychologist.' Ho ho ho.

As Judith and Fitz return home in a taxi, they pass some skinhead and Asian gangs barely being kept apart by the cops. Penhaligon stops the cab and looks in, surprised to see that it's Fitz. Judith eyes Penhaligon beadily: 'We've met.'

Fitz, in a bid for sympathy and an attempt to head off potential trouble at the pass, tells Penhaligon he's been in hospital. But he reckons without Penhaligon's anger at being stood up.

'Nothing trivial, I hope,' she spits. Judith catches the tone and the look that runs between Penhaligon and her husband.

In the cop shop, Penhaligon advises Bilborough on another psychologist. Fitz locates Harriman in the pub and gives him his view of the profile. When Harriman regurgitates it in a meeting the following morning, Penhaligon scoffs, 'How is Fitz?'

Bilborough invites Fitz into the case. The two have a huge row over Cassidy and the sacrifice of an innocent man in the previous Cracker story. As Fitz, out of guilt and a strong sense of injustice, goes for

Bilborough's jugular over the compromised Cassidy conviction, Bilborough turns the tables on Fitz by bringing up his dalliance with Penhaligon.

'You hurt her again and I'll out you in traction,' warns Bilborough.

'I can take a hint,' responds Fitz. Coltrane has got the wit of the born coward down pat. As if to prove he is good at something, Fitz goes all out in his interview with Azir, the murdered shopkeeper's daughter. She is convinced it is a racially motivated killing and is extremely militant in her views.

Fitz begins to figure out what happened and gives his imagined scenario to Bilborough: 'He goes home, shaves his head, comes back and kills him.'

Not surprisingly, Bilborough thinks he's gone mental and sends him home. There follows an extremely funny scene in a pub with Fitz looking ruefully at a bare handful of change before asking the barman. 'What's a large Scotch?'

The comically morose barman replies in drop deadpan: 'It's a well-known alcoholic drink.'

Fitz: 'Don't give up the day job.'

On hearing it is £1.20, Fitz says it sounds reasonable. 'It's Happy Hour,' says the barman, miserably.

The scene lasts about 20 seconds but McGovern's writing is as tight as a drum, and the performances are honed to perfection. There is hardly more than a joke in its motive but it feels so right – given everything we know about Fitz, his impecuniousness, his tendency to wind people up – that it seems a completely necessary scene.

Albie, meanwhile has traced the girl reporter who has been following the case.

Back at Fitz's house, Judith arrives to find Katie, who simply says: 'He's on the floor again.'

Fitz is wallowing in drink and self-pity. He can't bear being fired from the case and it has destroyed his last vestigial sense of self-respect. Judith attempts to comfort him. But she also wants him to stop drinking. She reveals his secret stashes of booze throughout the house to shame him into stopping. It doesn't work. Fitz is in denial.

'Look, I do not have to hide my booze, Judith. I am not an adolescent.'

They go for a walk in the park, where Fitz confesses. 'Look, I'm forty-five years old, I've finally discovered what I want to do with my life – can we slow down, please? – I want to work with the police. When I'm doing that everything is fine. When I'm not doing that I get bored and depressed and things go wrong.'

Coltrane is particularly fine in this moment. He conveys acutely Fitz's complex personality – the way he is genuinely revealing himself to Judith and also aware of the fact that he is attempting to win her over, to get her to see things from his point of view. There is a buried complacency in Fitz which is his least attractive trait. Judith is past being manipulated by Fitz, even at his best.

'I'm not leaving, Fitz,' she says later. 'I think it's unfair on Katie. I want you to leave.'

'I'm just going,' says Fitz, moving towards the door.

'For good.'

Fitz is absolutely gobsmacked. He simply cannot comprehend what Judith is saying to him. It's a mixture of incredulity and contempt.

It is while the cops are talking to the girl reporter that Fitz gets it; he understands the motivation behind the crime. It's all to do with Hillsborough.

'He's going to kill 96 people in revenge for Hillsborough. And if there's any justice on this earth most of them are going to be coppers.'

This is one of the most ominous lines McGovern ever wrote for Fitz. The full horror of the extent of Albie's potential crimes, and his reasons, charge this story with a tragic power unmatched by any other story in the series. Frankly, if it weren't for the fact that Coltrane, Eccleston, Somerville and Cranitch had established themselves with such authenticity, it would appear melodramatic. As it is, and thanks to Robert Carlyle's tremendously focused performance, we don't question it one iota. It's truly terrifying.

As McGovern turns up the heat, he also gives Fitz and Judith an opportunity to rekindle their passion. Engaged in a vivid intellectual argument, they are raking over the past, revealing small but telling details about each other and their respective pasts. Fitz suddenly stops and looks at her. 'Come to bed with me,' he says. 'Come to bed with me.'

'Only if you carry me up,' says Judith.

They are still passionate about each other – and it is the intellect, the intelligent argument and the fact that they can talk to each other (from time to time) that keeps their passion alive.

Afterwards, Fitz is singing in the bathroom. As he leaves, he says 'Bye.' Judith says 'Bye' but in a slightly different tone. We fear the worst, though Fitz, as usual, is totally oblivious.

As the police net widens and various people are questioned, Beck finds Albie and interrogates him in his house. Stupidly, Beck misses the picture on the wall that links Albie to the killing and swallows Albie's story that his hair has fallen out because of cancer and chemotherapy. It's a fatal mistake, a criminal lack of observation.

Fitz returns to the house, rubbing his hands and full of the joys of spring.

'Right, Jude,' he shouts. 'Upstairs on that bed stark naked. Right now.' Life is good again. Little does he know. Judith has gone and taken all her clothes. Fitz is devastated. Naturally, the first person he takes it out on is Mark and anyone else who gets in his way.

At the supermarket checkout he is told off by a woman for having more than eight items in his basket while waiting in the eight items only queue. Well, you know how annoying *that* can be. Fitz, of course, loses his temper immediately with the sheer pettiness of the woman's complaint, exacerbated by his own domestic crisis.

Meanwhile, Albie lures Bilborough into his house and stabs him with the bayonet. The remainder of this sequence is one of the most painful of the entire series as Albie leaves and Bilborough crawls across the room, calling for help on his radio. The trouble is, he has no idea where he is, and every time he moves blood gushes out. He knows he's dying and gives a dying man's statement over the radio, knowing it will stand up in court.

By the time Fitz and Penhaligon and Beck arrive on the scene, Bilborough is dead. Fitz, the man who has an answer for everything, just stands in the street, helpless. Coltrane lets his hands hang loose, as if they had suddenly become useless things; he looks like a spare prick at a wedding, which is what he is. He knows he can't do anything to save Bilborough, he can't do anything at all and he hates it. He presents a spectacle of a big intelligent man rendered completely powerless by life, or rather death.

DCI Wise (Ricky Tomlinson) is introduced immediately. He comes in to the crime scene and establishes his presence. The Chief Constable calls Fitz to ask him to talk to Bilborough's wife, Katrina.

Fitz is very sensitive here. He even suppresses his feelings about Cassidy's wrongful conviction in order to save Katrina from any more pain. It is one of the rare moments when Fitz acts completely without self-interest. When Katrina says that Bilborough wouldn't lock up an innocent man, Fitz replies: 'I know that. I was wrong. I'm sorry.' What's more, he makes her (and us) believe it.

Fitz is then brought in to meet DCI Wise, and the rapport between Coltrane and Tomlinson is immediately established. We know what it's going to be like.

'Your results are my results, OK?' says Wise. 'I get the Brownie points. You get the money.'

Fitz replies in his best Humphrey Bogart voice: 'This could be the beginning of a beautiful friendship.' But Wise isn't buying.

'I doubt it, lad,' he says. Wise is, uh, wise to Fitz's ploys. Mistrustful of anything other than good honest coppering, Wise nonetheless will use anything, including a bloody psychologist like Fitz, if he can get a result.

Fitz turns his attention to Albie's estranged wife. He shows her pictures of Bilborough, dead on the pavement. He plays her the tape of Bilborough's dying words. He gets her defences down, softens her up, and then proceeds with great care. Clearly, she is very shocked.

'How did you meet?'

'Hillsborough.'

'You still love him?' Coltrane drops his voice right down to a barely perceptible whisper. Here we see Coltrane giving Fitz an even more rounded characterization; Fitz doesn't just talk, he listens. And it is listening and watching that he does here.

After the questioning, Fitz brings Penhaligon some coffee.

'I'm sorry I hurt you,' says Fitz, genuinely contrite.

'You didn't,' she says.

'I did. He said I did.'

'The boss?'

'He said if I ever hurt you again he'd break both my legs.' Fitz then goes on to tell her that Judith has left him.

'I'll move in immediately,' scoffs Penhaligon, having learnt a thing or two about spiky ripostes from Fitz himself. 'It's one thing to be left at the airport, Fitz. But to be left at the airport by a big, fat, egocentric, middle-aged, married man – that's another thing altogether.'

Fitz counters with the cruellest cut of all, by telling Penhaligon what she is thinking about her chances of promotion in the wake of Bilborough's death.

Penhaligon is exasperated and hurt beyond measure. 'You're an emotional rapist, Fitz.'

'No, I'm saying I understand. These things are far better out than in.'

'You're an emotional bloody rapist.'

Later in the hunt for Albie, Beck sees him being put out of a football ground and gives chase. When he finally catches him he kicks the shit out of him, watched by all the others, who do not try to stop him.

Fitz comes in to see Albie and gets inside his head by shouting 'Chelsea!' at him over and over again. He psychs him out through the usual procedure, suggesting that he is trying to make a mark by killing others. To be a somebody. Albie and Fitz battle it out psychologically until both are scarred. It is a pure battle of wills.

Fitz figures out from what Albie is not saying that there is a bomb somewhere. Somebody walks into an office holding a jiffy bag. A bomb goes off in Albie's allotment without problems. Fitz walks into the street, satisfied that he has got to the end of Albie. The female journalist opens her jiffy bag. There is an explosion. Fitz stares up as he hears something in the distance.

This is a dark and brutal ending. Albie's reach extends far beyond his captivity. He gets the journalist who was working for the *Sun* at the time of the Hillsborough disaster, one of the most shameful pieces of reporting ever.

There is no doubt that this story was a very personal one for McGovern. Hillsborough was a terrible tragedy, and this is his *cri de coeur* as well as an attack on the media and the cops, who were disgraced by their treatment and handling of the disaster.

STORY 5 (SEASON 2) 1994
The Big Crunch

Having established their new hero, the surrounding characters and identified various themes in the first four stories, Jimmy McGovern and Gub Neal now felt confident enough to pass the script respon- sibilities over to other writers. McGovern was on hand to act as script editor, but the entire *Cracker* team by this stage had set the rules in stone. All the actors were comfortable in their roles and their on- screen relationships. A reality was established, a fictional universe which needed no further exposition. From now on, new writers brought in had a template from which to work. All they had to do was come up with some juicy stories.

Coltrane, in particular, had settled into the role of Fitz with almost supernatural ease. The research and study, the reading and lengthy conversations with psychologists and policemen had paid huge divi- dends. Fitz was flesh and blood – as easily identifiable a character as Sherlock Holmes and just as believable. On set, Coltrane could now indulge to the full, his capacity for entertaining the troops, even in between takes – cracking jokes, passing comments and performing his various vocal impressions to lighten the mood, before snapping straight back to Fitz at a moment's notice. By this stage, Fitz was Coltrane's second skin.

As soon as the first episode of Story 5 opened, however, there was a slight but discernible difference. Written by veteran television scriptwriter Ted Whitehead and directed by Julian Jarrold, *The Big Crunch* has an air of self-awareness – almost self-consciousness – that is not evident in the McGovern stories. Even Coltrane seems wrong- footed by the dialogue at times, and vaguely uncomfortable with the monologues to himself that Whitehead provides.

The change is evident from the opening music. The McGovern episodes almost invariably begin with upbeat, positive music, either rock and roll or something popular which is deliberately designed to lure the viewer into a false sense of security. It perfectly sets the tone for the switchback moods of the drama and comedy that follow.

Episode one of *The Big Crunch*, by contrast, begins with creepy music, played against the image of a woman walking through a wood.

There is menace, threat – the possibility of something nasty imminent. As it happens, she has come to spy on a couple making love against a tree. She takes photographs. Then we hear Fitz across the soundtrack, pleading and explaining to Judith about himself. He is pulling every Fitzian trick in the book, confessing, cajoling, being assertive, questioning. Finally we see that he is talking to himself in the bathroom mirror as he finishes shaving. Clearly, Fitz is preparing his speech for the arrival of Judith.

Aside from the rather unoriginal use of this device, there is something wrong about the scene; Fitz not only has his shirt on but is actually dressed in his suit, including jacket. I know of very few men who would perform their ablutions – especially shaving – in their own home while fully dressed.

Judith arrives with an estate agent, and it soon becomes clear that she intends to sell the house and divide everything up between her and Fitz. Fitz, who is confident that his silver tongue will once more win her over, is absolutely gobsmacked.

'I'm perfectly able to look after Katie. I expect you to do the same for Mark,' she says in a tone that brooks no argument.

In a behavioural switch that Coltrane now has down to a fine art, he changes tack, immediately going on the offensive.

'Oh, I see. You get the lochs and the glens and the mighty mountains, and I get the toxic waste dump. Is that fair?'

When Judith gives him a sheaf of legal documents to sign he performs a typical Fitz trick – he eats them. Aware that he is in no mood to be reasoned with, Judith and the estate agent leave, and she drives off with Fitz shouting after her: 'Bitch! Harridan! Witch! Harpy! Wife!'

There is a writerly archness about this line which doesn't quite ring true. But Coltrane manages to get away with it, pausing just long enough before delivering the final insult: 'Wife!' In a rage, he tears the For Sale board out of the ground and hurls it after the car. We watch Fitz's face as it turns from rage to horror as the inevitable crash of glass is heard over the soundtrack. Oops. He's in trouble now.

The following scene in the church of The Fellowship of Souls establishes the plotline. Kenneth (Jim Carter) is conducting a service, while among the congregation is Joanne (Samantha Moreton), whom we recognize as the girl engaged in sex in the woods. Clearly, this augurs badly for the religious community.

The next short scene reveals Fitz attempting to pick his daughter Katie up from school, only to discover that she has been taken away and put into another school. The battle between Fitz and Judith, we realize, is going to get really dirty. Even Fitz is shocked, unable to come up with any more witty rejoinder to cover his embarrassment and humiliation than: 'Ah, it was a shite school anyway.'

Meanwhile, Kenneth's wife is shown the photographs of her husband making love to Joanne in the woods by the woman who took the pictures. She picks the girl up from school.

Fitz is then depicted in a telephone box, receiver in hand, reading aloud the tart cards. 'Safe sex is breast worship. Come play in my wardrobe. I'll tie you and tease you till you say please.' Coltrane's double take indicates that someone has come to the phone and has been listening to at least some of this monologue.

'No this is not a dirty phone call. This is your daughter's erstwhile husband.'

Fitz is clearly trying to contact Judith and Katie, who are staying with Judith's parents. The phone goes dead. He dials again.

'Hello. Yes it's me again. Vlad the Impaler. Can I talk to my wife, please?' Clearly the answer is negative and he is left with a dead phone for the second time. 'A case for patricide in a nutshell,' he mutters.

This scene, I have to say, strikes me as particularly unconvincing and clumsy. Nobody reads the messages printed on tart cards aloud to themselves, especially in a public phone booth. It is too clearly a device to insert a little humorous aside. And the final line is similarly unconvincing; most people, Fitz included, would simply swear the place down under the circumstances. They certainly would not waste a line on empty air. Fitz, as has been established, likes nothing better than an audience; he talks to people, not to himself. Moments like these, and there are several in this particular story, sit uncomfortably with our understanding of Fitz's character. To his credit, Coltrane makes the most of them, but you can detect that he is not as happy with the dialogue now as once he was.

The wronged wife and her best friend, Norma (the photographer), grab Joanne and push her down into the cellar. The next scene establishes that Joanne is missing from home as Penhaligon questions the parents. The mother is worried. The father sits like a zombie with the remote control in front of the television. Penhaligon wants to bring Fitz in on the case to talk to the parents.

The timing is slightly odd here. Joanne is a schoolgirl, sure, but it is difficult to know how long has passed since she went missing and it is never explained.

Finally, Fitz is brought in to quiz the parents and looks at the school pictures while talking to the mother. Typically, Fitz attempts humour to get her to open up.

'Any boyfriends? Joanne, I mean.'

'Joanne's a good girl,' says Mum, without taking the bait and, of course, proving that she doesn't know her daughter as well as all that.

Fitz tries another tack by making it really personal. Having established that the husband is a dead loss – he remains glued to the television – he wants to get the woman on his side. He pulls a picture of his daughter Kate from his wallet and shows it to her.

'My Katie,' he says, with what appears to be genuine pride (as usual with Fitz, it is difficult to tell whether he is 'performing' or not). 'Kate is the goodest, most intelligent, the funniest, the most attractive girl the universe has ever seen. And one day she's going to be snogging on the doorstep with some spotty string of slime who's not good enough to clean her shoes. I know it. I know I'm never going to be ready for it.'

This is a classic Fitz speech and pumps some much-needed life and identity into what has so far been an intriguing but elusive episode. Coltrane seems to know it, too, and gives it the kind of impact that is painfully credible. It is at moments like this that we see just how far Coltrane has steeped himself in the character of Fitz. He is now able to control the climate of the dialogue in any scene, giving the lacklustre lines an extra twist, polishing the good stuff. This is the mark of a true talent and a confident actor, which Coltrane has clearly become.

Now that Fitz is bereft of Judith, of course, he must find others to act as his sounding board. In the pub after the interview with the parents, Fitz shamelessly asks Penhaligon to buy him (another) drink. 'I'm temporarily embarrassed,' he says, without much sign of embarrassment. We seem to be reaching another level of Fitz's emotional development; he is quite prepared to allow himself to fall into Penhaligon's power. He deploys the tactics of helplessness, partly out of necessity and partly because he knows (how could he not?) that by appearing vulnerable he will be more attractive to Penhaligon. Fitz is an emotional opportunist. This is made abundantly clear at the end of the scene, when Penhaligon walks out in a huff and Fitz goes to follow but is distracted at the last moment by a fruit machine. It's a beautifully orchestrated statement.

Fitz and Penhaligon meet later and go to the school, where Kenneth – who is the headmaster – welcomes them. Fitz lights up a cigarette and is immediately admonished by the school secretary. 'School,' he ripostes, 'is where I started.' Even Penhaligon tells him to put his cigarette out when one of the girls comes in to be interviewed.

Fitz later meets his daughter Kate who gives him a letter containing a ten-pound note. By now you can see the rage and resentment building up in him like a pressure cooker. Fitz offers to buy her an ice cream, and while he is in the queue some busybody parent fingers him as a pervert who's been hanging around the schoolyard. This is too much. Fitz pushes the bloke into some bushes and is immediately arrested for assault.

Although this is a potentially awkward scene, Coltrane and Tess Thomson (Kate) carry it off particularly well. Fitz's personal life is now becoming a real liability to his work, and Coltrane maintains the delicate balance between salvaging the last shreds of his self-respect through work, trying not to lose his family, struggling with his various addictions (although not very hard) and flirting with Penhaligon. It is inevitable that it will end in violence – though it is uncharacteristic for Fitz to use physical violence and, in truth, it is nothing much more than a frustrated shove. But the consequences are painfully humiliating as Judith is the one who has to bail him out. In order to cover his shame he emerges from the police station threatening all manner of legal action against the cops for wrongful arrest. It's bluster, of course, and both Fitz and Judith know it.

The humour in this scene is in sharp contrast to the scene that follows, which is one of the nastiest sequences in the series. While Norma and his wife hold Joanne down, Kenneth intones prayers and forces her to wash down scores of pills with neat gin.

Shortly afterwards, a big box is delivered by Kenneth's brother, Michael, to the crushing plant and left with Dean, the simple boy on night shift. Dean puts the box on the conveyor belt and starts the machine. Out of curiosity he stops it just before it tumbles over on to the whirling blades of the crushing machine and brings it back. When he opens it he finds Joanne, wrapped in a sheet and still, barely, alive. She has, moreover, cabalistic symbols and numbers written all over her body.

In the hospital, Fitz attempts to talk to Joanne. She has been silent since being brought in and is clearly in a bad way.

'Joanne,' whispers Fitz, 'my name is Fitz. I'm not a policeman, I'm a shrink. Which means you probably don't want to talk to me either.'

Fitz tries to get through to her, using all the subtlety and skills of which he is a master. This is a key scene in this story and both Coltrane and the young Samantha Moreton – whose big break came as the youngest prostitute in *Band of Gold* – are magnificent together. Fitz becomes ever more intimate: 'They blame themselves, your mum and dad. They didn't know you had a boyfriend, did they?'

But it is having the opposite effect to that intended. Joanne becomes increasingly agitated, almost hysterical, until the nurse comes in and throws him out.

We see a big chubby hand delicately put the needle on to a record. Fitz is copying down the numbers written on Joanne's body, using photographs taken of various parts of her body by the police photographer. Soon, he is snoring on the sofa.

Mark enters, waking Fitz. Coltrane does a great waking up double take, a big man's slide along the sofa to heave himself upright. His first words to his son are: 'I wasn't drunk.'

Mark looks at the numbers and the equations and explains the Big Bang theory to Fitz. The numbers and signs represent the beginning of life and the end.

In Joanne's case, it is literally the end. She dies in hospital and, in a remarkably moving scene, her father falls to his hands and knees in grief, having bottled it up since the beginning.

By contrast, we next see Fitz on the phone to his daughter. He is trying to explain himself, making excuses for not turning up to meet her as expected. Now that he and Judith have separated, Fitz spends more time trying to explain himself to his children than trying to talk Judith round.

'Katie, I was not pissed. Where did you learn that word? ...' The doorbell rings. It's Penhaligon. Fitz is caught between putting the phone down and trying to stall Penhaligon. Katie, we gather, is laying on the guilt big time at the other end of the phone.

As soon as Fitz opens the door he sees something is wrong.

'You all right?' he says to Penhaligon.

'Joanne's dead.'

'She was murdered,' says Fitz, all joking done with. This is one of Coltrane's most successful flips – from the whining, self-explanatory, wriggling, pitiful father to the ice-cool objectivity and razor-sharp brain of the professional psychologist.

In the cop shop, Fitz runs through the psychological import of the symbols on Joanne's body, photographs of which are pinned on the display board. While the cops look for Dean, the young simple guy who found Joanne in the box, Fitz and Penhaligon go and see Joanne's priest, Father O'Ryan, in whom she used to confide before being lured into Kenneth's sect. This sequence, with Father O'Ryan and Fitz verbally sparring, is absolutely wonderful, even if not entirely necessary. It certainly gives two actors a terrific opportunity to get their teeth into a sustained and articulate argument.

O'Ryan is also built on the generous side and looks like Coltrane's spiritual brother – which is, of course, the point. As Fitz and Pen-haligon approach the priest in his church, Fitz says under his breath: 'Why is it that whenever you're in church you always feel you're being watched?'

O'Ryan, of course, hears this. 'Because you are, Dr Fitzgerald,' he replies with great sang-froid. 'I saw you lecture once,' he continues. 'That level of cynicism must be hard to sustain.'

'Not at all,' Fitz ripostes. But he knows he's up against someone who can match him argument for argument, point for point. They are intellectual equals, two smart cookies rubbing up against each other. O'Ryan spots Fitz as a lapsed Catholic. Even in the humour stakes, O'Ryan can match Fitz.

'Bless me father, for it is 22 years since my last confession.'

'The next one should be worth hearing,' replies O'Ryan, totally unfazed. 'I shall look forward to that.' Fitz has met his match. They part as equals.

Fitz and Penhaligon then go to call on Kenneth, with Fitz explaining the psychology of letter-boxes to his amused colleague. Clearly, he's got to do something to recoup the ground lost during his extended encounter with Father O'Ryan.

Once inside, Fitz gives Kenneth a very hard time. He becomes quite intimidating, inferring all kinds of things about his position as headmaster and head of the religious sect. The oleaginous Kenneth bends but does not break, however, under Fitz's attack.

'Poor young girl. It's such a waste of life,' he says.

'Yes,' says Fitz. 'That's why we want to catch the maniac that did it.'

Fitz then goes through all the other suspects, and everyone connected with the case. He plays a brilliant cat and mouse game with Michael, Kenneth's brother, softening him up for later. He also finds time to put down the wretched Beck. 'You're a bit like a doctor, aren't you? You bury your mistakes.'

This is a clear reference to the death of Bilborough and Beck's contribution in letting Bilborough's murderer, Albie, slip through his fingers. Beck has been harassing Dean, who he thinks is involved in the abduction and (ultimate) murder of Joanne.

Fitz then talks to Dean and adopts a very different tack; he plays the sensitivity card and it is a rewarding, harrowing scene. He is not so well rewarded when news comes that Dean has hanged himself in his cell.

As Fitz passes Beck in the police station, Beck whines: 'You think I'm to blame for Dean's death?'

Fitz says: 'I'm not, but if I were I'd expect a bit of sympathy from you, Jimmy. You know exactly how it feels.' This reference to Bilborough's murder stuns Beck into silence. Even he can't think of a snappy comeback to that one. If he ever could.

En route to the pub, Fitz reveals to Penhaligon that he has no money at all and that he hasn't yet been paid for this gig. Penhaligon lends him £250 of her own money drawn from a hole in the wall. Shamefacedly, he accepts.

The next scene shows the growing intimacy between Fitz and

Penhaligon as they shop together in a supermarket. Something, clearly, is going on between them.

Back in his kitchen, with Fitz fussing about with red wine and microwaved pizzas, he blurts out: 'I think I love you.' Which annoys Penhaligon intensely. But not for long. This is one of the moments we have been waiting for, which the writers have taunted and teased us with for so long. Fitz and Penhaligon kiss and go to bed together. Mercifully, I feel, we are spared any lengthy sex scenes between the two. The subtlety here is that they not only wake up together but are caught by Mark, Fitz's own son. It's a reversal of how parents catch their own children at it in their teenage bedrooms, and Mark is not impressed by his father's blustering excuses about Judith having left him.

'You drove her away for being a dickhead,' Mark yells.

Fitz has more trouble to contend with back at the police station when DCI Wise (Ricky Tomlinson) tries to take Fitz off the case – saying that Dean's suicide is an expression of guilt. After a hectic piece of negotiation, Fitz is given an extra 48 hours to come up with someone else.

Fitz pushes it with Kenneth's wife. He nearly gets her but she proves, ultimately, resistant. He then talks to Joanne's girlfriend at school, leading her on. Next he has a long session with Norma, the friend who took the photographs. This is a tense, surprising and very uncomfortable scene, as the middle-aged Norma reveals her true colours under Fitz's relentless interrogation. She tries to flirt with him, and Fitz can see straight away that she is lying. He doesn't like it at all. She is, he says, obsessed with Kenneth; this is a suppurating wound of jealousy that goes back many years and has never healed.

Fitz then goes after Michael, knowing that he is the weakest link in the chain. Fitz plays on Michael's wife, Norma's obvious infatuation with Kenneth, stirring up jealousy and trying to humiliate him. Strangely, he can't break him.

A brief interlude – an emotional breather, in fact – occurs now as Fitz plays boogie-woogie piano and sings the blues for his son.

Finally, Fitz quizzes Kenneth very perceptively, very closely. He delivers the usual emphatic description of how it felt for a man of his age to have the carnal and emotional love of a girl less than half his age. Its great, Fitz on top form, but Kenneth won't break.

Finally, he confronts him in the church itself, during a service. Backed up by Michael, who brings in the incriminating pictures taken by Norma and shows them to the congregation, Fitz asks him questions in public which will surely be answered in the next weeks. Whatever else happens, it's the end of Kenneth's power in the church community and his career as a headmaster.

Finally, Fitz has the last laugh with Penhaligon. 'No, I know my limitations. What you see is what you get. Imperfect. A sex god. But imperfect.'

There is something oddly uncompelling about this story, my least favourite of the series. I suspect it is something to do with the slightly arcane language, the formal tricks of the writing that don't always ring true. Also, the tale of a community held in thrall by a small-time religious leader is unnecessarily melodramatic. That said, it contains some real dramatic highlights and some of the best performances, especially from Samantha Moreton as the ill-used Joanne. This is not vintage Coltrane, either, though it serves to show how he can hold the centre of a script together even when the cracks are appearing outside.

STORY 6 (SEASON 2) 1994
Men Should Weep

Jimmy McGovern returned to script this crucial story in the series. It was to prove a turning-point, not for Fitz but for the characters Jimmy Beck and Penhaligon. It also focused more than usual on the social activity and the deep-seated prejudices of the police themselves, especially about blacks and women. It not surprisingly outraged members of the police across the country, who felt they had been exposed to ridicule and that the suggestions of sexual and racial prejudice were exaggerated. Given the fact that this was written before the Stephen Lawrence enquiry, it appears that McGovern may not have been so wide of the mark.

It begins with Fitz in a radio studio. He's landed his own phone-in analysis show. Naturally, being Fitz, his advice is somewhat unconventional.

'You're depressed,' he says to a caller. 'How depressed? Suicidal?'

When the answer is in the affirmative, he asks how old the (female) caller is. 'Seventy-eight' comes the reply.

The caller is depressed because she's been done for shoplifting from a local supermarket. Fitz's sense of the injustice of the charge drives him to extreme measures. He broadcasts a call for everyone to go down to the supermarket and begin shoplifting, much to the alarm of the radio station boss.

Meanwhile, a coloured minicab driver, Floyd, is seen with his girl-friend Trish. Having been going out for three months she is having trouble persuading him to come to bed.

'You wouldn't like me naked,' he says, by way of explanation. Clearly, he has some kind of problem with sex. The hook of the theme is in. Fitz is next seen in a noisy pub where couples are dancing to a tango record. He spots Penhaligon dancing in the arms of a young, attractive man. A look of pure jealousy passes across his face. An old lady asks him to dance with her.

'Can you dance?' she asks.

'Can I dance?' replies Fitz. 'I taught St Vitus.'

On the dance floor he and Penhaligon exchange words. He leaves in a huff and goes home.

As he is pouring whisky into a half-pint beer mug, Mark walks in, sees what he's doing and walks out again. Fitz turns and directs a challenging glare to his retreating form.

Coltrane has now reached the stage where he can simply narrow his eyes, cock an eyebrow or shift into any number of facial expressions and reaction shots to achieve meaning without dialogue. Depending on the director, he will do more of these as the series progresses, so well does he know Fitz. Sometimes, a look or a gesture speaks volumes.

Floyd, meanwhile, attacks and rapes a woman in a public swimming pool. Unusually, he spends more time talking to her after the event than actually performing; it is as if he is talking to his girlfriend after they have just made love. He takes her (masked) into the swimming pool and leaves her alive.

Penhaligon arrives to pick up Fitz. 'There's been another rape.'

Fitz splashes water on his face and Penhaligon offers him some mints. 'Don't want you smelling of whisky.'

She tries to explain what she was doing with the bloke in the pub, but Fitz says there is no need. He gives her the cold shoulder treatment like a petulant little boy.

As they walk past the cops towards the pool, one of the cops (Bobby) mutters lewdly: 'Did the earth move?'

'8.2 on the Richter scale,' spits Fitz. 'And those Krauts are accurate.'

He interviews the victim with great sensitivity. First he establishes the basic MO to align it with previous attacks. Did he wear a mask? Yes. Did he put a hood over her head? Yes.

'Was there anything else?' asks Fitz. 'Sometimes, when someone is raped, things happen. Things that are very difficult to talk about. Was there something like that?'

Under Fitz's gentle probing she reveals that he combed her pubic hair afterwards.

The intermediate scene reveals that Floyd's victim is the wife of his minicab boss. It is some kind of power/revenge trip.

DCI Wise tells his boys to round up all the usual suspects, anyone with previous convictions for rape or sexually motivated attacks. This gives Beck and Co. carte blanche to go hunting for 'perverts'. They treat them all very roughly.

Beck, in particular, is very edgy. He has developed a very unhealthy pallor and his eyes have a glazed appearance. Is he cracking up? He is still suffering from guilt at the death of Bilborough and it brings out his worst side – his racism, his sexism.

Fitz knows the score on the attacker. 'So he combed your hair to get rid of his own. He dragged you into the pool to remove traces of his own semen.' Fitz deduces that he has been caught before and knows police procedure in these matters.

Penhaligon arrives at Fitz's house and asks to come in. She wants to explain about Peter, her old boyfriend with whom she was dancing. Fitz is immediately on the attack.

'Did you sleep with him? No. Sorry. Ignore that.' He delivers a small stream-of-consciousness self-analysis of sexual jealousy, exposing the mechanics of the male mind before returning to irrational form.

'No, sorry, it's not working. The green-eyed monster's growling. Ignore the sodding brain. Did you sleep with that man?'

Coltrane has got the rhythm of these exchanges down to a tee. McGovern's trick of getting Fitz to blurt out his feelings, then explain

Once a chauffeur during the Edinburgh Film Festival, Coltrane can now enjoy being driven – especially after a night on the town.

A fine Coltrane caricature by Ron McTrusty of the *Evening Standard*

Never one to shy away from a little fancy dressing, Coltrane goes for gold as Alonso Turner in *Perfectly Normal* in the company of co-star Michael Riley.

Playing to the gallery: as the opera-loving conman Alonso Turner in *Perfectly Normal*.

Coltrane pontificates as Pope Dave 1 in *The Pope Must Die*.

Cross dressing is one thing but religious cross dressing is a bad habit to get into as Coltrane and Eric Idle discovered in *Nuns on the Run*.

Coltrane and Rhona Gemmell oblige the photographers at the BAFTA Awards ceremony in London.

One lump or two? Pope Dave 1 takes tea in *The Pope Must Die* – which was retitled *The Pope Must Diet* in the U.S. to avoid offending Catholic sensibilities.

The trouble with cars today is that they're just not built for the man with the fuller figure. There is just never a vintage Cadillac around when you need one.

Coltrane and Eddie Izzard exchange views on the finer points of sartorial culture. Brown is the new black. And the boots, dear, the boots!

One of the planes in *Coltrane's Planes and Automobiles* flies a little too close for comfort.

Portrait of the actor sneaking a forbidden ciggie.

Right Above Not averse to expressing his opinions in public Coltrane airs his views on paparazzi who insist on getting the 'back seat' shot.
Right Below Sporting the latest thing in villainous facial hair – grown for his role in *The World Is Not Enough* – Coltrane accompanies Rhona Gemmell at the *Evening Standard* Film Awards.

Fitz and Bilborough (Christopher Eccleston) in one of their many head-to-head confrontations. In spite of the fact that Bilborough brought Fitz onto the team, his honest coppering was often at odds with Fitz's mercurial methods.

Fitz and Judith (Barbara Flynn) in a rare moment of marital harmony following the birth of their new baby in *Brotherly Love*. Normal service was resumed shortly thereafter.

them rationally, only to snap back into the emotional again is a clever device and one that suits Coltrane's particular style perfectly. Without needing to slip into a different accent or a funny voice, Coltrane can actually play two characters in one speech – a sort of dialogue between Rational, Intellectual Fitz and Irrational, Emotional Fitz.

Fitz has also spoken with Peter, to whom he refers as 'Fidel'. Not because he looks like Castro, one gathers, but because he is ever faithful to Penhaligon in spite of her errant ways with Fitz.

'He said you're a dirty old man, Fitz. The grave is beckoning and it's your last chance to get your hands on some firm young flesh,' Penhaligon scoffs.

Back at the pool, Beck and Bobby arrive to find Fitz and Penhaligon questioning James, the caretaker. Beck hauls him away in spite of Fitz's protestations that James is not the culprit. In a very funny sequence, Fitz and Penhaligon, Bobby and Beck march along with the hapless James between them while Fitz explains why James isn't the man. The man they are looking for, says Fitz, only rapes the kind of woman he is used to or to whom he aspires.

'Whereas James aspires to nothing and nobody. The man's a non-entity. He gets letters from *Readers' Digest* telling him he has not been included in the draw. Besides, the man we're looking for can swim, whereas...'

Without warning, Fitz pushes James into the pool, where he flounders fully clothed. Beck has to jump in and save him. It's a very funny scene and it looks as if Coltrane enjoyed it. There is a benign sadism about him that is perfect for Fitz. He'll do anything to prove he is right. Anything.

Later, Mark returns home and goes into the bathroom to walk straight into Penhaligon coming out dressed only in a towel. He and Fitz have a father and son chat – though, as usual, it is not altogether clear who is the father and who the son.

'Do you want Mum back?' asks Mark.

'Most of the time, yeah,' says Fitz with his usual candour. But he also wants the 'firm young flesh' of Penhaligon.

James the caretaker is then attacked by someone unseen and given a good kicking.

In a deceptively uncomfortable scene, all the cops, Fitz and

Penhaligon included, are at the pub enjoying an after-work drink and exchanging bawdy tales, rape jokes and other sexually offensive remarks. Penhaligon attempts to join in but the laugh dies in her throat. Fitz is again made to feel like an outsider, by Beck especially, who clearly wants to pick a fight.

Beck's assertion that women allow themselves to be raped ('You can't thread a moving needle') is too much for Penhaligon, however, who defends her sex and says he is talking garbage.

'Do you fantasize about rape?' asks Beck aggressively.

Penhaligon leaves the table. Wise goes over to her and tells her to rejoin her mates. He encourages her to be one of the 'boys'. 'Forget your feminists and hairy-arsed lesbians.'

Beck brings in the rape victim's husband for questioning on the attack on James. Wise and Fitz interrogate him.

'He's in intensive care. He's lying there like a cabbage,' says Wise.

'Well, he can't be that bad if he's doing impressions,' riposte Fitz. In spite of being in appalling taste, it is one of the funniest lines McGovern wrote for Coltrane.

'Bad taste?' he continues. And of course, it's his entrée into the husband, a method of getting to grips with him. He susses the guy out completely. It's not that he has to prove something to his wife, or himself, but to other men.

Fitz then goes into listening mode while the husband attempts to explain himself. 'I know exactly what you're feeling,' says Fitz. 'It's not very nice. It's not very PC.'

After a reconstruction of an earlier rape, Penhaligon drops off the victim at her block of flats and is attacked on the way back to her car. She is brutally raped. At first sight, it appears to be the work of the same guy. But some details are different.

Fitz is still hammering away at the husband. Finally, through the extensive use of empathy and all the other psychological tricks he keeps up his capacious sleeves, he gets him to confess to the attack on James.

As Penhaligon drives back from the scene of the rape clearly in some distress, Fitz is back on the radio with his phone-in programme. Floyd is on the phone to him with an affected Jamaican accent. He is responding to Fitz's remarks about rape and rapists, about the possibility of detection, that rapists will always be caught and that there is not much difference – in the sentencing – between rape and murder. He asks Fitz if the rapist should kill his victims.

'Show me a man and I'll show you a potential rapist ... I am one, for God's sake,' says Fitz before the caller is cut off.

Wise finds Penhaligon at her flat and she tells him she's been raped by the guy they are looking for. The knife and the mask lead her to the mistaken conclusion. Wise is shocked and as sympathetic as he can be. It's a terrific scene and lays the tone for the remainder of the story. Fitz, meanwhile, is preparing for a night of passion with Penhaligon by putting champagne in an ice bucket by the bed. He tries to phone Penhaligon but her line is constantly busy. The ironies are now coming thick and fast.

Penhaligon goes through the same series of tests experienced by the other rape victims. Then she goes home and burns all the clothes she was wearing at the time.

Fitz shows up, totally oblivious to what has happened, and starts making jokes about burning bras. His accidental crassness is, of course, toe-curling, although he is completely innocent in his ignorance of what has occurred.

'You're not going to burn that bra, are you? That's a bit Sixties, isn't it?' he quips. Receiving no answer, he blunders on. 'Oh well. Personally I'm greatly in favour of women's movements. I hate it when they just lie there. I think your phone's off the hook.'

She rebuffs him, and not gently. 'Hey hey hey,' he says, bewildered at her response. Coltrane has got the bewildered and baffled look down pat now. It's a particular Fitz quality that as a selfish, arrogant, know-all he cannot comprehend that he cannot comprehend. Knowing he is right is everything to Fitz; not knowing is anathema. He hates being mystified almost as much as he hates being wrong.

This has curdled to frustrated rage by the time he gets home, and he attacks Mark for having smelly feet and for not tidying the place up.

'You know you could be a member of the Lost Generation ... Personally, I think you're just a bone idle git!'

A black girl comes to the door to talk to Fitz. She has heard him on the radio and tells him she was an early victim of the rapist. She describes what happened, and it is clearly the same MO. She tells Fitz the perpetrator is black. She could tell by his voice.

In the police station, Wise and Fitz are waddling along a corridor. Fitz insists the rapist is black. Wise corrects him.

'Penhaligon says he's white. She should know.'

'Why?' asks Fitz. 'Why should Penhaligon know?'

Wise: 'Haven't you heard?'

Fitz: 'What?'

Wise: 'He raped her.'

This news hits Fitz right between the eyes. Everything falls into place, but at what a cost. Coltrane simply gapes; for once Fitz is speechless. This is another of the very rare occasions when Fitz is rendered completely helpless. Waiting for Penhaligon, he gives a little futile gesture of helplessness with his meaty hands. 'I wish you'd told me,' he says.

Fitz is at sea. He hesitates at the door of the office where Penhaligon is giving her deposition and – unusually for him – knocks before entering. Looking sheepish, he hesitates before taking his seat opposite Penhaligon. He is polite, courteous, shamed.

'Do you mind if I ask you something? You told your boss he was white?'

Penhaligon confirms her observation.

Fitz goes for broke.

'It's not the same man. The man we're looking for is black.'

Just to make sure he is right, he goes through the scene with her. Did he use water? No. It's a different MO.

'It's someone you know. That's why he didn't want you to hear his voice.'

Fitz gets it on the nose right away, causing Beck to fulminate about it being a load of bollocks.

Down at the DHSS office, Floyd pushes his claim one stage too far. The DHSS officer knows he has been driving a van and advises him to withdraw his claim. 'I know where you live,' says Floyd and leaves.

Fitz knocks on Penhaligon's door. She refuses to open it.

'I want to be alone.'

'Great Garbo.'

'Before my time.' She opens the door, nonetheless.

This is a beautifully acted scene by Coltrane and Somerville. It's not what is said so much as what is left unsaid. The baggage they both carry weighs heavily in every small gesture and nuance.

'I'm so sorry,' says Fitz on seeing her. Then, 'May I?' He holds out his arms, uncertain of the response. She allows him to hug her but pulls away after a short while. Pushing him away. He is, after all, a man.

'I want my dad,' she says, heartbreakingly. 'I blame you.'

Fitz is gradually regaining control. He slips imperceptibly into professional mode.

'I'm listening,' he says.

'You think it's someone I know.'

'Yes.'

'Then he's seen me with you. Overweight. Skint. Drunk. Middle-aged...'

'If she'll go with him she's anybody's.'

'Yeah.'

Fitz is almost back in control now. He risks a joke. 'I'll get you a white stick for when we're out together in public.'

She's not buying. She wants him to leave. But Fitz seizes his opportunity. He tells her to clench her fists, tightly. 'Trust me.' He tells her to imagine all her pain and anger in her fists. In spite of herself, she obeys. 'Tighter, tighter, tighter...'

Fitz comes good with some psychological healing. Fabulous.

A blonde woman (Deborah) we have seen in the back of Floyd's cab arrives home. She can't find her cat. The cat is shut in the lavatory with the lid closed. She releases him and comes face to face with the masked rapist. Alarmingly, Floyd pulls off his mask and reveals his face to her. She is the DHSS bloke's wife. We fear the worst.

'I've got to do it. I've got to hurt your husband.'

The next scene is one of the most unusual in the entire series. McGovern attempts an experiment which I am not sure is wholly successful. He lets us inside Fitz's head while he is making deductions from his analysis of Penhaligon. He takes her – via a process of hypnotherapy – through the events of the rape. He gets her to remember things, sounds, smells, details. 'I won't let anyone harm you. I promise. I promise,' he says to her.

As she describes the smell of leather gloves, whisky and cigarettes on his breath and an aftershave, we hear Fitz's thoughts on the soundtrack.

Fitz (VO): 'He's hurt someone I care about deeply. I'm going to catch this man. Leather gloves, drinks whisky. He's not short of money. He's got quite a decent job.'

Fitz tells her to remember the smell. It is the key to his identity.

'You will remember this smell. Remember this till we find him. And we will find him, believe me.' Fitz's assurance is given with more passion than usual. This time, it's personal.

Floyd is picked up by cops who want to book him for illegally soliciting fares on the street. Thinking they are after him for the rapes, he begins to laugh.

Later, at home, Fitz answers the phone. It's Floyd, who tells him he took his advice. If it is possible to enact a chill running down your spine, Coltrane does it here.

'I didn't give you any advice.'

Fitz is very alarmed but even so he doesn't forget his professional side. He retains the presence of mind to ask the caller if he raped anyone the previous evening in Bellvale, where Penhaligon was attacked. Floyd says: 'No.'

'You black?' asks Fitz, but it's a question too far. Floyd hangs up.

Now Fitz gets the blame for Deborah's murder. She is found in the bath, raped and murdered. The husband is distraught. Wise blames Fitz for being reckless on the radio. The husband addresses Fitz: 'Why kill her? He didn't kill the others. Why kill her?'

Fitz is laden down with guilt by this time. As if he didn't have enough. And, being a lapsed Catholic, he has nowhere to unburden it. No confessional, no absolution. This is part of the key to Fitz's character and his pattern of behaviour. As a result even Fitz is reduced to the simple level of his fellow police officers: 'We're going to get this man.'

Things are unravelling. Penhaligon won't answer to Fitz that night and he sadly takes the cab home, his face a mixture of guilt, pain, loss and helplessness.

Meanwhile, Beck is cracking up so badly he has telephoned the Samaritans. He is explaining about Bilborough's death and how he interviewed the killer before it occurred. He blames himself for having compassion for a man he thought had cancer.

'I showed a bit of compassion, you see,' he says. 'Compassion only gets you killed.' This is a marvellous piece of work by Cranitch, whose only equal in portraying this type of cop is the immortal Dennis Frantz from *Hill Street Blues* and *NYPD Blue*, in which he plays Sipowicz.

Following a series of heavy emotional scenes, McGovern lightens things up a little, before plunging us into the depths awaiting us at the conclusion of this story.

Fitz arrives home to find Mark and his pals hanging around outside the house. Fitz sees the car and asks: 'Is your mother here?'

Mark: 'Yeah. I think you're going to need a drink.'

He finds Katie on the phone and gives her a hug. As he walks away she says to her friend, explaining the interruption: 'It's only my dad.' Coltrane's reaction to that is an absolute picture.

But more surprises are to come. Judith is unpacking a box. She stands up. We see Fitz's face change from guarded pleasure to open-mouthed astonishment. It's an Oh My God moment.

Judith is very clearly pregnant. 'Five months,' she says.

Fitz, of course, pours a big drink. He starts calculating.

'I'll save you the arithmetic,' says Judith. 'It's yours.'

They hug each other. Then they circle around each other like old lovers and enemies. These are people who know each other too well.

'Are you pleased?' asks Judith.

Fitz says he is.

'Pleased about the baby or pleased that I've come back?'

'Both.'

Judith isn't fooled. 'I love you when you lie. When you're kind enough to lie.'

By this time, the police, with the help of a nosy old lady who took down the number of the minicab cruising past the murdered woman's house, are now fully aware that Floyd is the man they are after. Wise gets it immediately: 'You know what this means?' he says to Beck. 'Fitz was right. Penhaligon was raped by someone else.'

Fitz uses Penhaligon to break down Floyd's mother, Mrs Malcolm, by describing what happened to her. It's a device he has used before, but never on an occasion requiring such a sacrifice. He sits listening with his head in his hands.

'It can't be easy knowing that this ... this monster came out of your womb. Sorry, did that hurt you?'

Fitz is on absolutely solid ground now. He knows what he is doing. He just needs an explanation from Floyd's mother that will give the key to his motive. 'Every rapist, every killer in the world blames their mother, Mrs Malcolm. And it's all bullshit.'

He asks her if he has a scar of some kind. She tells him he was ashamed of being black and wanted to be white, like her. One day when he was nine she found him sitting in a bath of bleach.

When the cops go to arrest Floyd they catch him in the shower. Sure enough, his legs and posterior are hideously scarred.

Fitz is helping Judith take a mattress upstairs. He is being very solicitous. For once, Fitz is being a good guy; the baby and the vulnerability of his wife are making a new man of him. So far.

Just at this moment, Penhaligon – with spectacularly bad timing – comes to the door. The look that passes between Fitz and Penhaligon and their behaviour is immediately spotted by Judith, who, after all, has had the benefit of Fitz's training. She knows immediately.

'You're screwing her.'

Fitz, ever honest, looks down shamefacedly. 'I was. Yes.'

'Mark knows.'

Judith is shocked at how young Penhaligon is. Fitz launches into a self-analysis, pouring it out for Judith's benefit. It's the nearest thing he's got to a confession. Having unburdened himself, he says: 'Did I miss something out?'

'Do you love her?' asks Judith.

Fitz tries to sneer but it doesn't quite work. Coltrane reveals much in this; Fitz is in deep trouble. Caught between two women he 'cares about deeply'.

Penhaligon drives Fitz very fast in the rain with the wipers off. She scares the living shit out of him.

'Will you please slow down. I'm allergic to accidents. They bring me out in bumps.'

Back at the police station, Fitz goes straight for Floyd's jugular. He attacks him where he's weakest: his colour. He draws him out, empathizing with him as the fat boy at school who was always picked on; just like the coloured boy. Gradually, painfully, Fitz breaks him down.

'I know what you are thinking, Floyd. Look at me. Look at me!' he says. At this moment, Coltrane is very tough indeed. The look he gives Floyd on these last two commands is quite compelling and absolutely terrifying. For the first time in the series, Coltrane reveals – if only for a moment – something naked about Fitz. Underneath that cool, wisecracking, slippery, attractive exterior, lurks a real killer.

Fitz gets Floyd to the point of confessing when Wise comes in to say that his lawyer has arrived. Fitz is absolutely furious. He rages at Wise. Floyd is allowed to leave.

Beck arrives back at the station, having been to Bilborough's baby's christening. He is clearly very upset. Penhaligon hugs him and smells the aftershave. She knows he is the one who raped her. He tries to deny it, put on a brave face. She tells Wise, who wants evidence. He sees real trouble brewing for all of them. Matters are coming to a head.

Out in the main office Fitz is spouting forth. 'He's going to rape again. If not the previous victim, it will be the wife of some man he's got a grudge against. A white man.'

Suddenly, Fitz realizes what he is saying and rings Judith. She's OK. There is loud music coming from Mark's room, where he is canoodling with his girlfriend. In the background, Penhaligon is becoming increasingly distressed. This is a brilliantly choreographed scene, with several different dramatic signals being given at once. Everything that Fitz says now has an indirect effect on Penhaligon, especially the call to his wife.

A call comes in. Floyd has abandoned his car in Charlotte Road. Fitz is on full alert.

'That's my road. Phone my wife!' He runs for the door. Or at least does a passable imitation of running.

Fitz enters his house warily. He sees Floyd with a knife at Judith's throat. Coltrane looks down, so as not to challenge Floyd in the eyes, but also to avoid eye contact with Judith. He knows what he has to do.

'What do you want, Floyd?'

'You'll write about me one of these days.'

'Oh yes.'

Then Fitz plays his ace. He tells Floyd to kill her. 'We've been married over twenty years, I'm sick of it.' Judith is horrified. They move into the hall. Fitz keeps up the contemptuous babble as cops begin to surround Floyd. Mark is on the stairs just above him and smashes him over the head with a bottle. Fitz grabs Judith and Mark and hugs them to him. It's over.

Not quite.

Penhaligon is in Beck's house. She has found a gun, an old Colt .45 Peacemaker. Beck arrives and Penhaligon makes him lie down. She puts the gun barrel in his mouth.

As Fitz watches Floyd being led away, the phone rings. He picks it up. There is no answer. He waits.

'Who is this, please?' he asks.

'Jane Penhaligon. I need to speak to you.'

Fitz half turns towards the camera. Having just managed to save his wife from certain death he has another imminent crisis on his hands. And it's still personal.

STORY 7 (SEASON 3) 1995
Brotherly Love

Directed by Roy Battersbury from a script by Jimmy McGovern, this is one of the most controversial *Cracker* stories and brought howls of protest from viewers who considered it blasphemous or simply too violent for television.

It opens with Fitz in the back of a taxi reading the various signs prohibiting smoking, drinking, eating and putting feet on seats. As an act of defiance which is second nature to him, Fitz lights a cigarette. He is *en route* to the clinic where Jimmy Beck is 'resting' following a minor breakdown. At first, we think Fitz is just visiting, but it soon becomes clear he is on a mission.

'Why did you rape her?'

'Who?'

'Jane Penhaligon.'

'I didn't.'

Beck is in deep denial and Fitz knows it. Outside, on the streets of

Manchester, prostitutes barter with kerb-crawlers. One of them agrees to a 'Shirley Temple' and haggles over the price.

Beck and Fitz are talking at cross purposes. Intriguingly, as we near the end of the entire series, the close-ups become increasingly brutal. Often it's as if we are inside the character's minds, so close to their eyes do we get.

Also, Fitz's appearance has been subtly altered. His clothes are the same but his face and, particularly, his hair have become undeniably sexier. He looks, at the beginning of this story at least, like a man whose confidence has returned big time. It's a subtle juxtaposition; as Beck becomes greyer and more wild-eyed, Fitz looks better and better. It is almost as if Fitz were sucking the life out of Beck; an emotional vampire. Which isn't so very far from what Penhaligon called him in an earlier episode -'an emotional rapist'. Maybe this is Fitz's secret. If so, it's a profoundly disturbing one.

Beck uses spite to get at Fitz, telling him he screwed Penhaligon in the past, as did Bilborough. He reminds Fitz about that 'little tattoo on the inside of her thigh. You've kissed that tattoo, felt the hairs tickle your cheek.' Fitz doesn't want to believe this, but it is evident that the seed of doubt has been planted.

As Fitz leaves and is about to get into the cab, Beck sneers, 'Give her my love. And a big kiss.' Fitz cannot help himself. He nuts Beck in the nose and gets into the cab. The taxi driver says: 'If you want to smoke, you smoke.'

Given the fact that we have never seen Fitz demean himself by resorting to serious physical violence, this is a real shock. And all the more for the fact that Coltrane delivers the blow with what seems like professional ease.

Meanwhile, Jean, a prostitute, and Dave Harvey, her client, are arguing about money. Dave can't get any out of the ATM and she comes into his house while he is trying to get it from his wife, Maggie (Brid Brennan). Incensed that she should walk in, Dave drives her to a remote spot and beats her up very badly.

Fitz knocks at Penhaligon's door. All jokes are off now. This is serious. 'I've been to see Jimmy Beck,' he says.

'You weren't around when I needed you, Fitz,' she replies. 'I had to cope on my own.'

Fitz bites the bullet. You can see the doubt eating away at him. If only Coltrane were a different colour, he'd make a terrific Othello.

'I have to ask you this. Did you and Jimmy Beck, you know, ever …' he can't bring himself to say it. It is intense, awkward stuff. And surprisingly, Coltrane has rarely looked sexier than at this moment.

Dave is having a row with his brother, a local priest, Father Michael. Michael tells him he must inform his wife.

Having been through a hellish evening, Fitz returns home to find the entire family gathered in the living-room. He immediately senses trouble. 'What are you doing here? What's up? Is it Ma?' He fumbles for the whisky bottle. Any lingering doubts about Coltrane's ability to express intense emotion without 'acting' all over the place are dispelled in this scene and the story that follows.

'Don't say anything. It's bad news, I know that. I'm clutching at straws here. Serious illness? Operation required?'

Danny, Fitz's brother, tells it straight: 'She's dead.'

Coltrane flinches as if he's been struck. He tries to recover his composure with a typical Fitz tactic, by going on the offensive. And with grief and anger, his Scottish accent becomes more pronounced: 'How did you not phone me?' he says. Danny (Clive Russell) tells him he was never around, never went to see her. Fitz has to fall back on fraternal insult: 'You always were a sanctimonious wee shite.'

There are no jokes here. Coltrane – indeed, all of the assembled cast – are in deadly earnest. It is absolutely terrific drama.

A little later, Judith finds Fitz weeping on his own. She comforts him. But Fitz's burden of guilt comes pouring out in torrents. 'Grief's delicious, isn't it? Life's boring, banal. And then a parent dies and at last there's a genuine emotion, a profound emotion and you savour it. It's delicious.'

This speech, it has to be said, looks more like a writer's expression when written down than an authentic expression of grief. But in Coltrane's mouth it is completely credible.

The prostitute's body is found on waste ground. Fitz arrives sucking from a can of beer. He looks terrible. When DCI Wise remarks on his appearance, Fitz says simply: 'My mum died last night.' Wise backs off. 'Sorry, Fitz,' he says.

With almost offensive disdain, Fitz assesses the scene. There is a chisel embedded in the woman's vagina. Fitz shrugs. 'Prostitute,' he says.

Fitz and Danny see the priest – Father Michael (David Calder) – to arrange the funeral. They disagree over the details. Fitz doesn't want communion. 'Don't look at me like that.'

Back in the police station, Wise tells everyone that Jimmy Beck is coming back the next morning. Penhaligon rushes to the loo and is violently sick.

When Beck comes in the following morning, Wise crassly attempts to break the ice and keep things smooth. Penhaligon is very unhappy. Fitz looks on aghast.

Penhaligon and Beck are in the car; she questions him, asks him why he pulled the trigger when she put the gun in his mouth. He realizes she has a hidden tape recorder and goes mad. Later, while questioning a tramp, Beck is attacked and has his arm broken.

Fitz sets to work getting under Dave's skin. Fitz knows he is lying but pretends he thinks he is innocent. Dave reveals aspects of his visits to prostitutes which are overheard by his wife, Maggie.

'You have a wife. You have children. You wouldn't have unprotected sex with a prostitute.'

'Unprotected?' breathes Maggie.

'You Catholic? Me too. I'm totally convinced that you're innocent. We're not the most adventurous of people, sexually, I mean, are we? Personally, I've done it twice with the lights on, but that's just me being risqué...'

If there is one aspect of McGovern's scripts that Coltrane has really got the measure of, it's his use of industrial strength irony.

Dave is banged up. But while he is inside, another prostitute is horrifyingly attacked.

Meanwhile, Fitz is quizzing Maggie and he is being brutal. Part of his problem is the Catholic angle. As a lapsed Catholic, he views her devout following of the religion as responsible for all the frustrations and repressions that have caused the problems.

He moves on to Dave and unlocks him on the subject of married sex. Coltrane is very good here, knows his way around the subject, plays it light but is actually fuelled with contempt and loathing. Watching this interrogation closely, I realized that Coltrane was playing a warped variation on Satan's temptation of Christ in the Wilderness. The moment he whispers in Dave's ear, 'Say you did it ...', with an expression of almost obscene cunning on his face, is absolutely chilling. There is something perverse about it, almost as if Fitz was getting some kind of sexual satisfaction from it. Once again, Coltrane is subjected to the kind of close-up that might as well be an X-ray.

When the other prostitute dies in hospital, the pathologist concludes it was the same MO as the first, down to the chisel, and says it must be the same killer. Wise tells him it's impossible.

Penhaligon calls for Fitz and encounters Judith. In an attempt to undermine Fitz's image in her eyes, Judith says: 'He's on the lavatory picking winners.' It's a very bitchy line. When Fitz looks over the banisters and sees them, his eyes roll heavenwards. 'Beam me up, Scotty.'

The DNA report on the two murdered prostitutes reveals that they both contained the same semen. Wise is totally nonplussed. 'How do you murder a woman from behind bars?' 'Voodoo?' ripostes Fitz, who's paying more attention to the discussion taking place across the office between Judith and Penhaligon.

In a flight of pure fancy (and McGovern's logic goes AWOL in this story), Fitz proposes that brothers might have the same DNA. He knows the wife, Maggie, is the link to all this and goes after her. But she is tougher than she looks. She tells him there has been a mistake.

'A mistake,' roars Fitz. 'You call murder a mistake?' He then puts the boot into Father Michael, claiming that he has known all along about her husband's extra-marital visits. 'Father Michael has known for years, he's just not bothered to tell you.'

In this way, Fitz kills two birds with one stone: he is getting Maggie unnerved and suspicious about her husband while also eroding the foundations of her faith.

Fitz then goes to see Father Michael and begins by asking him to take his confession. This is one of the most famous – and oft-quoted – scenes in *Cracker*. Secretly, of course, Fitz wants to interrogate the priest.

'A few grubby sins to get off my soul. And it won't be a two-minute job with a damp sponge. More like two weeks' sandblasting.'

He confesses to adultery. 'Does your wife know?' asks Father

Michael. Strangely, Fitz is unprepared for the question and is somewhat taken aback.

'Yes. I am sorry about that. I'm sorry I hurt my wife.'

'Anything else?'

'I drink too much. I smoke too much. I gamble too much. I *am* too
much.'

Fitz then tosses a grenade into the conversation. Will he still be
absolved, he wonders, if the priest is involved in murder? Father
Michael ignores him.

'Why do you drink?' asks Father Michael.

'I'm easily bored.'

'Bullshit. So many drunks tell me that.'

Fitz is genuinely shocked at the priest's language and the vehemence
of his reply. By the end of the 'confession', Fitz is as cynical as ever
about the Church but he's quite as sure of himself over the priest.

The next big scene, and one of the most sustained and poignant
sequences in the entire series, is Fitz's mother's funeral. Fitz and Danny
are the leading pallbearers and Fitz even takes communion without a
fuss. Then he stands up to give an address to the congregation. In the
course of studying Coltrane's work for this book, I do not think I have
seen him do anything to equal this particular scene. So emotionally
honest is it, so brilliant a depiction of a man remembering his mother,
that I can hardly believe it was actually scripted. Coltrane pitches it
perfectly, stammering slightly, rambling awkwardly and losing his
place in an anecdote, struggling to maintain the empathy of the gathering. It is riddled with the embarrassment, affection, pity, guilt and
remembered joy that anyone who has ever witnessed a similar eulogy –
or, indeed, delivered one – will recognize as completely authentic. It
is a simply mind-blowing piece of acting and is alone worth all the
awards showered on *Cracker* and Coltrane.

After the funeral, during which the congregation also, hilariously,
play bingo, the mourners retire to the pub. Fitz and Danny become
progressively drunk and start rowing with each other. Fitz is awash in
self-pity and drunken, tearful rage and recrimination.

Meanwhile, Maggie has murdered another prostitute, brutally,
bloodily. Danny and Fitz, having sort of made it up, are annoying
passengers on a bus. A little while later, Fitz is in hospital having a

minor head wound attended to. 'I got hit by a mobile phone,' he quips. 'It was more mobile than I thought.' As the nurse plunges a needle into his behind, he yelps.

Things are now occurring thick and fast. Judith has gone into labour and Fitz assists at the birth. She wants Fitz to swear that he'll never gamble again. Unwisely, he does. It's a boy. Fitz is beside himself with pride.

As Danny takes pictures of Fitz and Judith and the family, Penhaligon arrives to drag him off to another murder scene. There is a wonderful exchange in the car.

'He's lovely,' says Penhaligon, warily.

'Got a fair-sized willie, too,' says Fitz.

'Well, never mind. He's got your eyes.'

'Seven pounds twelve ounces. That's the whole baby, of course. Not just the willie.' It's mischievous, priceless.

Penhaligon and another female cop disguise themselves as prostitutes to lure the killer out. As they stand in the police station, subjected to the usual ribald comments of their colleagues, Penhaligon challenges Beck on his relationship with one of the prostitutes. Beck stayed with her the night before because he was lonely. Penhaligon is merciless, humiliating Beck in front of everyone. Fitz watches the exchange with increasing alarm. He doesn't care for it. Even for him, this is sadistic.

Fitz takes Beck out for a drink and seems really concerned for his health. He pushes him to confess, to the extent that Beck hyperventilates and has a seizure. After helping him recover, Fitz listens as Beck finally fesses up.

The tables are turned once again. Fitz is the priest, the pub is his confessional. Beck makes him swear on the life of his newborn child not to tell anyone. He confesses that he raped Penhaligon. Fitz now carries Beck's guilt as well as his own considerable burden, but he doesn't betray Beck. He obeys the rule of the confessional, the patient/doctor vow of secrecy.

When Fitz and Danny are going over the contents of their mother's house and Danny offers Fitz a cheque for half of the proceeds from the sale (Fitz wants cash), he suddenly realizes, looking at the teacups, that the murderer is a woman. He gets on the phone to Wise, who is still tailing Father Michael. 'It's Maggie bloody Harvey,' he screams. 'Who else could it be, for God's sake?'

Beck manages to get there first and just saves the latest victim from Maggie's murderous attack.

Back at home, Fitz is eavesdropping on Judith, who is quizzing Mark on Penhaligon. Danny comes to the door with a bundle of cash for Fitz. He is full of contempt for his brother.

'You know everybody respects you. Everybody respects good old dependable Dan. But nobody loves you.'

Danny looks Fitz straight between the eyes. 'Nobody ever pitied my wife,' he says. It gets Fitz right where it hurts.

Fitz interrogates Maggie. In a very long scene, Coltrane and Brid Brennan collide and collude in an exchange of quiet, lethal intensity. Finally, she confesses to the murder of all three prostitutes. Fitz knows she is lying. Her husband killed the first one.

When it is clear that Dave Harvey is going to be released, all hell breaks loose in the station. Things come boiling to a head with Beck and Penhaligon, prompting Fitz to interrupt in an uncanny impersonation of Ricky Tomlinson's scouser accent: 'Hey, calm down. Calm down.'

But it's too late. Beck goes home and loads his gun. After a visit to Father Michael, Fitz goes home and picks up the cash. 'I'm going to make my mother a millionaire,' he says. Judith is furious. 'You promised you wouldn't gamble again.'

'This doesn't count,' says Fitz with the logic of the terminal addict.

Judith cries after him: 'Cheap sentimentality. Cheap sentimentality'

Beck picks up David Harvey in the street and 'arrests' him. He drags Harvey up to the roof of the Ramada Hotel, from where he says they are both going to jump because they are 'both guilty'.

Fitz and Penhaligon arrive first. Fitz takes the lift, Penhaligon the stairs. Confronting Beck on the roof, Penhaligon listens while Beck confesses he raped her. He gives a dying man's statement (just like his hero, Bilborough) before grabbing Harvey and plunging with him to their deaths.

Fitz pulls Penhaligon back from the edge and holds her as she wails in the agony of emotional release.

STORY 8 (SEASON 3) 1995
Best Boys

The penultimate *Cracker* three-parter, *Best Boys*, was scripted by Paul Abbott and directed by Colin McDougall. It opens with a young man, Bill Nash, being chased by girls around a factory floor and being debagged. The giggling women are introducing themselves to the new work experience person.

A tolling bell is heard on the soundtrack and a funeral procession appears. Among the floral tributes, one reads 'Jimmy'. It's the funeral of Jimmy Beck, Penhaligon's rapist, who jumped to his death at the conclusion of the previous story.

Fellow officers ask Penhaligon if she's OK. Fitz strides up, black suit crumpled, tie askew and puts on his Sean Connery voice: 'Oh for God's sake, Miss Moneypenny . . . you're a sour-faced bimbo.' Getting no response, he carries on as normal: 'Oh, come on. You must be fed up with all the platitudes, aren't you? They blame you anyway. You were there when it happened. But you didn't stop him jumping. Say it. Say it loud and be proud. I helped him to die. The Eddie the Eagle of the law enforcement agency.'

Coltrane's abrasive delivery and Abbott's hard-nosed humour gel perfectly here. He totally dominates the proceedings in an attempt to shift the mood away from guilt and self-recrimination.

At the wake Fitz stays off the booze, drinking water instead, until he meets Beck's sister. Surprisingly, she is rather attractive and wants to talk to Fitz. She tells him they didn't have frequent contact; he barely wrote letters and called infrequently.

'But,' she continues, 'your name came up most often. I just wanted to put a face to a friend.'

Is she being ironic? Coltrane gives a look which suggests he isn't quite sure if she's taking the piss. She could be telling the truth.

'To be honest,' she continues, 'I imagined you were Austrian. Fitz. Fitz the shrink. You obviously made an impact on him.'

Fitz is not sure how to react to this. In a fabulous close-up we see his eyes are suspicious but he makes the decision to tread carefully.

'We talked at length about many things,' he says, licking his lips in the hope that she won't ask him to be more specific. It is an interesting tête-à-tête, not only because it puts Fitz in a position where he considers it better to hide the truth for fear of hurting someone, but also because he is on the verge of a flirtation with a woman who is neither Penhaligon nor Judith.

Meanwhile, Penhaligon is getting pissed and starts becoming aggressive about wanting a promotion. Unaware of what is going on behind him, Fitz is trying to answer Beck's sister's questions as discreetly as possible.

'Did Jimmy go wrong?' she asks.

Fitz waits a long time before replying: 'Yeah.'

'Badly wrong?'

'Yes.'

When the sister tells him she's a barrister, Fitz splutters: 'Barrister? He told me you were a nurse.' Another example of poor old Beck's low self-esteem. A copper and a nurse are somehow more equal siblings than a copper and a barrister, especially as in Beck's case the barrister is the woman.

'Will you have a drink with me, Fitz?' she says, appreciative of his honesty.

Fitz, just happy he's got through it, replies: 'I'll have a double malt, thanks.'

It's a great exchange, very intimate – and is interrupted by Penhaligon shouting. Fitz stands, reluctantly taking leave of Beck's sister. 'Sorry, I'm going to have to go. It was really nice to meet you.' Amazingly enough, there is a sincerity in this remark that we have rarely heard in Fitz. Also, there doesn't appear to be any ulterior motive. It's as if Fitz has matured, is more centred, more solid in his family environment than he has been for a long time.

This is borne out by the next scene, in which Penhaligon comes on strong with Fitz, asking him to come home with her. Fitz refuses. The way Coltrane lays it, he seems amazed at himself, shocked at his own sudden strength of will. Penhaligon, who likes to think she is in control, hits him. She's drunk, unhappy and Fitz has just refused her. It has not been a good night for her.

'Oh piss off, Fitz. Just piss off.'

At the factory, there has been some kind of break-in. Factory charge-hand Stewart Grady (Liam Cunningham) discovers Nash asleep in an ante-room and doesn't tell the police. He takes him home, where Nash hints at an attraction for Grady.

We then see Fitz unwrapping a large picture while Judith looks on sceptically.

'It's for you,' says Fitz, without getting much response. 'I think there is a protocol here. "Thank you, darling." And a stiff drink.'

Judith is unimpressed. Fitz cannot buy his way out of trouble. 'If your mother's money meant sod all, how grateful were you looking for?'

'Wrong, wrong,' says Fitz. 'I put the deposit on this just after our last huge telephone bill. I squandered money on this when we were almost skint as a present for you.'

'Shucks,' says Judith. 'You shouldn'a.' She isn't buying the guilt trip Fitz is attempting to sell off cheap.

Back at Grady's rooms, the landlady Mrs Franklin comes calling for the rent. She gets very nasty with Grady for underpaying her, then goes completely ballistic when she sees he has a young teenage boy in his room. She immediately takes him for a rent boy and tells them both to get out. In a rage, Nash stabs her but she tries to crawl to the phone. Unsure of what to do, Grady takes the knife and kills her. Now they are colleagues in crime, mated in murder.

They put her in the basement. The husband comes home and starts calling for her. He hears something coming from the basement and opens the door. She is still alive and they fall together down the steps into the basement. It's a mess.

By the time Fitz arrives on the scene, DCI Wise just wants to know whether the husband is capable of murder.

There is the now customary exchange of fire between Fitz and the police pathologist. Each thinks the other is a wanker. Fitz usually gets the upper hand by the sheer force of his observation.

There is a brief but telling scene of Judith with the new baby in a supermarket. She looks washed-out, distracted and keeps bumping into other customers with her trolley.

At the police station, the husband is brought in to see Fitz, who stands and applauds him as he enters. This is Fitz (and Coltrane) playing to the crowd, putting the husband on the spot. He holds out his hand.

'Put it there, boy. Every normal man's fantasy. Give the bitch what she really wants. And finally, finally show her who really is boss. Stick her in the ground and say I did that. Rot in gaol with all the other brave men.' Fitz is in heavy irony mode.

Fitz pushes him hard. Challenges him on the same ground as his own. 'No more gambling for you, boy. No more drinking.' Imagine Fitz's surprise to learn that the man neither gambles nor drinks. Christ, what does he do?

The husband shows Fitz his stomach. He has an implant to stop him from drinking. Fitz is truly taken aback. 'Sorry,' he mumbles.

Fitz tells Wise in the loo that he is not the man they want. These exchanges are always good value, as Ricky Tomlinson's bluff, Liverpudlian copper is the perfect foil for Coltrane, especially when he is getting on his high horse.

'I'm saying we're looking for two people,' says Fitz. 'And he's not one of them.'

'Here we go again,' says Wise. 'Russell bloody Grant. Nothing's ever straightforward with you, is it? I bet you even piss sideways.'

With a look of utter exasperation, Fitz walks out.

At the post-mortem, Fitz tells the pathologist how the death occurred, much to his annoyance. There are, he observes, two different kinds of wound.

Fitz then delivers his profile at the briefing but gets it slightly wrong. He tells the cops they are looking for a man and a woman. He then tries phoning Judith but gets the answerphone. Fitz is concerned, trying to behave responsibly in his role as a fresh parent.

The Chief Constable gives Fitz the benefit of his opinion: 'You're only here because you're good for publicity.'

Fitz sneers back: 'The results don't count for anything then?' If there is one way to hurt Fitz it is to impugn his professionalism and his ability to create the right profile. It is, perhaps, the one aspect of his catastrophic life in which he can take pride.

When he arrives home, he is dismayed to find that Judith has passed out on the sofa. It looks as if he is going to have to take on a greater sense of responsibility than even he imagined.

A black social worker comes to see Nash to find out what is going on. Nash is harrassing his former foster family, who sent him back when the wife unexpectedly became pregnant. Nash, the cuckoo in the nest, has developed an almost psychotic sense of rejection as a result. Pushed beyond endurance, Nash and Grady kill the social worker.

When Fitz hears of the latest victim's profession, he spits: 'Oh, a social worker. And you're looking for a motive?'

He begins to revise his opinion about the killers. It occurs to him that it is two men: possibly father and son? While he is speculating on this at the murder scene he hurriedly returns to his car and brings out the baby, Jimmy. In an extraordinary moment which reveals as much about Coltrane as it does about Fitz, he cuddles the baby and bottle feeds him while simultaneously continuing to deliver his profile of the killers. It is one of the funniest moments in *Cracker*. This is a new kind of Fitz.

In stark contrast, the following scene shows him in all his latent fury. Fitz is struggling with a recalcitrant social security officer who will not yield the dead man's diary. Fitz, who clearly hates this kind of do-gooder, describes in lurid detail the wounds inflicted on the man as the woman pales. 'We think one of your "clients" did it. Now can we see the diary please?' Needless to say, he gets it.

Fitz has all the makings of a first-class bully, and it is to Coltrane's credit that he allows this side to pop out wherever necessary and sometimes when it is inappropriate. It marks him as the adolescent who has never quite grown up enough to handle his responsibilities, but also as a cunning psychological operator. At times his tactics seem laudable; at others, appalling.

There is more fun in the following scene, with Fitz at home in a pinny ironing baby clothes. It is a deliberately ridiculous image, though it is tempered with the reality of Fitz's concern about Judith's increasingly erratic behaviour. Judith, however, goes for him. She's had it with Fitz's irresponsible ways. 'You want things to get better so we can get back to your terminal 26-year-old crisis.'

At the police briefing, Fitz is sure of his behavioural profile. 'I was right. All I'm saying is that these two have just met. These are star-crossed lovers. This is *Death in Venice* before the hair dye.' This is a deliberately esoteric reference to Visconti's film. Fitz knows full well that most of the cops in the room won't have a clue what he's on about. The audience, however, being intelligent, perceptive, cultivated and altogether cine-literate, will get the reference, which allows us to feel smug about ourselves. A cunning line, Mr Abbott, if indeed you did write it. It smacks to me of a Coltrane ad lib.

Now that his domestic situation is in tatters, Fitz asks Penhaligon if she has a bed for the night, just somewhere to sleep. Ever the opportunist, however, he pushes it one stage further, chancing his arm.

'Although I could be harrassed into more. I would like more.'

'No,' says Penhaligon firmly. 'You don't like me pissed. Tonight might be a bit of a disappointment.'

Later, Grady is caught but Nash escapes the police net. Fitz interrogates Grady, beginning by singing 'If you were the only girl in the world and I were the only boy.' Taking a break from the questioning he has an argument with Danny, his brother, who is looking after the baby in the cop shop. Danny finally pushes Fitz over the edge. In a display of volcanic temper we have rarely seen in Fitz, he slaps the desk and shouts: 'Don't you dare tell me about my wife! You overgrown, underqualified shite!' It is a truly dangerous moment.

Back in the interrogation room, Fitz shows Grady a picture of a scantily clad woman, then a scantily clad man. He uncovers his past, creating the scenario on which his closet homosexuality is founded. Grady is backed into a corner.

'Come on, Grady. It's your one chance to let the light in.' Fitz walks around, casually changing tack. 'You love him, Stewart. And if you love him you must tell us where he is.'

Grady relents, and just as Wise leaves the room Grady tells them Nash has got his old service revolver. Wise insists that Fitz accompany them. Fitz is horrified.

'You must be bloody joking. That's my bit. I don't mind the occasional razor blade or perhaps even a rope. But I do not do guns.'

Fitz, of course, has no choice. Together with Grady, he approaches Nash in a local carnival, where the boy is holding his foster mother and her son hostage. Fitz briefs Grady on what to say and warns him not to tell the boy he's a psychiatrist.

'He's my lawyer,' says Grady.

'Thanks,' mutters Fitz.

As Nash starts to give the gun to Grady, the child and the mother slip out of his grasp and the police snipers shoot him down. The shock on Fitz's face is difficult to fake. 'God!' he says. Fitz can cope with many things, post mortem. But sudden death before his very eyes is still a shocking event. Even he can't rationalize his way out of that.

STORY 9 (SEASON 3) 1995
True Romance

The last *Cracker* episode proper before the obligatory 'Cracker Abroad' telefilm, *White Ghost*, which concluded the series, this draws on several moments of personal crisis to highlight the story.

Written by Paul Abbott and directed by Tina Fywell, it opens with Fitz sitting on the edge of a desk, dealing with a woman who appears to be a private patient. Coltrane, dressed as usual in a dark suit and red braces, looks like a professor gone to seed, with his black reading glasses perched on the end of his nose and the smoke from his cigarette curling up from between his fingers. The patient, having been given an exercise to figure out how much she loves her husband – two columns of twenty items each: things you hate about him, things you love about him – suddenly discovers (after getting to number four on the 'reasons I love him' list) that she is cured and gives Fitz a fistful of cash before leaving. Fitz licks a finger and counts through the cash as if in a betting shop.

The following scene shows Fitz and his wife in the street with a pram. They are arguing over money. This is to be a recurring theme throughout – money and children, the worth of each. 'You are worth more to me now dead than alive, Fitz,' says his wife, as she complains that the bank is now insisting that they return their Switch cards. In a gesture of typical Fitzian flamboyant rebellion, he takes the offending cards from his pocket and drops them in a waste bin. 'Done.' Needless to say, they are quickly retrieved.

Fitz is then seen lecturing psychology students in a big hall. This is where the plot kicks in. Fitz uses his own personal correspondence, bills, letters and so on as visual aids to illustrate the principles of psychology and determine what is real life and what is not. Amazingly, he also includes a fan letter – amounting to a love letter – that he has received from an anonymous admirer. He turns the matter into a joke by claiming it must have come from a psychology student, as only a psychology student would find a professor of psychology attractive.

Fitz is walking on dangerous ground here and Coltrane makes us aware of it, of his deeply unsettled nature. The fact that he exposes his own life – including his family's – to the analytical gaze of a bunch of students is shocking enough; the fact that he tosses in a recent personal letter is cavalier in the extreme.

In the bar afterwards, Fitz and his fellow psychologist professor Irene are chatting away when a girl member of staff joins them for a drink; she asks if anyone wants one and acts familiarly around them. Fitz is more than usually contemptuous and sneering, which does not seem to faze the girl at all. It is clear to us straight away that she is probably responsible for the letter. Coltrane almost overplays this scene, one of the few times when Fitz's contempt for his fellow creatures appears unbalanced. Clearly, Fitz has a lot on his mind, what with pressing debts, his wife about to walk out, children problems and so on, but his dismissal of the girl is a shade distorted. It also suggests, quite wrongly, that Fitz suspects that she may be the letter writer. Nothing could be further from the truth.

Early the following morning, Fitz arrives home and wakes his wife with a bundle of cash he has won gambling in the night. There is no joy in the transaction; Fitz simply uses it as a kind of weapon to stave off her anger at his addiction and irresponsibility.

That same night, the body of a naked boy is thrown from the back of a van. The phone rings for Fitz at the same time as he is handing the money over.

At the crime scene, the boy is established to have had sexual relations just before he died. 'Sex and death?' says the cop, looking at Fitz. 'Your favourite.'

Fitz goes through the motions of psychological profiling for the cops. Coltrane, by this stage, has reached an interesting level; Fitz is clearly brilliant at his job and it is the only thing holding him together – but there are signs that it is becoming increasingly insignificant to him. He sounds bored, as if being able to put this stuff together to impress the cops is a bit like putting on a show, a half-hearted conjuring show. He's good, but the magic has gone.

DCI Wise (Ricky Tomlinson) seems to spot something too and asks: 'Have you been drinking?'

Fitz protests that he hasn't.

'You want one?'

As they have a few drinks together in Wise's office, he reveals to Fitz that he has marriage problems and wonders whether he might not have a session with him. Fitz agrees and says it's £50 a session, at which Wise goes ballistic. Fitz tells him how to begin the analysis, by writing down the columns of Likes and Hates about his partner, and Wise realizes that his wife has already been to Fitz – she was the woman in the session at the episode's opening. Even Fitz realizes he may have been indiscreet, and Tomlinson sacks him on the spot.

The next few scenes are domestic, and Coltrane reveals once again his facility for working with young actors. First, we see him playing with the baby in a rocker while his wife berates him over the job situation. He says to the baby: 'You're the little miracle that was supposed to save our marriage. What are you now? Three months? Three months and she's using you like a weapon.'

To add to his woes, Fitz discovers his son Mark using a mobile phone and that he pays for it by having got a job in a hamburger joint. All of which is news to Fitz, another reason for his wife to berate him about his neglect of his family.

Fitz gets another love letter, but this one names the dead boy and describes him. He goes straight back to the cops. 'She's the killer,' he says without a shadow of a doubt.

Fitz goes to have a heart to heart with his son at the hamburger joint. Mark tells him that he got his girlfriend pregnant. Fitz interrupts with a moan, 'Oh no. I'm going to be a grandfather!' He changes his tune when Mark counters that she lost the baby and subsequently dumped Mark. This news softens Fitz a little and the mixture of relief and pity is perfectly captured in Coltrane's eyes. While he can't help leaving on a light note, we can see a serious shift in emotional perspective in Fitz: 'I know I said enjoy yourself, but put a bit of double glazing on the old todger, will you?'

The contrast between this scene and the following one could not be more marked. Fitz and the cops are questioning a young psychology student – the room-mate of the dead boy – who bears a resemblance to Mark, Fitz's own son. Fitz utterly destroys the boy by tearing into him over a paper in which he misquotes from one of Fitz's own books or papers: 'Memory serves fact not interpretation.' Fitz challenges him on whether he believes it or not, and the boy responds the only way he can: 'I used it so I suppose I must.'

Fitz plays a classic psychological trick, allowing the boy almost to leave the room before saying quietly to him: 'You're a liar. The actual quote is memory only serves its user not the truth. But that's OK. He was brighter than you. But he's dead so it's no use to him now. And like you say, you were good mates.'

Having slipped the knife in and twisted, Fitz now asks the question he really wants to know the answer to: 'You don't happen to know who he was sleeping with, do you?' There is a suggestion that Fitz is becoming increasingly brutal in his treatment of suspects, witnesses, almost anyone who crosses his path. Even Penhaligon is going down the same path. It is this subtle development of character that runs throughout the series, and the level of thought that has gone into cause and effect and character evolution, that makes Cracker so special. Few long-running shows of this nature get anywhere near to this kind of narrative subtlety – Callan is perhaps the one that comes closest.

Having led the questioning with the boy, Fitz now takes a back seat to watch Penhaligon have a go at the girlfriend. He reacts with some surprise to Penhaligon's cool, ruthless and far from sympathetic approach to the interrogation, which leaves the girl in tears. Has she learnt something from Fitz, or is she, too, just reacting over the job?

The following scene is almost indescribably painful. Fitz attempts to seduce Penhaligon in the students' common room as they sit and watch adolescent students getting to grips with each other. There is a sense of how frightened Fitz is of getting old and of Penhaligon's bitterness over betrayal.

This is followed by one of the most remarkable scenes in the entire Cracker series. Fitz, drunk and clearly distressed, is being psychoanalysed by his colleague, Irene. Within the space of a fairly brief scene, Fitz recounts the major emotional highlights of the entire series, from the murder of Christopher Eccleston's DCI Bilborough, through his affair with Penhaligon and her rape at the hands of Beck.

'Beck's suicide was the only highlight,' he concludes, with the kind of rough magic of which Coltrane is capable. 'She's absorbed all the guilt,' he adds. 'She gets the guilt. I get the blame.'

Fitz is by now drinking hard, mired in a pit of self-doubt, resentment and self-pity. The most remarkable feature of Coltrane's performance as Fitz – especially as the series draws to its conclusion – is his utter fearlessness in depicting every aspect of the character, however ugly it appears. If the keynote to Fitz is his honesty, the same can be said of Coltrane's acting. In *Cracker* it is brutally honest, abrasively candid. Which, oddly enough, makes him even more attractive.

Even his own profession – the one thing he can cling on to for emotional support – appears to be letting him down.

'Four decades of social science to sound like Esther Ranzten.'

'I paid for the takeaways,' says Irene. 'I can say what I like.'

At the police station, Fitz gets a good profile together, but then Penhaligon fingers him as the motive. 'She's killed three people for you.' This is too much for Fitz, who agrees to be taken off the case. It's too compromising. Irene is suggested as his replacement.

Meanwhile, Danny, Fitz's brother, is having a would-be romantic dinner *à deux* with Judith. There is clearly seduction in the air.

Fitz is then shown doing his radio phone-in show, but he is coming adrift. Irene, meanwhile, having been shown the photographs of the victims, nips off to the loo for a quick swig of something alcoholic; it appears that she may not stay the course.

A major crisis is looming, one of the worst that Fitz has ever faced. The two halves of his life – his personal life and his professional career – are now totally intermixed.

The killer then sends Fitz a fax revealing that her next victim is Fitz's son, Mark. Coltrane, who has improved steadily as an actor throughout the series, now delivers one of his most devastatingly authentic scenes. He sees the fax, realizes instantly what it means and almost completely loses control: 'Oh God, no. No. Oh God, no. No, please God.' This is acting of the very highest order.

Fitz, in a fit of irony, then goes on television to appeal to the killer. 'I love you, I love you, I love you,' he says. Then: 'No, it's not really working, is it?'

Finally, he cannot hide his true feelings from the woman any longer.

Flinging down the photographs of her other victims he storms: 'If that's the way my boy ends up I'll see you dead, you murdering bitch.' He goes off and grabs a drink.

When they eventually find Mark, Fitz collapses in tears. The sight of a big man brought down by emotional relief and a cathartic outpouring of grief is almost too much to bear.

The final scene has Fitz and Judith on either side of the sliding glass doors of the hospital. They are separated but can still see each other. An invisible barrier between them. It is a grimly effective symbol of their relationship.

Chapter 16

WHAT HAVE YOU GOT?

It is said that there is nothing more burdensome than great potential. If it is true, then Coltrane has had to carry a bigger burden than most. Here is a man who started off in the 'wonderful business we call show' somewhat late and has been struggling to catch up with himself ever since. Having attempted to establish the depth and breadth of Coltrane's talent, to figure out what makes him tick by simply observing him at work, I have reached two conclusions: firstly, that he is a vitally talented actor whose fear of vulnerability has often hindered his progress and is responsible for his tendency to change tack, become wilfully distracted (and distracting); in short, to fart about. The torrential wit, the accents and funny voices, the suspicion, aggression and wariness when faced with the press or the unknown all contribute to the feeling that, for much of his career, Coltrane has been uncertain of the volcanic talent that lies within him. And, just as clearly, for reasons that I have tried to explain, *Cracker* changed all that.

Secondly, Coltrane's evolution as an actor is far from over. Having studied the trajectory of his work I am convinced that he has more to give, even deeper resources on which to draw. *Cracker* should be seen as just the beginning. Now it is up to him to show us what he's got.

He could move in several directions. Some of the really big roles in theatre might be his for the asking – from Shakespeare to Pinter, from the Jacobeans to Mamet. Actors of his maturity, experience and, above all, theatrical presence are not as common as once they were. But I suspect that theatre is not his first love. He is a creature of the screen. It is a loss to theatre, but perhaps he will prove me wrong.

His natural habitat is the movies. Gone are the days when casting agents looking for a funny fat man would automatically think of Coltrane. He is beyond that now. Not that one would deny him his fun. Clearly, he had immense fun playing Valentin Zukovsky in the latest Bond movie, *The World Is Not Enough*. But he is worthy of more. Much more. He might not be physically appropriate for Bond or Hamlet, but he is certainly actor enough to carry a movie in a leading role. Frankly, there aren't many actors of his generation who combine warmth, charisma, sex appeal, wit, aggression, fallibility, danger and a psychic stillness. He may not be anyone's idea of a clean-cut hero, but who believes in those nowadays? As Fitz, Coltrane was the seminal anti-hero of our age; an age of uncertainty, of shifting social perspective, of besieged virility and intellect. Here was a man whose only bulwark against a world sinking into crassness, instant gratification and bastardized values was his extraordinary combination of keen intellect and destructive hedonism. Fitz, in his way, is as much an anti-hero as Sherlock Holmes and for many of the same reasons.

Yet his choice in movies has often proved erratic. Given that actors rarely have the chance to direct their careers, make selections based on aesthetic decisions rather than simple economic ones, and that what may read well on the page can end up looking dreadful on the screen, it may seem unjust to criticize Coltrane for the waywardness of his curriculum vitae. It is difficult now to imagine why he hesitated over *Cracker* when it was first presented to him; maybe he'd been disappointed once too often. It was an honourable, challenging project from the start, but nobody could foresee the impact and success it would eventually have.

One thing is certain: the stakes have risen as a result of *Cracker*. Coltrane can now command seriously good money for participating in films and television. He may not yet be a sure-fire marquee name, but his attachment to a project will substantially increase the interest, may even help get the film from script to screen.

Whether he likes it or not, he has a greater degree of responsibility now. His decisions will have a noticeable effect on the potential marketability of a movie. He is no longer just an accent for hire, a big funny guy who'll keep the set entertained between takes and will sort out your carburettor problems. He is an actor. No irony intended, none needed. His work over the next few years will determine his position in the rarefied arena of films. Hollywood likes him but remains tentative, uncertain. He has yet to be fully embraced by the bosom of Tinseltown. This, I suspect, is due as much to his own resistance to the viperish blandishments of the studios, the agents, the Hollywood system. But how terrific he would be trading dialogue with such as Danny DeVito or Bill Murray. How dangerous he could be sparking off Clint Eastwood or James Woods. And if Hollywood fails to tantalize him, what amazing presence and human authority he would bring to a Ken Loach film. The very fact that one can imagine him in these very different situations is surely a testament to his versatility.

The synthesis of Coltrane's career and character studies, hobbies and interests was to have arrived with *Butcher*, an American television series which cast Coltrane as a New York detective whose sideline is a delicatessen in a seedy New York backstreet. Conceived and developed under conditions of great secrecy, *Butcher* was created by the Granada team in America following the success of the American *Cracker*. Their basic idea was to create a vehicle for Coltrane which would carry over the success and some of the facets of Fitz and *Cracker* into another series.

This is personality marketing via creative teamwork. It happens all the time in the States and to a certain extent in the UK – Robson Green is a classic example of a leading television actor who has achieved such a level of success that series are now created around him, taking him from one character to the next in easy-to-swallow stages. While it might be said that *Butcher* would be considerably more of a risk and a greater leap for Coltrane, it should be remembered that *Cracker* owed much of its stylistic tropes and hardcore depiction of police works to American cop shows anyway; Coltrane would be simply shifting gear. The food angle might work well, as he clearly relishes good food, though one can hardly recall the detective/chef played by Richard Griffiths in a short-lived television series, *Pie in the Sky*.

Scheduled to be filmed on location in New York, *Butcher* will run initially for thirteen episodes. In many ways, it is a throwback to the cop shows of the 1970s, like *Kojak* and *Columbo*, rather than the ensemble pieces of *NYPD Blue*, *Hill Street Blues* and all the other

Stephen Bochco series based around urban policing. Whether *Butcher* would prove to be as popular as any of the above is anyone's guess. But there is a direct precedent that augurs well. *The Equalizer* was a hugely successful American New York-based television series starring a British actor, Edward Woodward, which traded off his earlier television incarnation as Callan. The McCall character was generically linked with Callan in the same way as *Butcher* is with *Cracker*, and it didn't do Edward Woodward any harm – beyond the odd heart scare due to the fact that he was, ironically, overweight.

Still, maybe Coltrane won't have to perform the kind of physical activity and heavy-duty violence that was McCall's stock-in-trade. It will almost certainly be like *Cracker*, a more cerebral character, whose greatest weapon is his smart mouth and fully loaded wit. As for the food side, it should prove the light side to the darkness of the detection.

It is an enormous gamble for Coltrane, who turned his back on a fortune by leaving *Cracker*, and no one is under any illusions about the size of the task confronting him.

'It is a huge risk,' said a Granada insider. 'There is no shortage of American cop programmes around and Robbie is not even American. But we are confident he can do it and that the series will be as good as *Cracker*.'

At time of writing, *Butcher* has been put on the back burner. The fact that *Fitz*, the American version of *Cracker*, was pulled from the schedules while there were still three episodes left to run may have had an indirect effect on the decision. Perhaps the greatest irony of all is that the concluding – and as yet unseen – episode of *Fitz* features Coltrane himself playing the villain. In the episode, entitled *Faustian Fitz*, Coltrane plays a larger-than-life Hollywood producer who becomes a murder suspect when a beautiful girl is found drowned in his swimming pool. Coltrane's appearance in an American version of a television series that made him famous illustrates his confidence, his playfulness, his egotism and, perversely, his humility. It is almost as good an idea as Sean Connery playing the villain in a James Bond film, a suggestion which has yet to be realized.

There can be little doubt that Coltrane's more settled domestic situation, his home life, his family, his impregnable fortress by Loch Lomond in Scotland, have had an effect on his aspirations. For all his past indiscretions and self-indulgent behaviour, Coltrane is at heart a romantic. He enjoys his family and he goes to considerable lengths to protect their privacy. While Rhona Gemmell will accompany him to premieres, film parties and other selected outings, she is very much in the protective circle which Coltrane throws around himself on such public occasions.

Willowy, red haired and beautiful, Gemmell has provided a remarkable stability for Coltrane's life. Her slight, almost ethereal appearance conceals a firm resolve and the sharp focus of a dedicated artist. She is clearly self-sufficient and maintains the family and a degree of privacy similar to that of Coltrane himself. Whenever he has to spend long periods away from home while filming, Coltrane makes every effort to bring Gemmell and Spencer with him; they are sure to be closer to him than many would think. Even to the casual observer, they are an extraordinarily integrated couple: he, dark, large and solid; she, fair, small and airy. The visual contrast could not be greater, yet they compliment each other perfectly. Whatever contribution she has made to Coltrane's development, both as actor and man, can only be guessed at. But clearly Coltrane values her psychological impact – quite apart from anything else – highly. And having spent so many years in fruitless pursuit of love he is not about to let anything, or anyone, threaten the personal harmony, the balance and the happiness he has discovered with Gemmell.

A higher profile would undoubtedly put more pressure on him; he would be called upon by the press and publicists and the whole marketing machinery of movies to perform with increasing regularity. He would be obliged to give more interviews, to give up more pieces of himself, his past, his family than he has done so far. He is, I am sure, painfully aware of this and may often debate the problem of incipient stardom; more correctly, the next level of fame. The increased intrusion and probing into his background and private life that would be the inevitable result would be anathema to him; he would resent it furiously. It's a problem and one which only he can solve.

This, of course, is my speculation. It is based on little more than observation of Coltrane at work and, occasionally, at play. I indulge in it for no other reason than to attempt to understand the landscape of Coltrane's career and to guess where it might go from here. I know he has more to offer, which is an exciting prospect for both the actor himself and those to whom he matters.

Perhaps the question one should ask of Coltrane now is not, as Brando's Johnny says, 'What have you got?' but 'What are you going to do with it?'

Appendix

LIST OF COLTRANE'S CREDITS

Robbie Coltrane's Film and TV Credits

The World is Not Enough (1999) – Valentin Zukovsky
   aka *Pressure Point* (USA) or *T.W.I.N.E.* (UK promotional
   abbreviation)
Alice in Wonderland (1999) (TV) – Tweedledum
Message in a Bottle (1999) – Charlie Toschi
The Ebb-Tide (1998 TV) – Chisholm
Frogs for Snakes (1998) – Al Santana
Montana (1998) – the Boss
   aka *Nothing Personal* (1998) (Australia: video title)
Buddy (1997) – Dr Lintz
Coltrane's Planes and Automobiles (1997 TV series) – himself
Cracker (1997 TV) – Fitz
GoldenEye (1995) – Valentin Zukovsky
Coltrane in a Cadillac (1993 TV series) – himself
Cracker (1993 TV series) – Fitz
The Adventures of Huck Finn (1993) – the Duke
   aka *The Adventures of Huckleberry Finn*
Boswell and Johnson's Tour of the Western Islands (1993) – Johnson
Oh, What a Night (1992) – Todd
Alive and Kicking (1991 TV) Liam Kane
   aka *Screen One: Alive and Kicking*
The Pope Must Die (1991) – The Pope
   aka *The Pope Must Diet* (1991 USA)

Triple Bogey on a Par Five Hole (1991) – Steffano Baccardi
Nuns on the Run (1990) – Charlie McManus
Perfectly Normal (1990) – Alonzo Turner
Where the Heart Is (1990) – uncredited

Notable TV appearances

Cracker (1997) – Fitz
Shooting Stars (1993) – himself
Clive Andersen All Talk (1996) – himself
The Comic Strip Presents (1982) – Arnold Silverstein in *Demonella*
   – Zarran/N in *Space Virgins from Planet Sex*
   – Speaker in *Red Nose of Courage*
   – Ken in *GLC: The Carnage Continues*
   – Max in *South Atlantic Raiders (2): Argie Bargie!*
   – Goldie/Dutch Celebrity in *The Strike*
   – Commander Jackson in *The Bullshitters; Roll out the Gunbarrel*
   – Max in *Gino: Full Story and Pics*
   – Gerald in *Susie*
   – Chief of Police in *Dirty Movie*
   – Mother in *Five Go Mad In Mescalin*
   – Desmond in *Summer School*
   – Kurt in *The Beat Generation*
   – *War*
French and Saunders (1987)
Thompson (1990)
The Lenny Henry Show (1984) in *Christmas 1987* and episode 2.5
Blackadder the Third (1987) playing Dr Samuel Johnson in *Ink and Incapability*
Girls on Top (1985) – Morris in *C.O.D.*
The Young Ones (1982) – Captain Blood in *Time*
   – Dr Carlisle in *Bambi*
Danny, The Champion of the World (1989 TV) – Victor Hazell
Bert Rigby, You're a Fool (1989) – Sid Trample
Henry V (1989) – Falstaff
Let It Ride (1989) – Ticket Seller
Slipstream (1989) – Madeleine

Blackadder's Christmas Carol (1988 TV) – The Spirit of Christmas
The Fruit Machine (1988) – Annabelle
  aka *Wonderland*
Tutti Frutti (1987 TV series) – Danny McGlone/Big Jazza
Eat the Rich (1987) – Jeremy
Mona Lisa (1986) – Thomas
Absolute Beginners (1986) – Mario
Caravaggio (1986) – Scipione Borghese
European Vacation (1985) – Man in the Bathroom
  aka *National Lampoon's European Vacation* (1985)
Defence of the Realm (1985) – Leo McAskey
Revolution (1985) – New York Burgher
The Supergrass (1985) – Troy
  aka *The Comic Strip Presents The Supergrass*
Laugh? I Nearly Paid my Licence Fee (1984 TV series) – various roles
Chinese Boxes (1984)
Krull (1983) – Rhun
  aka *Dragons of Krull, Dungeons and Dragons, The Dungeons of Krull, Krull: Invaders of the Black Fortress*
Alfresco (1983 TV series) – various roles
Scrubbers (1983) – Puff Guts
Ghost Dance (1983)
Loose Connections (1983)
Britannia Hospital (1982) – Picket
Kevin Turvey: The Man Behind the Green Door (1982 TV) – Mick
Flash Gordon (1980) – Man at Airfield
La Mort en Direct (1980)
  aka *Der Gekaufte Tod (West Germany), Death in Full View, Deathwatch*

INDEX

Abbott, Paul 202, 208
Absalom, Steve 27
Absolute Beginners 41, 104–5, 222
accents 4, 5, 40, 114, 122, 134
acting
  early days 21, 34–46
  first stage appearance 13
  future prospects 214–19
  inspiration 14–15
Adventures of Huck Finn, The 118–20, 220
Alfresco 222
Alice in Wonderland 220
Alive and Kicking 4, 66, 220
Amish community 92–3
art school 15, 19–20, 61

Bambi 221
Barton, Nicholas 58
Battersbury, Roy 194
Berry, Michael 77
Bert Rigby, You're a Fool 111, 222
Best Boys 202–8
Big Crunch, The 173–82
Billen, Andrew 25
Blackadder the Third 221
Blackadder's Christmas Carol 129–31, 222
Blank Generation, The 33
Bliel, Ted 94–5

Bond films 14, 31, 86, 215
Boorman, John 113
Boswell and Johnson's Tour of the Western Isles 56–8, 220
Branagh, Kenneth 109
Brando, Marlon 14–15, 53–4, 89
Brennan, Brid 195
Britannia Hospital 222
Brotherly Love 194–201
Buchan, Alasdair 105
Buddy 121–5, 220
Burn, Gordon 26
Butcher 216–217
Byrne, John 21, 56, 58

Calder, David 197
Canada 113–17
Canter, David 76–7
Caravaggio 51, 103–4, 222
Carlyle, Robert 162, 169
Carrington, Paul 86
cars
  Coltrane in a Cadillac 88–99
  mechanic skills 4, 7, 36, 70, 114
  vintage American 4, 88
Carter, Jim 174
childhood 10–19
Chinese Boxes 36–40, 222
Cinderella 131–3
cinema *see* movies

223

Index

Clarke, Frank 106
Clive Andersen All Talk 221
Coltrane in a Cadillac 30, 88–99, 220
Coltrane, Robbie
  accents 4, 5, 40, 114, 122, 134
  birth 12
  characteristics 10, 12–14, 16, 24, 29–30, 95
  childhood 10–19
  depression 7–8, 22, 30, 61
  dieting 3, 25–30, 59, 63
  drinking 3, 27, 28, 59
  future prospects 214–19
  hobbies 4, 86, 88
  homes 6, 217
  name change 21, 53
  nicknames 17, 47, 54
  parents 10–11, 21
  real name 10
  roles 5, 55, 215, 220–2
  size 2–3, 5, 8, 23–31, 59
  smoking 3, 25–6, 29, 63, 83
  workaholic tendencies 12–13, 30
Coltrane's Planes and Automobiles 220
comedy
  acting 41
  childhood talent 12, 17
  Peter Sellers award 4
  views on 2, 7, 49, 70, 95–6
Comic Strip, The 43, 47, 48, 49
  Eat the Rich 105, 222
  list of credits 221, 222
  The Pope Must Die 4, 49, 50–1, 221
commercials 4, 7, 54–5
Connery, Sean 8
Cowley, Elizabeth 58
Crace, John 70
Cracker
  Best Boys 202–8
  The Big Crunch 173–82
  Brotherly Love 194–201
  casting as Fitz 25, 64–71, 134–5
  end of series 86–7
  first series 135–62
  list of credits 220, 221

The Madwoman in the Attic 66, 135–44
Men Should Weep 182–94
One Day a Lemming Will Fly 155–62
  preparation for part 72–9
  scriptwriters 65–6, 173, 202, 208
  second series 85–6, 162–94
  third series 194–213
To Be a Somebody 162–72
To Say I Love You 76, 144–55
True Romance 208–13
  US version 79–80, 82, 83–4
White Ghost 208
Cranitch, Lorcan 155, 161, 191
Cunningham, Liam 204
Curry Boys, The 18

Dahl, Roald 107
Danny, the Champion of the World 107–9, 221
Deathwatch 32, 222
Defence of the Realm 41–2, 126, 222
Dent, Mary 21
depression 7–8, 22, 30, 61
dieting 3, 25–30, 59, 63
Disney film 118–20
Dougary, Ginny 30
drag roles 49, 105–7, 112
drinking 3, 27, 28, 59
Drury, David 41

Eat the Rich 105, 222
Ebb-Tide, The 131, 220
Eccleston, Christopher 136, 155
Edinburgh Festival 21, 32
education 13, 16–20
Elliott, Peter 123
European Vacation 222
Eyre, Richard 36

Fat Rab 17, 18
film noir 33–4
films *see* movies
Fitz 80, 83–4, 217
Flash Gordon 32–3, 222

Index

Flynn, Barbara 137, 153
Foreigner, The 33
forensic psychology 73–7
Fraser, Simon 131
French and Saunders 221
French Toast recipe 26–7
Frogs for Snakes 220
Fruit Machine, The 23, 49, 105–7, 222
future prospects 214–19
Fywell, Tina 162, 208

gambling 70, 72–3
Gemmell, Rhona 6, 27, 59, 62–3, 218
Ghost Dance 35, 222
Girls on Top 221
Glasgow Art School 15, 19–20, 61
Glenalmond public school 13, 16–19
GoldenEye 31, 86, 220
Grieve, Alex 17
guns 91

Hannibal 97–8
Head, Sally 64, 66
Henry V 26, 109–11, 222
heroes 14–15, 19, 53–4, 57
Hibbert, Tom 54
Hignett, Sean 20
Hollywood 4–5, 87, 111, 121–8, 216
Hudson, Hugh 43

Idle, Eric 47–8, 112

Jardine, Cassandra 49
Jarman, Derek 51, 103
Jarrold, Julian 173
Johnson, Dr Samuel 56–7
Jones, Simon Cellan 157

Kael, Pauline 5, 54
Kansas 93–4
Kerr, Euan 17
Kevin Turvey: The Man Behind the Green Door 222
Kral, Ivan 33
Kroger, Jane 94

Krull 36, 222
Kurtz, Gary 111–12

La Mort en Direct 222
Laugh? I Nearly Paid my Licence Fee 222
Lean, Sir David 8
Leith, William 17, 30
Lenny Henry Show 221
Let It Ride 4, 112, 222
Lietzes, Jennifer 125
Lindsay, Robert 65–6, 111
Loose Connections 36, 222
lorries, interest in 12, 17
Loughley, Catherine 21
Lurie, John 34
Lynch, Susan 144
Lynn, Jonathan 47, 48, 112

machinery, interest in 4, 36, 50, 70
MacMillan, Annie Rae 12, 19, 22, 30
MacMillan, Ian 10–11, 14, 21
MacMillan, Jane 21–2
MacMillan, Jean 10–11, 13, 22
MacMillan, Spencer Coltrane 18, 27–8, 53, 62, 218
Madwoman in the Attic, The 66, 135–44
Maltin, Leonard 32
marriage, views on 60
Mason, Robert 21
McDougall, Colin 202
McGovern, Jimmy
  acceptance of Coltrane 68–70, 79
  Brotherly Love 194
  Cracker scriptwriter offer 65–6
  Men Should Weep 182
  movie references 152, 155
  replaced as scriptwriter 173
  To Be a Somebody 162, 172
  To Say I Love You 144
McMaster, Gordon 55–6
McMullen, Ken 35
Men Should Weep 182–94
Message in a Bottle 126–8, 220
Millar, Gavin 107

Index

Missouri 94–6
Mona Lisa 39, 40–1, 100–3, 222
Montana 125–6, 220
Moray House College of Education 20
Moreton, Samantha 174, 178, 182
movies
  Cracker references 152, 155
  early films 32–46
  future prospects 215–16
  Hollywood 4–5, 87, 111, 121–8, 216
  interest in 14–15, 16, 33, 49–50, 53
  later films 100–20
  list of credits 220–2
Muhammad Ali 54
music 53, 70

National Health Service 6, 7
National Lampoon's European Vacation
  43, 222
Neal, Gub 64–6, 69, 77, 84, 173
New York 33–4, 89, 98–9, 113, 216
nicknames 17, 47, 54
Norman, Neil
  accepts biography commission 1–2,
  8–9
  interview with Coltrane 2–8
Nothing Personal 220
Nuns on the Run 7, 23, 47–8, 112–13,
  221

Oh What A Night 113–16, 220
One Day a Lemming Will Fly 155–62

Paine, Robin 59–62, 63
painting 15, 19–20
Parkinson, Michael 95, 96
Pastorelli, Robert 79–80, 82–4
Paterson, Peter 58
Pearce, Garth 14
Pellay, Lanah 105
Perfectly Normal 2, 5, 54, 116–17, 221
Permutt, Stewart 131
Perry, David 18
Peter Sellers prize for Comedy 4

Petit, Chris 36–7, 39
Poe, Amos 33–4, 99
politics 6–7, 47, 54, 56
Pope Must Die, The 4, 49, 50–1, 221
Pressure Point 220
psychology 72, 73–7
Pykta, Joe 112

radio, *Cinderella* 131–3
Red Robbie 47, 54
Reid, Beryl 148, 155
Reiner, Carl 111
religion 10, 47, 50–2
Renton, Nick 131
research 51, 57, 73–5, 106, 173
Revolution 43, 222
Richardson, Peter 43, 44, 47, 50, 105
Robinson, Lucy 105
Rogano's restaurant 2–4, 54
roles refused 55–6
romance 59–63, 218
rugby 17, 18
Russell, Clive 196

Sadwith, Jim 83, 84
Salt Lake City 90
Saville, Philip 105, 106
school 13, 16–20
Scrubbers 34–5, 222
Sessions, John 56, 58, 59, 62
Shakespeare 26, 109–11
Sholokian, Ed 89
Shooting Stars 221
Slab Boys, The 21
Slipstream 34–5, 111–12, 222
smoking 3, 25–6, 29, 63, 83
Somerville, Geraldine 139, 141, 155
sport 17, 18, 29
Stephen, Ian 74–5, 76
Strike, The 43
Subway Rider 33–4, 99
Supergrass, The 43–6, 100, 222

Tavernier, Bertrand 32

teacher training 20
television
see also Cracker
Blackadder's Christmas Carol
129–31
Boswell and Johnson's Tour of the
Western Isles 56
Butcher, The 216
Coltrane in a Cadillac 30, 88–99,
220
early appearances 43
Ebb-Tide, The 131
list of credits 220–2
Temple, Julien 104
theatre 5, 21, 56, 214
Thompson 221
Thompson, Caroline 123
Thomson, Tess 177
Tiernan, Andrew 144, 154
To Be a Somebody 162–72
To Say I Love You 76, 144–55
Tomlinson, Ricky 171, 181, 205, 210
transvestite role 105–7
Triple Bogey on a Par Five Hole 221
True Romance 208–13
Tutti Frutti 43, 222
T.W.I.N.E. 220

underground films 33, 35

United States
Adventures of Huck Finn 118–20
The Butcher 216–17
Coltrane in a Cadillac 30, 88–99
Coltrane's interest in 88–9
Coltrane's popularity 4–5
Cracker 79–80, 82–4, 217
Hollywood 4–5, 87, 111, 121–8, 216
Let It Ride 112
New York 33–4, 89, 98–9, 113, 216
Unmade Beds 33

Welles, Orson
admiration of 19, 54, 80
comparisions to 5–6, 54, 80–1
imitation 37, 39, 40
Where the Heart Is 113, 221
White Ghost 208
Whitehead, Ted 173
Winterbottom, Michael 135, 155
Wonderland see Fruit Machine, The
Woolley, Stephen 37, 39, 40–1, 100
World is Not Enough, The 31, 215, 220

Yates, Peter 36
Young Ones, The 221
Your Obedient Servant 5, 56

Zetterling, Mai 34